Morality in the Marketplace

# Morality in the Marketplace

*Reconciling Theology and Economics*

*By*

Paul van Geest

BRILL

LEIDEN | BOSTON

Cover illustration: New York 1927 St. Patrick's Cathedral.

Library of Congress Cataloging-in-Publication Data

Names: Geest, Paul van, author.
Title: Morality in the marketplace : reconciling theology and economics / by Paul van Geest.
Description: Leiden ; Boston : Brill, [2021] | Includes bibliographical references and index.
Identifiers: LCCN 2021044519 (print) | LCCN 2021044520 (ebook) | ISBN 9789004501744 (paperback) | ISBN 9789004501706 (ebook)
Subjects: LCSH: Economics–Religious aspects. | Economics–Moral and ethical aspects.
Classification: LCC HB72 .G39 2021 (print) | LCC HB72 (ebook) | DDC 201/.73–dc23
LC record available at https://lccn.loc.gov/2021044519
LC ebook record available at https://lccn.loc.gov/2021044520

Typeface for the Latin, Greek, and Cyrillic scripts: "Brill". See and download: brill.com/brill-typeface.

ISBN 978-90-04-50174-4 (paperback)
ISBN 978-90-04-50170-6 (e-book)



This book is printed on acid-free paper and produced in a sustainable manner.

Printed by Printforce, United Kingdom

This book makes a wonderful case that the conceptual frameworks developed by theologians over the centuries can fruitfully broaden and enrich the conceptual and analytical frameworks of economists, business leaders and other leaders of society. It provides an innovative vision of the possibilities that the interaction between theology and economics offers for deepening our understanding of the phenomenon of humanity.

JAN PETER BALKENENDE, Professor of Governance, Institutions & Internationalisation', Erasmus University Rotterdam; Prime Minister of the Netherlands from 2002 to 2010

•••

As an economist ( and a catholic) I find Paul van Geest's book impressive and convincing in emphasizing the indispensable relationships between theology and economy.

ONNO RUDING, former Minister of Finance of The Netherlands from 1982 to 1989, Chairman of the Christian Employers' association (NCW), COO of Citibank Europe; corporate director and non-profit director on several supervisory boards (Centre for European Policy Studies, NIBC Bank and the Tinbergen Institute)

•••

In this beautiful and well-crafted book, the leading scholar Paul van Geest guides the reader through a journey to bring economics and theology as scientific disciplines back together. This book is a must-read for anyone interested in progress in economic analysis.

PHILIP HANS FRANSES, Professor of Applied Econometrics and Marketing Research at the Erasmus University Rotterdam, Dean of the Erasmus School of Economics from 2011-2020

•••

Paul van Geest wrote this thought-provoking book at an opportune time. In part due to the rise of behavioral economics, economists are searching for a richer anthropology of their discipline. The rich treasure trove of ideas from this book should give economists plenty of inspiration.

LANS BOVENBERG, Professor of Economics at the Tilburg University and Erasmus University Rotterdam. He was awarded the Spinoza Prize in 2003

•••

In his book Paul van Geest invites, in a very well thought-out and original way, economists to enrich their own perspectives and assumptions with insights from the history of theology. He offers theologians insights from economics that can enrich their discourse on the sacred. His approach brings together the sacred and the profane. It is inspiring and should stimulate others to follow suit.

DEIRDRE NANSEN MCCLOSKEY, Distinguished Professor Emerita of Economics and of History, and Professor Emerita of English and of Communication at the University of Illinois at Chicago

•••

This impressive book by Paul van Geest is an important contribution in the search of a dialogue between Economics and Theology. Economics, in fact, needs theology for understanding its origins, its classics (from Smith to Wicksteed), its failures; but theology also needs economics, in particular behavioral economics which is offers empirical bases of and new lights to some classical concepts of theology, i.e. trust, reciprocity, love.

LUIGINO BRUNI, Professor of Economics at Lumsa University, Rome

# Contents

CHAPTER 1

# Introduction

History shows that economic prosperity nearly always entices policy makers and politicians to treat economic systems as isolated forces. This is both understandable and puzzling. Understandable, because as soon as an economic system brings the greatest possible welfare to the greatest possible number of people, it becomes nearly impossible to distance ourselves from the 'liberal' notion that we should by all means let the market do its job. At the same time this 'autonomous market thinking' is puzzling, because the market functions due to the fact that people consume; consume more and more and along the way sometimes discover that they are losing the freedom and autonomy they hope to find.

Politicians and policy makers are not alone in being susceptible to the strong formative impact autonomous market thinking has in times of prosperity. Economists, too, are greatly influenced by the spirit of their times and the vision of the market that come with it. Economist and Nobel Laureate Ronald Coase implicitly drew attention to the puzzling nature of this phenomenon by noting that economic science tends to describe economic activity without reference to its institutional context, consumers without mentioning human character, companies without reference to organizational structure and trade without mentioning market order.[1]

However, exclusive belief in autonomous market thinking loses ground in times of crises. Whether this be a crisis like the Great Depression that followed the October 1929 Wall Street crash, a crisis like the 2008 financial crisis or the recent Covid 19 crisis, all crises bring about a realization that an exaggerated belief in autonomous market thinking is defective, if only because the economy is more than just the market economy. The economy is a social practice in which people should be seen not just as consumers, but rather as relational beings.

This was a realization that emerged within economics as a scientific discipline. As a result, the idea began to take hold that other branches of

1 R. Coase, 'The relevance of transaction costs in the economics analysis of law', in: F. Parisi, C. Kershaw Rowley (eds), *The origins of law and economics: essays by the founding fathers* (Cheltenham, UK: Edward Elgar, 2005), 200: 'exchange takes place without any specification of its institutional setting. We have consumers without humanity, firms without organization, and even exchange without markets'. See also: R. Coase, *The Firm, the Market and the Law* (Chicago: University of Chicago, 1988), 5 and passim.

 | DOI:10.1163/9789004501706_002

science could contribute to the development of a well-constructed view on economics and the economy. In economics, human beings are seen as creatures whose economic activities add value to society. These activities are not an isolated objective, however. Although the instrumental reasoning that economic thinking requires helps us to do our work in a practical, efficient and hopefully sustainable way, these economic virtues need to go hand in hand with other virtues even in trade relations. Behavioral economist Paul Zak argues that if economic development is to really stand a chance of success, any form of trade involved should be accompanied by honesty, reliability and empathy.[2] In other words: when other virtues than just those of the *homo economicus* are at play in economic relations, this will almost certainly contribute to a society with a culture of reciprocity, respect, trust, love and reciprocity. Of course, love and reciprocity are very complex concepts that have layers of meaning that are almost contradictory. There is selfless love, but there is also such a thing as possessive love, in which, ultimately, the 'love' of the persons so afflicted has as its only purpose to strengthen their ego. Somewhat similarly, there is also a calibrated reciprocity dominated by economic and material aspects, which may conditional with regard to time, object, quality and quantity, and there is a negative reciprocity characterized by deception or exploitation.[3] And there is a reciprocity distinguished by altruism. In this book, love and reciprocity are viewed throughout as positive forces.

Prior to the emergence of economics as a field of study in its own right, during the 18th century, economic questions used to be discussed as part of treatises on God, Creation, humankind and its downfall, the salvation of humankind in Christ and life after death, that is, in theological tracts. Questions pertaining to human behavior, virtues and vices in social and economic relations were treated within the wider context of religion and theology. In the second chapter of this book we will give a broad outline of the way the philosophy of antiquity, Judaism, and particularly the works of Church Fathers and scholastic, reformation and counter-reformation theologians, dealt with economic issues in their respective treatises on virtues and vice, the restoration of relationships broken by fraud, and remission of sin. With the advent of economics as an independent scientific discipline, however, God disappeared from this field of study. In our third chapter we will present a number of reasons why the resistance to a theological contribution to scientific reflections

2 P. Zak, *Moral Markets. The Critical Role of Values in the Economy* (Princeton: Princeton University Press, 2008), passim.

3 D. Pessers, *Liefde, solidariteit en recht. Een interdisciplinair onderzoek naar het wederkerigheidsbeginsel* (Amsterdam: Universiteit van Amsterdam, 1999), 79f.

on economics seems understandable. Even merely associating with theologians seems to entail risks for economists. Aside from the fact that from the Enlightenment onwards the theological sources in which economic issues were discussed seem to have lost their relevance, the epistemological assumptions underlying theological research are largely incompatible with the assumptions that underlie economic theories. Mutual reconciliation between the most important basic principles of economics and theology seems out of the question, considering the great differences in terms of their objects of knowledge, methodology and epistemology.[4]

In spite of all this confusion, economists, urged on by their own doubts as to the appropriateness of the concept of a rational and ever-consistent *homo economicus* as the point of departure for their models, have looked to theologians and practitioners of other scientific disciplines. A brief summary of these attempts at rapprochement will be given in chapter four. It may be advantageous, or even necessary, to renew the old ties between economics and theology as scientific disciplines so as to arrive at a deeper and richer anthropology than which still underpins economic research.

As it turns out, modern economists have begun to think about notions like 'gratuity', 'trust', 'inner motives and intentions', notions that theologians have been reflecting on tirelessly throughout the ages. The economists concerned seem to have taken up the suggestion made by Daniel Kahneman towards the end of his book *Thinking, fast and slow*, where he calls for the development of 'a richer language' for reflecting on economic processes. He sees this as a potentially great tool for the skillful practice of constructive criticism: much like medicine, 'the identification of judgment errors is a diagnostic task, which requires a precise vocabulary.'[5]

In addition to the dubious viability of the current view of humankind, there is yet another justification for a rapprochement and dialogue between economists and theologians. At the level of explanation and in-depth study of notions current within their respective fields of study, they could mutually support and inspire each other. Taking Kahneman's advice to heart, we will try to show in the fifth chapter of this book that theology could be helpful to, or even indispensable for, the development of a language that takes into account the complexity of human beings and could help broaden the economic analytical framework. An advantage of interdisciplinary research by economists

4 See for the essential definitions of interdisciplinarity: T. Wilthagen, E. Aarts, P. Valcke, *Tijd voor interdisciplinariteit. Een essay over de meerwaarde van samenwerking voor wetenschap, universiteit en maatschappij* (Tilburg: Tilburg University Press, 2018), 11–14; 17–23.

5 D. Kahneman, *Thinking fast and slow* (London: Penguin Books, 2011), 8.

and theologians at the level of clarification of terms or conceptual definition ('Begriffsklärung') is that it makes it possible to circumvent differences in objects of knowledge, methodology and epistemology, as we will show later in this chapter. As an illustration of the usefulness of – and the need for –discussion on the meaning of key terms we will discuss the works of economists Luigino Bruni, Alessandra Smerilli, Bart Nooteboom and Samuel Bowles. In their recent work they interpret gratuity, trust and morality in motives as virtues that are essential for social and economic innovation.

Three economists do not a summer make, however. Bruni, Nooteboom and Bowles may be the proverbial exceptions to the rule that theology is of interest to economists because theology is heir to a centuries-old history of thinking about notions that economists find important for economics. In chapter 6 we will therefore discuss notions like *bounded morality, bounded rationality* and *bounded willpower*, that have all become crucial concepts in economics. Together these notions play a key role in behavioral economics, a relatively new branch of economic science. The attention these key concepts receive implicitly shows that economics has been taking the imperfection of the individual human being more seriously than it had until very recently . The emphasis was traditionally on the ability rather than the inability of rational human beings to evaluate or handle matters in the best possible way. More recently, however, behavioral economists have pointed out that our limited brain capacity in itself already means that our rationality is limited. This inherent limitedness can moreover be demonstrated experimentally as an inability to accurately process large amounts of information and to take into account all possible alternatives to a decision. The ease with which people yield to temptations that distract them from their original goals has in turn be seen as proof of the *bounded willpower* and, by extension, the *bounded morality* of human beings. The latter can even be seen to manifest itself in the human ability to justify one's own moral failures. In Chapter 6 we will try to show that, when we fully think through the notions of *bounded rationality, bounded morality* and *bounded willpower*, theologians have a useful and necessary role to play in answering Daniel Kahneman's call, particularly in those forms of economics where the model of the *homo economicus* is being challenged and attempts are being made to design an economy that puts human relationships before economic transactions.

We will argue in the epilogue that cross-pollination between economics and theology holds the promise of value creation and that theologians and economists have more in common than may seem to be the case at first sight.

This book owes its conception to many conversations that I was privileged to have as a theologian with economists. I am very grateful to my colleagues –and friends– Lans Bovenberg at Tilburg University and Harry Commandeur and Philip Hans Franses at Erasmus University Rotterdam for these conversations. Generous support from the *Goldschmeding Foundation* and the *Templeton World Charity Foundation, Inc.* permitted Lans Bovenberg and me, in the context of our respective teaching and research remits at the *Erasmus School of Economics* and the *Erasmus School of Philosophy*, to dedicate time to issues at the interface of theology and economics. My colleagues at the Faculty of Theology and Religious Studies at KU Leuven, Johan Leemans, Thieu Lamberigts and Anthony Dupont, gave me access to the perfect place to do literature research in Leuven. Finally, I would like to thank Ard Jan Biemond, Philip Hans Franses, Ingrid de Groen, Eric Holterhues, Eduard Kimman, Kees van der Kooi, Bert Jan Lietaert Peerbolte, Giulio Maspero and Onno Ruding for their comments on earlier drafts of this book.

The recently founded *Erasmus Economics and Theology Institute* now allows us, in conjunction with other theologians, philosophers, economists and business administration experts, to research notions from theology that have been influential in the history of the economy and of economics. One example of such study is the metaphor of the invisible hand that supposedly guides a free market economy towards a positive outcome. We are examining economic notions of which theologians suspect that theology can contribute to a better and deeper understanding. In addition, we are looking at how theology and world views are influenced by economic and social developments. Economic systems like feudalism, communism or capitalism not only mirror the spirit of the times, but have also left their mark on theological language and thinking about God. To what extent can economic insights help us to deepen our knowledge and understanding of the language of the Bible and the theological tradition (patristic literature, Middle Ages and Protestantism)?

This book can be taken as a foretaste of the research that lies ahead of us. As such it is a plea for cooperation between theologians and economists in an attempt to achieve a closer match between the image of the human being as *homo economicus* and the unruly and imperfect creatures that actual human beings are in real life. Of course, ultimately the theologian's research topic is not humankind but conceptions of God . But they who attempt to interpret the dealings of human beings in the light of Eternity may well be uniquely equipped to appreciate trends and tendencies in economic life. No less an authority than John Maynard Keynes essentially encouraged this approach by observing in his *A Tract on Monetary Reform* (1923), 'In the long run, we are all dead'. He wrote these famous words to point out to his fellow economists that there was no use in looking too far into the future, as the world in which he lived was changing rapidly. But paradoxically, at the same time these words emphasize the relativity and transitoriness of all human considerations and actions: one of the few concepts that recurs constantly in the sources of theology and is based on empirical observation.

CHAPTER 2

# The Relationship between Economics and Theology as Scientific Disciplines through the Ages

## 1 How God Appeared in the Economy (and Economics) of Antiquity, Judaism and Early Christianity

A copper engraving of Leiden University's first library on the Faliede Begijnhof tells it all. Theologians at the academy saw their market share dwindle after the Enlightenment came to dominate academic life in Europe. The copperplate by Willem van Swanenburg, dated 1610, shows that the collection of books for the use of the *literatores* around this time filled two bookcases, that of the *mathematici* just a single bookcase, that of the *historici* four, of the *medici* two, the *philosophi* two and the *iurisconsulti* five. But they were dwarfed both literally and figuratively by the theological collection: no fewer than six bookcases were reserved for books by and for *theologi*.[1] In Leiden at the time, the principle, inconceivable to us, was that all scientific disciplines culminated in theology. On the authority of the Scriptures, it was assumed that God was the origin of all that could be measured and verified in time and space. The *manus domini*, the hand of God, both imperative and invisible, was the prime, if not sole, subject of reflection. Van Swanenburg's copperplate also shows us that no shelf room at all was dedicated to 'the economy'. At the European universities, economics had not yet become a scientific discipline in its own right.[2]

There was no need for independence at the time. Up until Adam Smith (+1790) the founding father of economics as a scientific discipline, thinking about money, property, labor, trade, market processes and the behavior that people display and develop while making use of more or less scarce goods and services, had been the domain of philosophers and theologians. Admittedly, pamphleteers like the mercantilists created a political philosophy which also included economic theories and this relatively independently from theology. The mercantilist hypothesis that the wealth of a nation is related to the supply

1 R.E.O. Ekkart, 'De Leidse Bibliotheek in 1610', in: *De Boekenwereld* 1 (1984–1985), 13–17.

2 Cf. M.I. Finley, *The Ancient Economy* (London: Chatto & Windus, 1973), 17 and passim; H. Landreth, D. Colander, *History of Economic Thought* (Boston-Toronto: Houghton Mifflin Company, 2006. Fourth edition), 32–34. See also: R.M. Cook, 'Speculations on the Origins of Coinage', in: *Historia: Zeitschrift für Alte Geschichte*, 7, no. 3 (1958), 257–62.

 | DOI:10.1163/9789004501706_003

of capital and that the volume of international trade is fixed, so that one country's gain is another country's loss, are distinctly economic in nature. The same is true for the resulting conclusion – drawn mainly in England and France – that export must therefore be stimulated and import be discouraged by a protectionist state. In John Locke's wake, Smith, for instance in his *An Inquiry into the Nature and Causes of the Wealth of Nations*, criticized mercantilism because he too believed that the wealth of the world was not fixed but could be increased through human artifice. Similarly, German cameralism was an economic doctrine, mainly focused on organizing the government of the state in such a way as to fill the coffers of the seventeenth- and eighteenth-century German princes. Its object was not so much the development of trade but the perfection of taxation, at a time that German universities saw the endowment of the first chairs in economics, for instance in Halle in 1723.

Be this as it may: theologians still had a strong voice in debates about the economy even in this period. In his standard work *History of Economic Analysis* Joseph Schumpeter even observed that Adam Smith in his book *The Wealth of Nations* articulated no analytical concepts that had not already been devised by scholastic authors in the centuries before.[3] Schumpeter argued that the concepts that modern economics uses had already been discussed by philosophers and Church Fathers before these scholastic authors.

Thus in the fourth century BC, Plato, in his work *Laws* talked in a way that is still recognizable to us even today about property, fraud and the need for an efficient division of labor in production processes that are supposed to benefit welfare within a state.[4] In his *Nicomachean Ethics*, Plato's student Aristotle wrote about money as a means of exchange and payment, as a unit of account and as a unit for measuring the value of goods and services.[5] Interestingly, both

---

3 J. Schumpeter, *History of Economic Analysis* [edited from manuscript by Elizabeth Boody Schumpeter] London-Boston-Sydney: Allen & Unwin 1986 (paperback edition), 184. If Schumpeter had studied the early Christian authors, he would have noticed the same, as is shown by: J. Hengstmengel, 'The Paradox of Value in the Teaching of the Church Fathers', in: *European Journal of the History of Economic Thought*, in press. The work of these authors shows that the assumption that Adam Smith in *Wealth of Nations* I.iv.13 was the inventor of the classical value paradox (necessary goods like water are cheap and luxury goods like diamonds are very expensive) is wrong. Although Smith did not consult these works by early Christian authors, they do contain many passages that refer to this paradox.

4 Plato, *Laws* XI, 913 a–c; 914a–d, on property; *Laws* XI, 916d; 917a–d, on fraud; and *Laws* XI, 918b–c, on the necessity of having an efficient division of labor in a production process to benefit prosperity in a state.

5 É. Helmer, 'Platon et Aristote ou les pouvoirs politiques de la monnaie', in: *Revue du Mauss* 2015/2 (n° 46), 363–384.

Plato and Aristotle attempted to link economic transactions to the practice of virtue. Indeed, these classical philosophers emphasized that trade activity as such should sometimes be seen as a necessary evil: inferior even to cultivating land and the capture of land and goods from opponents. Retail trade in particular was associated with fraud, deceit and greed. This may have been due to the fact that in both Plato's and Aristotle's view, property and material goods were not seen as necessary preconditions for attaining a happy life. For Plato, and for the many early Christian thinkers who drew inspiration from his philosophy, the inconstancy and transience of matter implied that happiness did *not* to lie in those preconditions. Having said that, the acquisition of property and money was not always considered to be a 'bad' activity. Provided they were not gathered to excess or for their own sake, money and property were seen as necessary for an orderly and virtuous life. Money and material goods also enabled their owner to practice and hone virtues like moderation and generosity. Trade at a macro level, on the other hand, stood in high esteem as a way to allow city states to procure goods that would otherwise remain unavailable to their citizens.[6] Both at the level of personal life within the household (*oĩkos*) and the level of life in the city state (*polis*) the aforementioned virtues, along with justice and good understanding or judgment, were deemed indispensable for obtaining a healthy economy'. Anyone who practiced these virtues in their economic actions, so the ancient philosophers reasoned, contributed to a society in which at least no harm was done to others.

During this same period, Xenophon – like Plato a student of Socrates – reflected upon ruling (*nemein*) the household (*oĩkos*) and management of the forms of collaboration inherent to it.[7] The administration of moveable property and real estate that belonged to the 'extended family' was considered to be part of this household, as were childcare and managing the family's slaves. With or without help from bookkeepers or stewards, the pater familias acquitted himself of the task of securing an income and establishing and nurturing contacts that were economically relevant. All this in order to secure the continuity of his *oĩkos*. The idea that *oikonomia* was about managing collaboration can thus be traced back to Xenophon's work. In fact, his ideas amounted to a kind of 'science of collaboration', meant to generate wealth for a household or region, province or nation by making well-considered choices and collaborating constructively. Incidentally, the idea of a state economy, and of the *political economy* as a field

6 D.A. Irwin, *Against the Tide: An Intellectual History of Free Trade* (Princeton NY: Princeton University Press, 1996), 11–15.

7 Xenophon, *Oeconomicus* 4.2–3; 6.5–10.

of study, would not arise until much later, during the advent of the first nation states in post-medieval times.[8]

Xenophon's work paved the way for a whole genre, *peri oikonomias* ('about the economy'), in which systematic consideration was given to the essence of property and its acquisition, preservation and shared use. In addition to Xenophon's own three treatises on this subject, the Pythagoreans Bryson and Callicratides, the stoic Hierocles and the epicurean Philodemus of Gadara wrote treatises on the same subject matter. A further work in this genre, *Oeconomica*, has been attributed to Aristotle's student Theophrastus, while several fragments dealing with economic issues from the work of Dio of Prusa have survived. Aristotle's first book, *Politica*, became the most influential representative of this genre.[9]

The economic treatises of these authors differ as regards the attention they devote to various aspects. Callacratidas mainly writes about the conditions under which the continuity of a household is guaranteed, Aristotle writes about relations that can be interpreted as economic, Xenophon about balancing income and expenditure and how surpluses can be used to help the poor. Just like Aristotle, Philodemus talks about the ultimate goal of the economy: securing as much leisure time as possible, to enable free men to either lead an active social and political life or lead a life of contemplation in which they could reflect in the company of friends on the purpose of life and the essence of happiness, truth and beauty.[10] This leisure time (*otium*) was thought to be more essential than trading and working hours. *Neg-otium* was in fact little more than a negation of more essential activities.

The crucial books of the Jewish and Christian tradition treat less systematically with the issues that are now the remit of economics as a scientific discipline. All the same, both the Old and the New Testament articulate basic assumptions and principles that later became key subjects in economics. In Genesis 1, for example, the primeval condition of humankind just after its creation is described in terms of economic abundance. After all human beings are given possession of seed-bearing plants in order to supply themselves with food, although they find himself faced with the task to process the fruits of

8 For an overview of this development see: T. Hutchison, Before Adam Smith: *The Emergence of Political Economy*, 1662–1776. New York: Basil Blackwell, 1988.

9 J. Fitzgerald, 'Chapter 2: Early Greek economic thought', in: D. B. Hollander, Th. R. Blanton IV, J. T. Fitzgerald (eds.), *The Extramercantile Economies of Greek and Roman Cities. New Perspectives on the Economic History of Classical Antiquity* (London-New York: Routledge, 2019), 30–48 (*Routledge Monographs in Classical Studies*).

10 J. Hengstmengel, *De homo economicus. Een familiegeschiedenis* (Amsterdam: Boom Uitgevers 2020), 34–39.

nature (Gen. 1:29). After the Fall – a situation humans brought upon themselves through their desire to be both omnipotent and invulnerable – the situation in which humankind finds itself becomes significantly less paradisiacal. The first human beings are told that what the earth's surface offers them as food will only become theirs through heavy labor (Gen. 3: 17); 'By the sweat of your face will you earn your food, until you return to the ground, as you were taken from it' (Gen. 3:19, New Jerusalem Bible).

In the Old Testament, 'poverty' in the sense of the absence of consumption goods is seen as negative. Ideally it does not occur (Deut. 15:4). It is the king's duty to help the poor (Ps. 72: 12–13). Similarly, the tithe system, in which wine, grain and cattle carry a levy of ten percent, which is spent on aid to the Levites and the poor, was a form of poverty reduction (Lev. 27: 30; Deut.12: 6; 14: 22–29; 26:12). The effects of shortages of food, clothing and housing were seen as lamentable. Social disdain, isolation (Prov. 14:20; 19:7), the fear of being enslaved and the accompanying separation from one's children (Deut. 15: 16) are counted among its possible consequences. In the Old Testament, material wealth is seen in a more positive light: the wealth Abraham's herd brings him, for example, is seen as a blessing from God (Gen. 24: 35). Even the courage to invest and enjoy the affluence it brings are valued as positive traits. In the Book Ecclesiastes, on the other hand, we come across a successful man who very poignantly points out the relativity of wealth and of earthly existence (Eccl. 1: 1; 3: 22; 5: 17–18; 11: 1–6 and passim). Greed and infringement on private property are condemned in the Decalogue (Ex. 20:15; 20:17).

The same tenor concerning poverty and wealth can be observed in the New Testament. Poverty is unwanted, and in a call to his disciples to help combat it, Jesus identifies with those who need help in their material need: 'For I was hungry and you gave me something to eat ... I needed clothes and you clothed me ... whatever you did for one of the least of these brothers and sisters of mine, you did for me (Mat. 25: 35–40). The courage to make the most of one's talents –both a unit of account and a means of payment –is also praised by Jesus (Mat. 25: 14–30). The story of the wedding at Cana teaches us that the early Christian circles from which the gospel according to Matthew originates did not look down upon great wealth and prosperity. Nonetheless, halfway through his Sermon on the Mount, Jesus reflects upon the relativity of transient wealth when he points out that life entails more than just food and clothing, and that people should try to adopt the carefree attitude towards tomorrow that birds have, who do not store away things in barns=. (Mat 6: 23–35; Lk. 12: 22–34; cf. 1 Tim. 6: 17–19). For Paul in particular, greed is the root of all evil (1 Tim 6: 10; cf. 1 Kor. 5: 11). He strongly condemns infringing upon private property (Eph. 4: 28). But there is a paradox in Luke's view on money and property, one which he makes no attempt to resolve. Implicitly and explicitly his gospel suggests that wealth leads to isolation and that the capacity of the wealthy to see the needs of others and work for the restoration of social relations declines. (Lk. 5: 27–32; 6: 27–38; 7: 40–43; 7: 47; 16: 9; 16: 13; 16: 19–25; 19:1–10; 19:11–27. Their wealth means their morality is 'bounded': their capacity to make ethically responsible choices becomes impaired. People must free themselves from the pernicious influence of their possessions by giving it away to the poor (Lk 18:22). But in addition to Luke's view that money and property are obstacles on the way to the freedom and carefreeness that are characteristic of disciples of Christ, he presents money and property in various long stories as useful and necessary to put virtues such as mercy, confidence and forgiveness into practice. Wealthy characters such as the Samaritan and the prodigal son's father are portrayed as perfectly indifferent to their money and possessions (Lk 10:30–37; 14: 12–24; 15: 11–31) But at the same time, they use their wealth to 'bring the good news to the poor', in the words of Jesus' summary of his program in Lk 4:18, and to help mend family relations.[11]

As a final surprise, the books of both the Old and the New Testament contain several mentions of norms that seem to belong to a form of capitalism that simultaneously help form. In trade, properly calibrated scales and accurate weights have to be used (Lev. 19: 36; cf. Deut. 25: 13–16; Prov. 20: 10). The message that people deserve fair pay for their work is hammered home in several places (Lev. 19: 13; 1 Cor. 3: 8; 1 Tim. 5: 18; 2 Tess. 3: 10).[12]

To summarize: in spite of the absence in the Bible of any systematic writing on issues that are now current in economics as a scientific discipline, there are places in the Scriptures where principles are enunciated that would later become the subject of extensive economic study. The need principle, to name but one, is mirrored by the exhortation to supply the poor with basic necessities and pay workers without undue delay. An echo of the capability principle as later introduced by the economist Amartya Sen can be found in the urge not to restrict oneself to supplying the poor with food, which would prolong their dependency, but to support them in their self-improvement and enable them to build a free and dignified life.[13]

11 P. van Geest, 'The Fundamental Paradox in Luke's Perception of Money and Property', in: L.J.B. Lietaert Peerbolte, A. van Wieringen (eds), *On the road with Luke-Acts. Perspectives from biblical Texts and Early Christian Writings.* (Leiden: Brill, 2021), in press (*STAR*).

12 See also: J. Graafland, *Het oog van de naald. Over markt, geluk en solidariteit* (Kampen: Ten Have 2007), 88–94; 206–214; 216–229; 313–314; 319.

13 Cf. L. Bruni, *The Economy of Salvation. Ethical and Anthropological Foundations of the Market Relations in de First Two Books of the Bible.* Heidelberg: Springer Verlag, 2019 (*Virtues and Economics* 4); S.A. Wagner-Tsukamoto, *Is God an Economist? An Institutional*

### 1.1 *Excursus: An Attempt at Economic Exegesis*

There is a noticeable tendency in the works of economists like Amartya Sen and Luigino Bruni to mine scriptural passages for *incentives* for a type of economic interaction that takes values into account. In the story of the good Samaritan (Luke 10: 25–39), Bruni finds an *incentive* to enrich the 'market theory as a morally neutral zone' with a 'grammar of trust' for economic and business relationships.

Economically speaking, both the Samaritan and the innkeeper take a risk. They are both vulnerable to opportunist behavior on the part of their counterpart. On the other hand, true relations –which this famous parable advocates – tie the parties involved closer to each other's interests. In addition, non-exchangeability in relations has an intrinsic value for the partners. They have a mutual responsibility towards and significance for each other because from a certain point onwards, after the injured man has been given into the care of the innkeeper, they cannot simply be replaced by others. The contractual agreements thus made between the Samaritan and the innkeeper for the care for the injured person are therefore ideally based on trust. The Samaritan needs to have faith that the innkeeper will indeed spend the money received on his care for the injured victim, while the innkeeper has to trust that the money paid will actually cover the nursing costs. The innkeeper could opt to act opportunistically, as no agreements can be made that the innkeeper can be institutionally forced to hold.[14] Precisely because there is nothing in the parable that shows that the arrangements are fixed in detailed contracts, the conclusion of the 'economic exegesis' of the parable is that trust and generosity are important market virtues. At the same time, the mutual trust people express by binding themselves to each other is a token of appreciation. It gives people a sense of security and belonging. Usually within relationships, not only material services are exchanged and experienced, but also meaning and appreciation.[15] In fact, in an early allusion to economic classification made in 1975, the

*Economic Reconstruction of the Old Testament*. Basingstoke, UK- New York: Palgrave Macmillan, 2009.

14 L. Bruni, 'The Samaritan's Trust Game', in: *Journal of Economics, Theology and Religion* 1(2021), in press. See also L. Bruni, R. Sugden, 'Fraternity: why the market need not to be a morally free zone', in: *Economics and Philosophy* 24 (2008), no. 1, 35–64.

15 L. Bruni, L. Stanca, 'Watching Alone: Relational Goods, Television, and Happiness', in: *Journal of Economic Behavior and Organization* 65 (2008), 506–528; C. J. Uhlaner, 'Relational Goods and Participation: Incorporating Sociability into a Theory of Rational Action', in: *Public Choice* 62 (1989) no.3, 253–285; L. Bruni, *The Wound and the Blessing: Economics Relationships and Happiness*. New York: New City Press, 2012.

good Samaritan was characterized as a pragmatic, non-strategic altruist of a kind we as 'modern men' no longer recognize.[16]

This 'economic exegesis' of the story of the good Samaritan complements the existing 'theological' exegesis. After all, the latter prefers to stress the fact that of all people someone of a lower rank than the temple priest and Levite in the social hierarchy of the time in fact practices a higher and more valuable virtue than the priest and the Levite. In this story charity towards a fellow human being is in fact ranked above the virtue of fulfilling cultic or temple duty, a virtue that the priest and the Levite practice and which at the same time prevents them from seeking a higher good. In this way both the continuity and the discontinuity between Jesus and the Jewish tradition were elucidated. There was continuity in the sense that Jesus reminds the existing ranks and orders of their responsibility. And discontinuity in the sense that he puts their core competencies into perspective and values the lower-class person: he is the one who sets the ethically best-considered example, while the others painstakingly adhere to the laws on worship. There was also discontinuity in the sense that Jesus changes the order in which virtues are ranked in value. This concludes our first example of the way dialogue between economists and theologians can be mutually enriching.

## 2 Market and Morality in the Works of Church Fathers

In the more clearly 'economic' passages in their work, the first interpreters of the Scriptures, the Church Fathers, focused mainly on the pericopes from the gospel according to Matthew and Luke which point out the moral hazards of trade. [17] Irenaeus of Lyon, for example, does not hesitate to describe the later also much-quoted passage from Luke's gospel on the 'Mammon of injustice' – the hunger for money – (Luke 16:9; cf. Mat. 6:24) as abject, because it fuels the craving for money that hinders a person's relationship with God.[18] According to Tertullian, trade can be traced back directly to the vice of greed, and should therefore to be characterized as idolatry.[19]

16 J. Buchanan, 'The Samaritan's dilemma', in: E.S. Phelps (ed.), *Altruism, Morality and Economic Theory* (New York: Russel Sage Foundation, 1975), 71–85, quote 74.

17 See for instance Leviticus 19:35–36; Deuteronomy 25:13–16; Ezekiel 45:9–12; Hosea 12:7–8; Amos 8:4–6; Micah 6:10–11; Proverbs 11:1; 11:26; 16:11; 20:10, 14, 23.

18 Irenaeus, *Adversus Haereses* 4.30.1.

19 Tertullian, *De Idolatria* 11.

Augustine, on the other hand, did not qualify money used as a means of exchange and payment as intrinsically immoral. In the hands of good people, money is good because it allows them to practice charity, while it is bad in the hands of bad people because it arouses their greed, and thereby their isolation.[20] Nor does he exclude the possibility that virtuous traders will virtuously pay a fair price for goods and warn sellers who unwittingly sell below the price.[21] In his view, it is honorable to make profit in order to make a living.[22] On the other hand he recognizes that traders often commit fraud and perjury for the sake of trade, and lie about their merchandise.[23] It is clear that he judges the perverting of commercial transactions very severely from his unconditional statement that whoever commits fraud will be punished by God.[24] Stoically, he also stresses that they who lose themselves in *neg-otium* run the danger of overreliance on the results of their own labor and of a loss of the awareness that most things were given to them; and that there is not much that they did not receive.[25] In Augustine's view it is undesirable for people to think in an overly meritocratic vein. Moreover, the term *neg-otium* also implies the negation of the tranquility found in houses of prayer, a tranquility that is indispensable for human well-being. It was this realization, Augustine observes, that prompted Jesus to drive away the traders from the temple complex.[26] The so-called cleansing of the temple to which Augustine refers (cf. Mat. 21:12–17; Mk 11:15–19; Luke. 19:45–48; John 2:13–16) was the starting point for his criticism not just of tradespeople, but also of bishops, priests and deacons who were guilty of usury. Incidentally Jerome, too, is vehemently opposed to this practice.[27]

Early Christian views on overseas trade were subject to development. The Church Father and jurist Tertullian stated that the sea was not created to allow profit-seeking traders to sail to trading partners, to which Ambrose added that the sea was created to provide humankind with fish.[28] In the fourth and fifth century, however, a number of mainly Greek bishops began to regard over-

20 Augustine, *Sermo* 50, 3–5, 8 and passim.

21 Augustine, *De Trinitate* 13.3.

22 Augustine, *De opere monachorum*, passim.

23 Augustine, *sermo* 302.16: 'Oppressit me, cum essem negotiator. Tu ipsum negotium bene egisti? In ipso negotio fraudem non fecisti? In ipso negotio falsum non iurasti? Non dixisti?'

24 Augustine, *Enarratio in Psalmum* 33 2.14: '... non potest negotium esse sine fraude. Sed fraudem punit Deus. Time Deum"; *Enarratio in Psalmum* 70.1.17.

25 Augustine, *Enarratio in Psalmum* 70.1.18.

26 Augustine, *Enarratio in Psalmum* 70.1.15.

27 Augustine, *Tractatus in Euangelium Johannis* 10.4.

28 Tertullian, *De patientia* 7.12; Ambrose, *De Helia et Jejunio* 19.70–71.

seas trade as part of the God-given order because, in the spirit of Greek rhetor Libanius of Antioch, they saw this foreign trade as something that enhanced mutual dependency and connectedness between peoples and as a vehicle for the exchange of goods for which a trade partner had a greater need.[29] The conviction that God, in his design for the world, had provided for international trade as an activity that connected people and fostered a more even distribution of money and goods can also be found in many early Christian 'economic' texts.[30]

## 3 Economics as a Component of Theology in Scholasticism

Early medieval Europe witnessed the rise of an agrarian feudal society. In Flanders around 1300, for example, over 80 per cent of the population still lived in rural areas. Serfs were tied to the land of their feudal lord, whose task it was to protect then in times of war, in exchange for a fixed proportion of their harvest, labor or money. On the other hand, they were mobile in the sense that they could be moved by their lord or could try to 'free' themselves and leave his patronage. Under Charlemagne and his son Louis the Pious, monastic living according to the Rule of Saint Benedict spread far and wide across Europe. The large sums of money and real estate that the richer monasteries received from rulers and landowners who donated money or property during their lifetime or in their will, as a kind of insurance policy for their admission to heaven, meant that the feudal power of these monasteries rose. Abbeys that were

29 J. Hengstmengel, *De homo economicus. Een familiegeschiedenis* (Amsterdam: Boom Uitgevers 2020), 70–74, for evidence.

30 For a range of Scriptural proofs see Tomáš Sedláček, *De economie van goed en kwaad. De zoektocht naar economische zingeving van Gilgamesj tot Wall Street* (Schiedam: Scriptum, 2015), 160–206; for proof from patristic sources: J. Hengstmengel, 'Wealth-Poverty', in: D. Hunter, P. van Geest, B.J. Lietaert Peerbolte (eds), *Brill Encyclopedia of Early Christianity* (Leiden: Brill), in press; S.R. Holman (ed.), *Wealth and Poverty in Early Church and Society* (Grand Rapids: Baker Academic, 2008), passim (*Holy Cross Studies in Patristic Theology and History*); J.L. Gonzalez, *Faith and Wealth. A History of Early Christian Ideas on the Origin, Significance, and Use of Money*. San Francisco: Harper & Row, 1990; see also: A. Schüle, "Do not sell your soul for money"; economy and eschatology in biblical and intertestamental tradition', in: J. von Hagen, M. Welker (eds), *Money as God? The Monetization of the Market and its Impact on Religion, Politics, Law, and Ethics* (Cambridge: Cambridge University Press, 2016), 365–378; E. Lupieri, 'Businessmen and merchants will not enter the places of my Father', in: *ibidem*, 379–413; J. Hengstmengel, 'Trade', in: D. Hunter, P. van Geest, B.J. Lietaert Peerbolte (eds), *Brill Encyclopedia of Early Christianity* (Leiden: Brill), in press.

founded in the High Middle Ages in reaction to decadence within the church as offshoots of the poverty movement, like those of the Cistercians, gradually became powerful themselves. Agricultural methods and irrigation techniques were invented in both existing and new abbeys and technological innovations such as the mill, the wheel plow and the forge were introduced.[31]

In the ensuing period, the old Europe gradually changed from a feudal agrarian society into an urban capitalist society. From the moment the first hawker set up a stall on the market place goods like food and raw materials had begun to be brought in by farmers and traded at the city market. Cities grew in importance through their increasing wealth, which allowed their citizens to build imposing stone houses in the recently arrived Gothic style as well as facilities such as a weighing-house, covered meat markets and a Latin school in the heart of their cities. In Northern and Central Italy, where commodity markets and factor markets began to thrive for the first time, purchasing power is estimated to have been between 1000 and 1500 dollars per capita around the year 1300. Holland, the northwestern part of the Low Countries, saw the advent of thriving markets that help explain the increase of per capita gross domestic product to 1500 dollars around the year 1500.[32]

Benedictine monasteries, having amassed fortunes during the feudal era, funded or co-funded the building of a Gothic cathedral in many cities. At the same time, Gothic was the vehicle par excellence for the expression of the citizenry's self-confidence and the new social, institutional and economic order.[33] The guilds played a crucial part in this, both as a training ground for young craftsmen and as institutions that enforced standards of quality and offered their members social security.[34] Citizens who organized themselves into guilds were free men who were no longer at the service of a lord, and their cities gradually became home to political, economic and religious authorities too. In Western Europe, where the wool trade was booming, clothing, wood and arms

31 K. Schelkens, P. van Geest, J. van Gennip, *Het Katholicisme in Europa. Een geschiedenis* (Amsterdam: Boom, 2021. Second edition), 137–190.

32 B. van Bavel, *De onzichtbare hand. Hoe markteconomieën opkomen en neergaan* (Amsterdam: Prometheus, 2018), 145–183; 225–248 [transl. of *The Invisible Hand? How Market Economies Have Emerged and Declined Since AD 1500*. Oxford: Oxford University Press, 2016. The Dutch edition is an expanded version.

33 Cf. F. Braudel, *Beschaving, economie en kapitalisme (15de-18de eeuw)*. Amsterdam: Uitgeverij Contact, 1989. 2 vols. [transl.]. Vol 1: *De structuur van het dagelijks bestaan*, 471–498; vol. 2: *Het spel van de handel*, 19–211; A.E. Monroe, *Monetary Theory before Adam Smith* (Harvard: Harvard University Press; Reprint 2014), 14f (*Harvard Economic Studies* 25).

34 J. Lucassen, T. de Moor, J. Luiten van Zanten, 'The return of the guilds. Towards a global history of the guilds in pre-industrial times', in: *International Review of Social History* 53(2008), 5–18.

became the main export products to the Byzantine Empire. Within this changing society, religious orders that responded to evolving conditions within the church, such as the Franciscans and Dominicans, emerged as an offshoot of the European medieval reform and poverty movements that denounced the decadence that manifested itself among people of property. No longer tied to one particular monastery as the monks of the old orders were, they settled in the cities, where they set up universities. Thus, not only cities and guilds, but new religious orders similarly left a heavy imprint on the economy, religion and culture in the High and Late Middle Ages.

At the universities founded by priests, such as the one Robert de Sorbon founded in Paris, theology became the queen and mother of all sciences. Theologians at the time were familiar with the word 'economy' mainly through its use as the word for 'domestic science' by Xenophon and Aristotle. Together with philosophers and jurists, theologians were the scholars to whom it fell to discuss the sweeping consequences of the transition from a feudal agrarian society to an urban capitalist one for trade, interest and market mechanisms.[35] Having said that, it was never much at the forefront of their attention. Their handbooks were mainly concerned with the essence and actions of the Trinitarian God. The economic themes just mentioned were dealt with briefly in those parts of their works that discussed the remission of sins.[36] At the university of Paris, a hub of theological scholarship in medieval times, economic questions appeared as part of philosophical and theological commentaries on the integral translation of Aristotle's *ethica* and *politica* that had by then been published in the Latin-speaking western world. The commentaries by St. Albert the Great, Henry of Ghent and Albert's student Thomas Aquinas were particularly important in introducing the economic principles articulated by Aristotle into scholastic theology.[37]

Thomas Aquinas is generally seen as the architect of 'scholastic economics'. Economic questions are addressed in those places in his *Summa Theologiae* and *Summa contra gentiles* where he explains justice within the framework of the natural order that is inherent in creation. In Thomas's view, the common good (*bonum commune*) was the central concern because, within this natural order, human beings are first and foremost seen as social creatures, who are

35 Cf. O. Langholm, *Economics in the Medieval Schools: Wealth, Exchange, Value, Money and Usury according to the Paris Theological Tradition, 1200–1350* (Leiden: Brill, 1992), 8.

36 Cf. O. Langholm, *Economics in the Medieval Schools*, passim and O. Langholm, *The Legacy of Scholasticism in Economic Thought: Antecedents of Choice and Power*. Cambridge: Cambridge University Press, 1998.

37 Langholm, *The Legacy of Scholasticism*, 27, 198–274 (Thomas).

capable of conceiving valid universals about reality and therefore of assigning a 'natural' value to any given good.[38] The value that is thus assigned must be ethically justifiable. Economic interactions therefore, as human interactions, cannot be seen in separation from ethics. Virtues are just as important to business as they are to every other sphere of human conduct.[39] Thomas therefore levels fundamental criticism at the behavior of those who focus too strongly on the realization of their personal, material well-being, and in not a few cases his comments relate to what we would now call economic actions.[40] He warns his readers against an all-too dependent attitude towards traders. He emphasizes that acquiring and fostering personal property is inherent to human nature, and therefore inherent to the social order that is attuned to it. A society becomes more well-ordered if each person is responsible for their own property and satisfied with what is theirs.[41] With regard to transactions, finally, Thomas focuses mainly on their justice, and much less so on the consequences for market processes or their efficiency.[42] He frowns upon the charging of interest on loans because he feels that in doing so people are not asking money for a service, but for something that is no longer theirs.[43] This claim attracted criticism. If everybody were to forego interest on loans, no one would offer this service to the economy and society any longer because the risk that the money would be lost still existed. It remained a desideratum to differentiate between interest and usury. It has been pointed out that the meaning of the word 'usura' is context-dependent in the work of Clement of Alexandria, Ambrose and Augustine, or Robert de Courçon, Thomas of Aquino, Hincmar of Rheims or Raymond of Penyafort, and is often much more nuanced than later interpreters were prepared to admit in their eagerness to substantiate

38 Cf. C. Dierksmeier, 'Scholastic Business Ethics: Thomas Aquinas Versus William of Ockham', in: C. Lütge (ed.), *Handbook of the Philosophical Foundations and Business Ethics* (Dordrecht - New York: Springer, 2013), 159–178.

39 C. Dierksmeier, 'Thomas von Aquin über Gerechtigkeit als globale Wirtschaftstugend', in: R. Schönberger (eds), *Die Bestimmung des Menschen und die Bedeutung des Staates. Beiträge zum Staatsverständnis des Thomas von Aquin* (Baden: Nomos, 2017), 195–226 (*Staatsverständnisse* 103).

40 Thomas Aquinas, *Summa Theologiae*, II-II, Q. 183, A 2.

41 Thomas Aquinas, *Summa Theologiae* II-II Q 66, A 1(S Th II-II Q 66, A 2 (necessary for human life).

42 Thomas Aquinas, *Summa Theologiae* II-II, Q 77 A1 – A2. See also D. Koehn, B. Wilbratte, 'A Defense of a Thomistic Concept of the Just Price', in: *Business Ethics Quarterly* 22(3), 501–526.

43 Thomas Aquinas, *Summa Theologiae* II-II, Q 78 A1; *Summa Theologiae* II-II, Q. 78 A 4.

the theoretical foundation of the medieval ban on usury.[44] Be that as it may, Thomas's misgivings about interest that borders on usury cannot be explained away. However, in his *History of Economic Analysis* Schumpeter writes:

> 'St. Thomas ... was indeed interested in political sociology, but all the economic questions put together mattered less to him than did the smallest point of theological or philosophical doctrine, and it is only where economic phenomena raise questions of moral theology that he touches upon them at all'.[45]

Schumpeter's observation is right on the mark. It is therefore only logical that fundamental criticisms continue to be made on the basis of Thomas's *Summa* of the ethical shortcomings of capitalism, utilitarianism and the rational choice model. From Thomas's view of the good life, the rational choice model in particular is an obstacle to the pursuit of happiness because it ignores many aspects of human life that are equally relevant. [46] This conviction will be substantiated further in various ways later in this book.

Thomas was not alone in his wish to interpret economic interactions strictly within a virtue framework. The Franciscan John Duns Scotus (1266–1308), for example, stated in his *Ordinatio* that voluntary transactions contain an element of charity because they include the following tenet of natural law: 'treat people the same way you want them to treat you.'[47] During this period of Scholasticism, the Dominican Giles of Lessines (1235–1304) and the Franciscan Richard of Middleton (1249–1308) similarly sought to promote justice in trade.[48] Bishop Nicole Oresme and the priest Gabriel Biel also devoted treatises to the

44 G. Todeschini, 'Usury in Christian Middle Ages. A Reconsideration of the Historiographical Tradition (1949–2010)', in: F. Ammannati (ed), *Religione e istituzioni religiose nell' economia Europea. 1000–1800 - Religion and Religious Institutions in the European Economy. 1000–1800. Atti della Quarantaquattresima Settimana di Studi 8–12 maggio 2011* (Firenze: Firenze University Press, 2012), 119–130.

45 J. Schumpeter, *History of Economic Analysis*, 90.

46 M. Hirschfeld, *Aquinas and the Market. Towards a Humane Economy* (Harvard: Harvard University Press, 2018), 34–65 and passim.

47 John Duns Scotus, *Opus Oxoniense* IV.15.2.15 (cf. Odonis, *De contractibus* 3; Johannes Nider, *De contractibus mercatorum* IV; Bernardinus of Siena, *Sermones* XXXV.1.2; Antoninus van Florence, *Summa theologiae* II.1.16.3).

48 Giles of Lessines, *De usuris in communi et de usuram contractibus* IX en III; Richard of Middleton (Richardus de Mediavilla), *Commentum super quarto Sententiarum Petri Lombardi* III.33.3.4.

use and power of money and to fraud committed with money as a means of payment. Their work will be discussed in greater detail elsewhere in this book.

O. Langholm has given a summary of the various strands of thinking about wealth, trade, money and interest within the different schools in the Parisian theological tradition of the Franciscans and the Dominicans, and of the way they were interconnected. In their interpretation of economic processes as part of their portrayal of a God-oriented society, some of these thinkers were driven by idealism, others by realism.[49] But no matter how rich and varied the views on interest presented in William of Auxerre's *Summa* or Alexander of Hales' *Summa*, in Bernard of Auvergne's *quodlibeta*, the *libri confessionales*, Lessines' economic work or Remigius of Florence's or John of Naples' commentaries on Thomas, no matter how richly layered the image they sketched of the relationship between private property which they deemed to be necessary for all and the accumulation of wealth by a few, all these authors regarded private property and a certain measure of wealth as the necessary material foundation for a good and virtuous life.[50] They all deemed justice to be the essential starting point as well as the goal of the production, distribution and consumption of goods. In addition, their reflections on the economy were invariably linked to personal choices in which justice as a *conditio sine qua non* and good will towards others were regarded as self-evident. They certainly did not see the economy as a system of supra-personal mechanisms in which personal motives were irrelevant.[51] On the other hand, the individualistic view on the economy was based upon the implicit assumption that human beings should assess themselves particularly within the perspective of a wider social association. A final striking characteristic of these authors was their occasionally ambivalent attitude towards wealth. The Franciscans, themselves heirs of the poverty movements that had denounced the excessive wealth within the church, pointed to the dangers of excessive wealth as an obstacle to the practice of virtue. At the same time, they were very much aware that their chosen poverty meant that they were taking bread out of the mouths of people who were involuntarily poor and that they were thus disrupting the economy.[52]

49 Langholm, *The Legacy of Scholasticism*, 565.

50 Langholm, *The Legacy of Scholasticism*, 572–573; 586–588, 591. Cf. ook J. T. Noonan, *The Scholastic Analysis of Usury* (Cambridge, Ma: Harvard University Press, 1957), 82–99 (just price), 249–268; 340–364 (interest).

51 Langholm, *The Legacy of Scholasticism*, 568–573; 595.

52 Langholm, *The Legacy of Scholasticism*, 567.

## 4 Market, Morality and Anthropology during the Reformation and Counter Reformation

Even when other departments at European universities were becoming increasingly prominent, when it came to economics, the theologians' views remained influential. This was partly due to the fact that theologians concerned themselves a great deal with issues like the organization of public administration and public finance, and John Calvin is a prime example of this.[53] Calvin explicitly addressed property and human relationships in the light of the sovereignty of God as the proprietor of the earth and master of all that lives and moves upon it.[54] To him, this meant that no individual could claim anything as their absolute property. In this way he also substantiated his view that people are not born for themselves, not even as economic beings. By extension, therefore, he saw justice not as a virtue that had to be briefly recalled when contracts were being signed.[55] The *habitus* of the contracting parties –their inner constitution and attitude to life –had to be marked by this justice at all times. The conviction that God is sovereign and that the earth belongs to Him enables them to enter into a deal in which self-interest is far from being the dominant consideration.

Calvin clarified this *habitus* in his discussion of the issue of interest. In doing so he broke away from the age-old church tradition based upon Exodus 22:25, Leviticus. 25:35–38 and Deuteronomy 23: 19–20 of a ban on interest, as articulated most succinctly and comprehensively by Thomas Aquino. Calvin's break with the customary view on interest was mainly driven by his deep social and socio-economic consciousness. In his day the closed economy, in which products were meant for local consumption only like in feudal agrarian times, had come to an end. As the demand for products and goods grown or produced outside the local region increased, the need to invest in transportation grew. It was precisely because Geneva, Calvin's city of residence, was evolving into a transportation hub that he became acutely aware that the evolution from a closed economy into an open economy would require novel ways of financing. The need for banks and investors grew.[56] Convinced that it was unfair to refus-

53 Cf. C. van der Kooi, 'Protestant thinking on markets, morality and money: Calvin, Kuyper, and the Ecumenical Movement', in press.

54 John Calvin, *Responsio ad Sadoleti epistulam* (1539), in: *Ioannis Calvini Opera Selecta* (ed. P. Barth). Vol. I (München: Kaiser Verlag, 1926), 463.

55 G. H. Haas, *The Concept of Equity in Calvin's Ethics* (Waterloo, Ontario: Wilfrid Laurier UP, 1997), 2; A. Biéler, *Calvin's Economic and Social Thought* (Geneva: World Alliance of Reformed Churches, World Council of Churches, 2005), 139–179.

56 Biéler, *Calvin's Economic and Social Thought*, 145.

ing to compensate the risk-taking investor, Calvin refined his view on interest.[57] Usury, however, remained strictly forbidden.[58] In Calvin's view, economic relations were first and foremost social relations that should be marked by love and fairness. He even believed the state should set the preconditions for this. This idea was taken up by later reformers.[59] Incidentally, a loving and fair relationship for Calvin was connected to the human capacity to open up to God as a loving Father instead of a vengeful God.[60]

Late scholastic Thomism began to thrive during the Counter Reformation. In his commentary on Thomas Aquinas's *Summa*, Cardinal Thomas Cajetan, the principal theologian of this movement, saw the growth of personal wealth as a favorable consequence of a person's rise on the social ladder. Unlike Thomas Aquinas, who was more radical than his interpreter and who pointed out that possessions could encourage the vice of greed, Cajetan denounced neither growing prestige nor the accumulation of property. In an attempt to make business loans acceptable, Cajetan differentiated between business loans and loans to consumers. Once again unlike Thomas, but like Calvin, he argued that interest was acceptable. But Cajetan's approval of charging interest was criticized in the similarly Thomistic-scholastic school of Salamanca by Domingo de Soto, who referred to a passage from Luke's gospel 6: 35.[61] In Luke's rendition, Jesus explicitly says, 'But love your enemies, do good to them, and lend to them without expecting to get anything back. Then your reward will be great, and you will be children of the Most High, because he is kind to the ungrateful and wicked.'

Incidentally, Cajetan did not reduce value to existing demand and supply, but to market expectations. Thus, this eminent theologian became the founding father of the economic *expectations theory*.[62] More influential than the wish to clarify expectations, however, was the intention of scholastic economists to

57 Biéler, *Calvin's Economic and Social Thought*, 139–179; C. van der Kooi, 'Calvin and the Ban on Usury', in: M. Wijlens, V. Shmaliy, S. Sinn (eds), *Churches and Moral Discernment.* Vol 2: *Learning from History* (Geneva: WCC, 2021), 40–49 (*Faith and Order Paper* 229).

58 John Calvin, *Commentaries* 3, 131. Cf. L. Schulze, *Calvin and "social ethics": his views on property, interest and usury.* Pretoria: Kital, 1985.

59 Cf. Bieler, *Calvin's Economic and Social Thought*, 421.

60 C. van der Kooi, *As in a Mirror. John Calvin and Karl Barth on Knowing God. A Dyptich*, (Leiden-Boston: Brill, 2005), 136–138; J. Blosser, 'Christian Freedom in Political Economy. The Legacy of John Calvin in the thought of Adam Smith', in: P. Oslington (ed.), *Adam Smith as Theologian* (New York-London: Routledge, 2011), 46–60.

61 See for the late Spanish scholastic theologians for instance: M. N. Rothbarth, *Economic Thought before Adam Smith. An Austrian Perspective on the History of Economic Thought* (Auburn, Alabama: Ludwig von Mises Institute, s.a.), 99–133.

62 Hengstmengel, *De homo economicus. Een familiegeschiedenis*, 100–101.

treat market relations as personal relations that are morally justified because they are governed first and foremost by the virtues of charity and justice. In addition, scholastic economists stressed the importance of awareness of personal motives in economic relations as a way to prevent people from hiding behind the idea of an impersonal market. Finally, in their view of the interaction between human behavior and the creation of a just society, they conceived of merchants' sense of duty towards the community as a whole as a crucial factor.[63] Whatever the changes in trade practices and in views on money that occurred in the five centuries during which the scholastic economists since Thomas Aquinas, and regardless of the extent to which they took account of this in their economic thinking– even to the point of changing their view on interest–[64] they stayed true to these principles. They are a textbook case of how theological insights determined economic views, rather than the other way round. We will limit ourselves in the following to a single example of this.

A late member of the Salamanca school, Domingo de Bañez (†1604), argued in the spirit of the later Augustine that humans were incapable of doing anything good, or even aspiring to anything good until God bestowed his grace upon them. Bañez's view was shared by the Leuven professors Michael Baius (†1589) and Cornelius Jansenius (†1638), who were equally somber when it came to the situation of humankind after the Fall and the necessity of God's grace. In his *Concordia liberi arbitrii cum gratiæ donis* (1588) the Jesuit Luis de Molina (†1600) was more optimistic. Although he was censored by Bañez, he took courage from the early works of Augustine, in which this Church Father, still in the early stages of his thinking about free will, contended that people themselves are able to muster the strength to aspire to do good and then to do it. Considering his theological principles, it is self-evident that Molina would disapprove of governments setting exchange rates and official prices for agrarian goods. He would rather see them determined by the dynamics of supply and demand, on the assumption that people, using their free will and common sense, would make balanced decisions on these matters.[65] The Jansenists, who were named after Jansenius, with the Augustinian Pierre Nicole (1695) and Jean Domat as prime examples, criticized his optimism, although they were not explicitly reacting to Molina. They pointed to the many sins related to usury

63 W. Decock, 'Lessius and the Breakdown of the Scholastic Paradigm', in: *Journal of the History of Economic Thought* 31(2009), vol.1, 57–78.

64 F. Monsalve, 'Late Spanish Doctors on Usury, and the Evolving Scholastic Tradition', in: *Journal of the History of Economic Thought* 36 (2014), Number 2, 215–235.

65 For price controls by the state see: Hengstmengel, *De homo economicus. Een familiegeschiedenis*, 113–114.

and interest in the Catholic tradition. They regarded these as grounds to view self-love as a poison to society, but paradoxically also as a remedy for society.[66] In addition they thought God uses this self-love, often hiding under the cloak of the virtue of charity, to create something good and orderly at the level of society.[67] It was no great leap to move from this idea to Bernard Mandeville's (1670–1733) observation that vice can benefit the well-being of society.

Incidentally, variations on Nicole's and Domat's theories can be found in the works of the priest-economists Ferdinando Galiani (†1787) and Antonio Genovesi (†1767). In his five-part *Della moneta* (On Money) Galiani stated that it is thanks to God's *suprema mano* ('upper, sovereign hand') that people's selfish, relentless and 'filthy' pursuit of profit nevertheless does not lead to chaos, and that market equilibrium, just relationships and happiness are not jeopardized. He was guided first and foremost by the spirit of the times that left its mark on the theology of his days. During the sixteenth and seventeenth century, God's providence in particular had been transformed into a more abstract and impersonal causality, which naturally moved the focus away from the human freedom.[68]

In his *Lezioni di commercio o sia d'economia civile* (1765) – the first treatise on the Italian national economy –Genovesi argues that self-love (*amor proprio*) should in fact go hand in hand with acquiring the virtues that serve the common good. In his view, personal happiness is fundamentally linked to the happiness of others. Self-love can therefore only be linked to *l'amor della spezia*: love for the species, even in economic relations. Although Genovesi, in the spirit of Nicole, Domat and later Mandeville, accepted that a vice like greed could indeed lead to great and good things – for instance the foundation of a hospital even if the donor's primary goal is to gain prestige– he places a different emphasis. For him, the market is a place where the self-interest that is the initial motive is ultimately joined by an attitude to life marked by virtues like trust, helpfulness and friendship resonate.[69]

66 D. Gilles, 'Le remède et le venin, « Vrai mal dont Dieu tire de bons effets » Prohibition de l'usure et valorisation de l'intérêt à Port-Royal', in: L. Brunori, S. Dauchy, O. Descamps, X. Prévost (eds), *Le Droit face à l'économie sans travail*. Vol. 2: *L'approche internationale* (Paris: Classiques Garnier, 2020), 107–133 (*History of Law* 7).

67 Gilles, 'Le remède et le venin', 127.

68 D. Fergusson, *The Providence of God: A Polyphonic Approach*. (Cambridge: Cambridge University Press, 2018), 110–133 (*Current Issues in Theology* 11); J. Hengstmengel, *Divine Providence in Early Modern Economic Thought*. London: Routledge, 2019.

69 Cf. M. L. Perna, 'Genovesi Antonio', in: M. Caravale (ed.), *Dizionario biografico degli italiani* (Catanzaro, 2000). Vol. 53, 148–149.

It should be clear by now that Galiani in particular, as an economist-theologian, still looked to theologoumena like God's providence, expressed anthropomorphically in the phrase 'God's hand'. More so than was the case with his predecessors, Galiani's views on the economy were rooted in the theology of his day. What did not change was that theologians continued their search for an intrinsic relationship between morality and the market, driven by a belief that each and every human person had been created in God's image and likeness (Gen. 1: 26–28). Because of the intrinsic dignity of every person that was thus guaranteed, the pursuit of justice and charity be more important in economic relations than the pursuit of wealth from pure and insatiable greed and that was detrimental to others. The latter devalues this same intrinsic dignity of every human being: the truth that is born and created into people without exception and regardless of any achievement or standing.

## 5 How God Disappeared from the Economy

The times when philosophers and theologians pointed to vices like greed and virtues such as temperance as benchmarks for evaluating the morality and utility of certain economic developments or actions are gone, as are the days when all branches of science culminated in theology. A number of factors can explain this.

First of all, economic transactions and relations in early modernity were no longer, as they had been in Scholastic times, subjected to a value judgment on the basis that human beings would have to justify themselves *coram Deo*, before God. As early as the Renaissance, humanists like Pico della Mirandola (†1494) placed the human being at the core of their description of creation and the world, instead of God as the Creator and Organizer of all things and all creatures in space and time. Human freedom, reason and desire to comprehend God, the world and humankind became the crucial subjects. In his *Oratio de hominis dignitate* ('Oration on the Dignity of Man') Della Mirandola posited that human beings had been destined by God to be the shapers and creators of their own lives.[70] And Desiderius Erasmus (†1536), although he saw human freedom as a gift from God and as something that is sustained in a life led in accordance with the gospel, considered liberation from religious authorities as inherent to a Christian humanism which would protect the freedom and

70 Pico della Mirandola, *Rede over de menselijke waardigheid*. Vertaald en van aantekeningen voorzien door Michiel Op de Coul, met een inleiding en nawoord van Jan Papy (Groningen: Historische Uitgeverij, 2008), 48–51 (*Filosofie & Retorica* 2).

autonomy of the individual. A short time later the jurist and theologian Hugo Grotius (†1645) argued that it was necessary to design a view of society and a legal system *etsi Deus non daretur* (as if God did not exist). No longer was everything within the scientific and broader world interpreted as if it all rested upon God, and no longer were all things and all creatures traced back to God as the ultimate goal.

Secondly, the change of perspective in scientific and social thinking that occurred from the sixteenth century onward led to the marginalization of theology, because it came to be seen as naïve to appeal to a dogmatic tradition of revelation. God was increasingly discussed in deistic terms: philosophers of the Enlightenment such as Locke (†1704), Hume (†1776), Newton (†1727), Voltaire (†1778) and Rousseau (†1778) assumed there was a Godhead who had started the universe but who subsequently no longer interfered with the process of the laws of nature. God became *le Dieu horloger*, who made his watch, that is, Creation, so that it would work independently. Thus, Locke's compatriot Isaac Newton (1642–1727), himself a devout Christian, contended that the laws of physical reality could be discovered without resorting to religious premises: *etsi Deus non daretur* in a second sense.

The idea that humankind could plumb the depths of creation without leaning on Christian dogmas was nothing less than revolutionary.[71] It also constituted a serious challenge for theology. Step by step, God vanished from scientific hypotheses and thereby also from the economy (and economics): *etsi Deus non daretur* in a third sense. At universities across Europe theology was moving ever closer to the margins of the academy.

There was also a third reason. The need to take account of the common good was felt less strongly in economic thinking than during the heyday of Scholasticism, when guilds tried to guarantee a good standard of living for their members and offer them social security. Particularly in the mercantilist era, which began in the early sixteenth century, there were merchants who put their own gain before the common good of the society to which they belonged. Following naturally from the Renaissance outlook on humankind, some mercantilists even assumed that human nature was guided by self-interest in everything human beings did, not just in economic transactions. This growing economic individualism was increasingly seen as a positive drive, in part, incidentally, because it could lead to economic gain for a larger number of people. Even though mercantilism never completely ignored the respecting other people's interest, in fact, mercantilists, influenced by scholastic thinking

71 K. Schelkens, P. van Geest, J. van Gennip, *Het Katholicisme in Europa. Een geschiedenis* (Amsterdam: Boom, 2021. Second edition), 269–270.

about economic relations, portrayed merchants who focused on their own individual interest positively and approvingly. Gradually mercantilism pushed economic thinking and behavior in an unmistakably amoral direction. The exercise of virtues and economic actions were no longer seen as related issues. One consequence was that the role of normative theologians became ever more marginal. So marginal even, that anyone who searches the catalog of the library – or *E-learning center* – of Erasmus University Rotterdam today looking for theology will do so in vain.[72] God has not only vanished from the economy, but also from the university library.

72 Thanks to the mediation of J. Jüngen, the librarian of Rotterdam University Library, the EUR's theological collection was donated to the Tilburg School of Catholic Theology at Tilburg University in 2015.. Cf. J. Jüngen, 'UB wordt E-learning center: de eurolib-projecten van de UB-EUR', in: *Informatie professional* 7(2003), no. 10, 18–23.

CHAPTER 3

# Theology as a Coldshouldered Participant in Economic Discussion

## 1 Preamble: Religion and Economy or Theology and Economy?

We can conclude on the basis of the previous chapter that the relationship between economics and theology as scientific disciplines in history has rarely been the object of serious scholarship. The simple reason is that there was no need for this. Up until the Enlightenment, there was no autonomous discipline of economics, and when economics and theology went their separate ways, no effort was understandably made think about why interdisciplinarity between the two fields might be desirable. The relationship between theology and economics finally began to be investigated in the early twentieth century, albeit almost always as part of studies of how religion influenced individual and collective economic behavior.

One of the most widely discussed works in this genre was written by the founder of modern sociology, Max Weber. The first edition of his *Die protestantische Ethik und der Geist des Kapitalismus* was first published in 1905. Weber argued that Luther's idea that people are not just called to pray for mercy and hope for the best, but also have to establish a certain degree of dignity through their daily labor itself, strongly influenced the work ethic of what later became Protestantism.[1] In the famous thesis that bears his name, Weber did not therefore argue that Calvinism had stood at the origins of capitalism,[2] which would have been a misconstruction anyway. In the previous chapter we have seen that the transition from an agrarian-feudal to an urban capitalist society had already been completed before Pope Leo X excommunicated Martin Luther in 1521. Research of the key indicators of economic growth for 272 cities in the German territories of the Holy Roman Empire between 1300 and 1900 also showed that

1 M. Weber, *The Protestant Ethic and the Spirit of Capitalism* (London: Unwin University Books, 1930), 40–44 (First German edition *Die protestantische Ethik und der Geist des Kapitalismus* (*Archiv für Sozialwissenschaft und Sozialpolitik* 20 (1904) and 21 (1905).

2 Economic historians criticized Weber's study for its lack of source documentation and pointed out that capitalism originated centuries before the Reformation. Cf. R. Stark, *The Victory of Reason: How Christianity Led to Freedom, Capitalism, and Western Succes* (New York, 2005), xii. But Weber was aware of this, see Stark, *The Victory of Reason*, xxxiii.

 | DOI:10.1163/9789004501706_004

the Weber thesis can not be upheld.[3] In addition, it was recently established that scholars such as, for example, the influential Jesuit and Leuven professor Leonardus Lessius (+1633), contributed to the sanctioning of a capitalist economy, although he didn't write books that defended or denounced capitalism. There is 'evidence for the thesis that the spirit of commercial capitalism may have been fostered by Catholic theologians rather than by Reformers'.[4] Weber was convinced, however, that the puritan form of Calvinism facilitated a more modern form of capitalism. This form of capitalism focused to a greater degree than its predecessors on the rational use of capital and other production factors. For Weber, the new capitalism ushered in by Calvinism implied the rationalization and institutionalization of profit making based on exact calculations and a more transparent way of bookkeeping.[5]

Weber thus largely explained the emergence of this new form of capitalism from people's ability to develop behavior that is both practical and rational. He saw ascetic Protestantism as the main source of this behavior, because the attitude to life that it inspired was supposedly characterized by capacity for hard work, determination to stick to one's word, and temperance. This ascetism in turn helped safeguard the continuity of enterprises.[6] Protestant temperance and frugality, together with the willingness of entrepreneurs and employees to work harder than was strictly necessary for their subsistence, meant that money earned could be reinvested in the business. This was what turned a business into a success. Although Weber regarded the reluctance to enjoy accumulated wealth as a puritanical trait, economic success was regarded in Protestantism as a form of election.[7] This is why Weber regarded it as plausible that Protestant asceticism had fashioned a new economic-capitalist order.

R.H. Tawney, in his *Religion and the Rise of Capitalism*, another classic study of the influence of religion on social and economic practices, pointed out that both the capitalist spirit and the Protestant ethic were actually more complex than Weber had assumed.[8] Much later, D. McCloskey argued that the version of

3 D. Cantoni, 'The Economic Effects of the Protestant Reformation: Testing the Weber Hypothesis in the German Lands' [Job Market Paper] https://web.archive.org/web/20121119001845/http://www.people.fas.harvard.edu/~cantoni/cantoni_jmp_2_7_1.pdf

4 W. Decock, 'The Catholic Spirit of Capitalism? Contrasting Views on Profit-Making through Capital Investment in the Age of Reformations', in: W. Decock, J. Ballor, M. Germann, L. Waelkens (eds), *Law and Religion: The Legal Teachings of the Protestant and Catholic Reformation* (Göttingen: Vandenhoeck und Ruprecht, 2014), 22–44, quotation: 42.

5 Weber, *The Protestant Ethic*, xxxvi.

6 Weber, *The Protestant Ethic*, xxxix.

7 Weber, *The Protestant Ethic*, 111.

8 R. Tawney, *Religion and the Rise of Capitalism. A Historical Study* (Peter Smith; Reprint Edition 1962), 317.

capitalism that Weber had studied to support his thesis was not representative of the capitalism of the era he described.[9] Be that as it may, both Weber's work and that of his critics had a limited starting point and aim: they were all hoping to explain trade on the basis of religious or ethical motives. Max Weber's thesis on the interplay between puritan Calvinism and modern capitalism was the most specific elaboration of the idea that religion and economic behavior are closely connected.

The relationship between the economy, and specifically capitalism, and religion was subsequently approached from a different point of view. Thus, Walter Benjamin suggested that capitalism had been able to replace religion because it dispelled the same worries, fear and anxiety that religion had previously allayed.[10] Inner peace was now purchased through insurance policies rather than indulgences. And the Russian priest Pavel Florensky pointed to the similarities between religion and the economy, albeit with the proviso that the language of economics is ill-suited to describe God, beholden as it is to the concept of return on investment, a decidedly non-divine principle.[11]

Weber's book in particular marked the start of a deluge of studies of the interaction between religion and the economy, which has been ably surveyed by Oslington, Williams and Hirschfeld.[12] The criticisms that Weber's study of the relationship between Protestantism and capitalism attracted inspired research of the influence of religion on economic behavior and economic developments (1).[13] Thus, Bateman and Banzhaf observed on the basis of Durkheim's and Weber's theory of secularization that the secularization of the economy in highly developed societies, in which social institutions have a marginalizing effect on the role of religion and its institutions, certainly did

9 D. McCloskey, *Bourgeois Equality: How Ideas, Not Capital or Institutions, Enriched the World* (Chicago: The University of Chicago Press, 2016), xiv.

10 W. Benjamin, '*Fragment* 74, "*Kapitalismus als Religion*", in: W. Benjamin, *Gesammelte Schriften*. Ed. R. Tiedmann, H. Schweppenhäuser (Frankfurt am Main: Suhrkamp Verlag, 1991), 100–103.

11 P. Florensky, *Early Christian Writings 1903–1909*. Transl. B. Jakim. Grand Rapids: Eerdmans, 2017.

12 P. Oslington, P.S. Williams, M. Hirschfeld, 'Introduction. Recent Developments in Economics and Religion', in: P. Oslington, P.S. Williams, M. Hirschfeld (eds), *Recent Developments in Economics and Religion* (Cheltenham: Edward Elgar Publishing, 2018), 1–23 (*The international Library of Critical Writings in Economic Series* 341), divides historiography into the following parts: historical relationships; religious economics and its critics (including church teaching on economics); religion, capitalism and development; economics of religion; economics and Biblical studies. See also A.C.M. Waterman, 'On Economics, Theology, and Religion', in: *Journal of Economics, Theology and Religion* 1 (2021), no. 1, in press.

13 Cf. M.L. Stackhouse, 'Weber, Theology and Economics', in: P. Oslington (ed.), *Oxford Handbook of Christianity and Economics* (Oxford: OUP, 2014), 107–336.

not mean that these societies developed strictly secular economies from the nineteenth to the mid-twentieth century. Historians have rediscovered the importance of religion in the history of the modern economy.[14] And although the definition of 'religion' was never unambiguous, research focused on parallels between the economy and religion (2) as they manifested themselves in their institutional forms.[15] Many studies have been dedicated to the way in which (3) religion, specifically theological themes, influenced economic theory formation. One consistent subject in the field has been the question how Adam Smith's economics relate to his moral philosophy and theology. There is no unanimity as to the answer.[16] J. Everett's book on the impact of religious assumptions in the work of John Bates Clark, Richard T. Ely, Simon N. Patton may serve as an early example of this kind of research.[17]

Initially, the focus was primarily on the influence of Christianity on economic behavior and economic theory formation. More recently, however, (4) substantial studies have appeared of the impact of ideas from Judaism, Buddhism, Hinduism and Islam on the economy and on economic thought.[18] Research of the 'Islamic economy', Islamic banking, monetary policy, debt financing and fiscal policy has shed light on the tension between rationality,

---

14 H.G. Brennan, A.M.C. Waterman, 'Introduction', in: H.G. Brennan, A.M.C. Waterman (eds), *Economics and Religion: Are They Distinct?* (Boston: Kluwer, 1994), 3–15; L. Bruni, S. Zamagni, *Civil Economy: Efficiency, Equity, Public Happiness*. Bern: Peter Lang, 2007; B.W. Bateman, H. S. Banzhaf (eds). *Keeping Faith, Losing Faith: Religious Belief and Political Economy*. Durham, N.C.: Duke University Press, 2008; id., 'In a Space of Questions: A Reflection on Religion and Economics at the Beginning of the Twenty-First Century', in: *History of Political Economy* 43 (2011), no. 2, 389–411; J.M. Dean, A.M.C. Waterman (eds), *Religion and Economics: Normative Social Theory*. Dordrecht: Kluwer Academic Publishers, 1999; see also contributions by Bridges, Mixon, Solari and Sandonà on the Puritan and Catholic views of capitalism, respectively. F.G. Mixon, 'Introduction to the Symposium on the Economics of Religion', in: *Forum for Social Economics* 49 (2020), no. 4, 345–356. See also: B.M. Friedman, *Religion and the Rise of Capitalism*. New York: Knopf, 2021. And P. Oslington, P.S. Williams, M. Hirschfeld, 'Introduction', in: *Recent Developments in Economics and Religion*, 2, 4 for further references.

15 See p. 58 of this book.

16 SeeP. Oslington, P.S. Williams, M. Hirschfeld, 'Introduction', 1–2 for references to the relevant literature by Viner, Hill, Waterman, Long, Harrison, Oslington, Arbo.

17 J. R. Everett, *Religion in Economics. A Study of John Bates Clark, Richard T. Ely, Simon N. Patton*. New York: King's Crown, 1946; P. Jackson, Chr. Fleischer, 'Religion and Economics. A Literature Review', in: *Religions and Development Working Paper 3*. University of Birmingham, 2007.

18 A. Levine (ed.), *The Oxford Handbook of Judaism and Economics*. Oxford: Oxford University Press: 2010; H.D. Vinod (ed.), *The Oxford Handbook of Hindu Economics and Business*. Oxford: Oxford University Press, 2012.

ethics and morality on the one hand and an economy based on risk sharing and prosperity on the other.[19]

The emergence of this fourth strand of research has not prevented studies of the interaction between Christianity and the economy (5) from continuing to highlight the intrinsic connections between religion, morality and the economy. The utility and necessity of this connection were (a) explored at the theoretical level. The underlying hypotheses of such studies was that incorporating Christian values into economic theory formation was not incompatible with objectivity in economics.[20] Writings of a more adhortative nature (b) similarly pointed to this intrinsic connection. Thus the social encyclicals of Popes John Paul II, Benedict XVI, and Francis - recently summarized in *Oeconomicae et pecuniariae Quaestiones* – are based upon the premise that a morality that believes it can dispense with the technical knowledge of economic laws is not morality but moralism, and that economic laws may not cause the rich to become richer and the poor ('immoralità prossima').[21] Moreover, certain contributions that are situated in between a and b also argue that the economy can be improved through the influence of religious traditions on economic thinking. These contributions (c) are premised upon religious views or theological notions. Thus, in this line of research, Catholic and Protestant academics assess economic developments in the light of Scriptural, Aristotelian-Thomistic and Calvinist ethics.[22]

Finally, a number of studies have appeared (6) that use economic theories and methods, such as rational choice theory or theories based on supply and demand, to chart the economics of religion, the economic stability of religious communities, the competitive religious market, the motives of people's religious and economic actions or the economic consequences of religious

---

19 H.M. Kabir, M. K. Lewis (eds), *Handbook on Islam and Economic Life*. Cheltenham/Northampton: Edward Elgar, 2014; H. M. Kabir (ed), *Handbook of Empirical Research on Islam and Economic Life*. Cheltenham/Northampton: Edward Elgar, 2017; N. Maghrebi, a.o. (eds), *Handbook of Analytical Studies in Islamic Finance and Economics*. Berlin: De Gruyter, 2020.

20 J. Henderson, J. L. Pisciotta (eds.), *Faithfull Economics. The Moral Worlds of a Neutral Science*. Waco: Baylor University Press, 2005.

21 L. Ladaria, P. Turkson, *Oeconomicae et pecuniariae quaestiones* (Roma: Libreria Editrice Vaticana, 2018), sections 2–16.

22 See P. Oslington, P.S. Williams, M. Hirschfeld, 'Introduction', 1–2 for references to relevant literature by Amagni, Bruni, Curran, Cavanaugh, Gregg, Finn, Bruni, Waterman, Lonergan, Ormerod, Oslington.

motivation in many countries.[23] Such studies can help theologians to understand the economic aspects of a life of faith.

A very recent study by Eugene McCarraher is *sui generis*. Based on a study of historical developments in the United States, he concludes that capitalism itself is a perversion of religion. In his view, the Mormon obsession with gold and the alliance between puritans and theologians to legitimize the slave trade, for example, led to a mechanism in which capitalism afforded money a central role as a deity, thus perverting religion. Other values than the God-ordained order of creation took center stage. Precisely because 'the American way of life' is untenable, McCarraher believes, humankind should return to the 'sacramental understanding of reality' which it had known through religion as a way of giving meaning to life that enables human beings to rise above the material world.[24] McCarraher fails to mention that the financing of American faith-based institutions, like monasteries, schools and hospitals – institutions that certainly accepted the sacramentality of life– was a fruit of capitalism; that is data that does not fit his model. But this criticism does not take from McCarraher's apt portrayal of the harm that the interaction between religion and capitalism has done in many respects.

However, no matter how intertwined they may be, religion and theology are two different things. Broadly speaking, religions are based on revelation and extraordinary experiences of the transcendent by a select group of intermediaries. Theology is the academic discipline that studies the religious content involved in this revelation.

The fact that the object of theological study originates in 'revelation' appears to be sufficient grounds for some to disqualify theologians as equal partners in a dialogue with economists. In the next section we will look more closely at this purported unsuitability of theologians as interlocutors for economists

---

23 P. Oslington (ed.) *Economics and Religion*. 2 vols. Cheltenham/Northampton: Edward Elgar, 2003; J.-P. Carvalho, I. Sriya, J. Rubin (eds), Advances in the Economics of Religion. London: Palgrave Macmillan., 2019; L. R. Iannaccone, W. Sims Bainbridge, 'Economics of Religion', in: J. Hinnells (ed.), *The Routledge Companion to the Study of Religion* (Abingdon: Routledge, 2010), 461–75; R. McCleary (ed.), *Oxford Handbook of the Economics of Religion*. Oxford: Oxford University Press, 2011; L. Obadia, D.C. Wood (eds), *The Economics of Religion: Anthropological Approaches*. Bingley: Emerald, 2011; J. Rubin, 'Introduction to the special issue on the economics of religion', in: *Journal of Demographic Economics* 86 (2020), no. 3, 2007–211; R. McCleary, R.J. Barro, *The Wealth of Religions. The Political Economy of Believing and Belonging*. Princeton/Oxford: Princeton University Press, 2019.

24 E. McCarraher, *The Enchantments of Mammon. How Capitalism became the Religion of Modernity* (Cambridge, MA-London: The Belknap Press of Cambridge University, 2019), 6–13; 663–679.

within the academe. We will do this by further elucidating the history of theology as an academic discipline, its scholarly premises and its epistemology.

## 2 The Course of History as a Prelude to the Disqualification of Theology

As the previous chapter shows, the notion that each human being would have to answer before God disappeared from economic transactions in early modernity. Developments within society, the laws of nature and the legal system were no longer derived from God as their source and goal, while mercantilism gradually but undeniably pushed economic thinking and behavior into an amoral (not immoral) direction. Theology became increasingly marginalized.[25] It is true that Christian values like solidarity, compassion, individual freedom and equality had firmly taken root in the history of the Western world. But from the Enlightenment onwards, these values emancipated the modern world from the institutional forms of religion within Christianity that the early theologians in particular had helped shape. The Catholic philosopher Charles Taylor has pointed out the paradox that Christian values were expressed more convincingly in post-Enlightenment Western society than in the days when the world was still Christian, and popes were the most powerful rulers on earth. To illustrate his claim, he mentions things like the recognition that all persons, no matter where they live, have the same rights, as well as the abolition of slavery and the works of charity in the form of humanitarian aid in times of war and natural disasters. Why then would economists take an interest in ecclesiastical authors whose descriptions of creation, society and economic associations or the legal system, however fascinating, were based on an outdated world view?

In addition to this, there is another historical reason, which was already mentioned briefly in the previous chapter, why theology was considered – and appeared - as a discipline from which little of value to economics is to be expected. Before the break that John Calvin effected, theologians generally refused to see interest as a morally justifiable remuneration for the lender of money. They were afraid that interest would lead to usury, and subsequently to blind greed, and believed that making money through money was forbidden. After all, acquiring money without labor could also lead to laziness and indolence.[26] In addition, the *Summae* contained numerous tracts, sermons and

25 See p. 26–28 of this book.

26 Cf. Noonan, *The Scholastic Analysis of Usury*, 82–99 ('just price') 249–268; 340–364 (interest).

*distinctiones* in which theologians described interest as a sin against charity that threatened the sense of community and could throw a society out of balance. By flatly portraying anyone who charged interest as a usurer, theologians ignored the key role banks played in the internationalization of trade and in the transition from a closed economy to an open economy. The economic revolution of the sixteenth and seventeenth century required a different view on money and the morality of its use than contemporary theology had to offer. This episode in history seemed to offer additional proof that theologians were disqualified as serious interlocutors for economists, because they failed to pay sufficient attention to changes in the market in their moral judgments on certain forms of economic behavior. In short: history does not seem to offer economists any reason to actively seek dialogue with theologians.

Another historical reason for economists to disqualify theologians as worthy conversation partners for economists is the fact that whenever theological issues of great economic relevance were at stake in the past, theologians either kept silent or their comments were inconsistent and contradictory. This obfuscation manifested itself particularly when slavery became rampant.

In 1545, the Dominican Juan Ginés de Sepúlveda published his *Democrates secundus, sive de iustis causis belli apud Indios*. Based on his reading of Aristotle's *Politika,* he argued that there were people with a 'servile soul'. This was a soul, he claimed, that made them subservient to people with a free soul. By portraying the indigenous people of Central and South America as servile souls and the Europeans as possessed of a superior soul, he sought to legitimize the enslavement of 'weak and imperfect' original inhabitants by 'strong and perfect' European colonists. Sepúlveda sought to condone social and racial inequality as a natural phenomenon on philosophical and theological grounds, like the Delft jurist Hugo Grotius did in his *De iure belli ac pacis* (1625), published at a time when the slave trade by the Dutch East Indies Company and West Indies Company had become much more than just a lucrative sideline.[27]

Bartolomeo de las Casas, another Dominican, together with his fellow Dominican Francisco de Vitoria, gave Sepúlveda's view on the Indians as *natura servi* or slaves by nature short shrift. His adage was: 'No-one is a slave by nature'. Up to the arrival of the Spanish, he argued, the Indians had always been free people, perfectly able to support themselves. Sepúlveda and De las Casas locked horns during the Valladolid controversy, with the latter emphasizing

27 M. Vink, 'Freedom and Slavery: The Dutch Republic, the VOC World, and the Debate over the 'World's Oldest Trade', in: *South African Historical Journal* 59 (2007), no. 1, 19–46, especially 30–37.

that he had not been able to find even a single passage in Scripture that offered support for Sepúlveda's Aristotelian outlook on humankind.[28]

The fact that theologians of the past held fundamentally different opinions on fundamental notions within their field of expertise –like the nature of humankind in the above example – could be a reason to disqualify them as conversation partners within universities today. Their status is further diminished by the fact that, at a time when the conquest of the Americas enriched the usurpers through the repression of the original population and the enslavement of people from Africa, most theologians shied away from condemning this and adopted a naïve or aloof stance in their sermons on the kingdom of God.[17] The latter objection may perhaps carry less weight as a reason for or against an academic interdisciplinary collaboration. A counterargument that could be raised here is that Pope Paul III stated in *Sublimis Deus* (1537) that Indians and Europeans had equally sensible souls, and that the enslavement of the former was therefore unjustified. Much later, in the Pastoral Constitution of the Second Vatican Council, *Gaudium et Spes* (1965), a few thousand bishops well-versed in theology condemned slavery and equated it with mutilation, deportations and the traffic in women and children.[29] Besides, essential differences of opinion on crucial notions in the history of a particular discipline do not necessarily mean that its present practitioners should be discounted as interlocutors. It is food for thought, though, that certain strands in debates on crucial notions in theology, such as the nature of humankind, permitted themselves to be influenced by the dominant pursuit of economic gain, rather than the words about human beings and their souls recorded in Scripture.

Aside from the fact that theologians' past performance could give economists ample reasons for doubting the feasibility and purpose of interdisciplinary collaboration, the position that modern theologians take does not do much to assuage their understandable reserve. Even now theologians themselves seem more intent on maintaining than demolishing the barriers to fruitful dialogue with economists.

Not infrequently theologians addressing large audiences still claim that money, which they call Mammon following the gospel of Luke, is a force for evil. In this context, the economy and *finance* are often referred to as 'Mammon's modern aliases'. The perpetrator is allegedly so dominant in modern society, that these theologians believe that the only way out is to try and

28 See P. van Geest, 'Onenigheid en tweesporenbeleid. De visie op en omgang met slaven in de katholieke kerk tot de achttiende eeuw', in: *Nieuw Letterkundig Magazijn* 38 (december 2020), 6–11.

29 See *Gaudium et Spes* 27.

dethrone Mammon to prevent this dark force from corrupting the values and preferences of our civilization.[30] Now it is true that, as Augustine says, financial concerns must not come to dominate life.[31] And when we are faced with choices in daily life, reading texts that invite us to engage in thorough self-evaluation can be both upsetting and healing. It seems less promising, however, as the point of departure for a dialogue between theology and economics.

Moreover, as soon as theologians begin to reflect on the scientific bases of economics on a more academic level, they often create an opposition between economics and theology that puts economists at an early disadvantage.

In the same vein as the scholars just mentioned who regarded the economy as a substitute for (Benjamin) or even a perversion of religion (McCarraher), some theologians have come up with theological critiques of modern economics. They contend that economists have devised a 'rival theology' in an efforts to answer questions that lie beyond their traditional research remit of the production and consumption of goods. A number of ethical theologians in the United States have accused economics of being based upon a view of humankind and of the world that is at odds with the world view and anthropology that has evolved within Christianity. By treating everything that lives and moves in the world's flora and fauna as things that can be exploited, consumed and traded, they have argued, the 'economically religious person' subjects the natural environment to market forces. As a consequence, people are no longer able to experience themselves, as part of the whole of nature, and creation as a gift from God: a way of experiencing for which they credit Christianity. They interpreted the practices that economically thinking and believing human beings developed as sinful and abject from a Christian perspective. A theologian like John Milbank has stated unequivocally that, just like the other social sciences, economics should take its guidance from theology, the 'Queen of the Sciences'. Only then can the world, very tentatively, begin to experience the real meaning of salvation by God.[32]

But such criticisms have been entirely unavailing, precisely because economists were not convinced by the theologians' description of 'the market', and believed that the theologians were forcing market mechanisms onto the Procrustean bed of their own moral theology. Admittedly, economists sometimes

30 Cf. for instance Justin Welby's spiritual-exegetical work: *Dethroning Mammon. Making Money Serve Grace. The Archbishop of Canterbury's Lent Book 2017* (London-Oxford-New York-New Delhi-Sydney, 2017), 59–83; 131–158, esp. 135.

31 See p. 120 of this book.

32 Cf. D.S. Long, N. Ruth Fox, *Calculated Futures: Theology, Ethics, and Economics*. Waco: Baylor University Press, 2007; J. Milbank, *Theology and Social Theory: Beyond Secular Reason*. Malden-Oxford: Blackwell Publishing, 2006. Second edition.

all too easily speak of the efficiency of the market, and show little awareness of the extent to which market dynamics are influenced by human motives. On the other hand, theologians have sometimes denounced ethical shortcomings of modern capitalism in a manner that reveals a poor grasp of economy and economics, and without any real understanding how individual behavior is influenced by the market. This was yet another reason why interdisciplinary collaboration has not materialized.

## 3 The Irrelevance of Theological Sources

There seem to be still other reasons to keep theology at arms' length when reflecting on the economy. One of them has to do with the sources created by theologians themselves, for instance in the of autonomous treatises on subjects that are related to economics. At a time when theology was regarded as the source and goal of all scientific endeavor, various theologians wrote separate treatises on subjects that are now on the curriculum of faculties of economics rather than of theology. But these treatises have now lost their former status as valid sources for reflection upon economics. A few examples can serve to illustrate this. Around 1360, Nicolas Oresme, a philosopher, mathematician, physicist and trailblazer for the heliocentric theories of Copernicus and Galilei, and also bishop of Lisieux, wrote *De origine et Natura Iure et Mutacionibus Monetaram.*[33] In his *Collectorium circa quattuor libros Sententiarum*, Gabriel Biel, the first ever professor of theology at the university of Tübingen, devoted a *quaestio* to economic issues.[34] In 1516 the jurist Johannes Adler refashioned

33 Nicholas Oresme, *De Moneta of Nicholas Oresme and English Mint documents.* Translated with introduction and notes by Ch. Johnson. London,-Edinburgh-Paris-Melbourne-Toronto-New York: Thomas Nelson and Sons, 1956 (*Medieval texts*). For his personality, see: Ch. Johnson, 'Introduction', in: *De Moneta of Nicholas Oresme and English Mint documents*, ix–xii. See also: A. Labellarte (ed), *Nicola Oresme. Trattato sull'origine, la natura, il diritto e i cambiamenti del denaro*. Bari: Stilo Editrice, 2016.

34 Gabrielis Biel, *Collectorium circa quattuor libros Sententiarum*. Auspiciis Hanns Rückert. Collaborantibus Martino Elze Volker Sievers et Renata Steiger. Ediderunt Wilfridus Werbeck et Udo Hofmann. Tübingen: J.C.B.Mohr (Paul Siebeck), 1973–1992. 4 Vols. Vol. IV/2, *Libri quarti pars secunda* (*dist. 15–22*) (Tübingen: J.C.B. Mohr (Paul Siebeck), 1977), 175–189. In *distinctio* 15 of the fourth book, a treatise on penance and forgiveness (sic), Biel addresses a number of (*quaestiones*) on economic issues. Thus he discusses restitution after robbery or theft (*quaestio* 3), exploitation of local and foreign workers (*quaestio* 5), corruption in obtaining ecclesiastical positions and negligence (*quaestio* 8), counterfeiting (*quaestio* 9), fraud in transactions and labor (*quaestio* 10), interest and usury (*quaestio* 11), acquisition through prescription (*quaestio* 14). Although *quaestiones* 5, 8 and 10 contain

Biel's treatise into a separate work called *De potestate et utilitate monetarum*.[35] Even a cursory reading of these treatises tells us that on those rare occasions that theologians wrote separate treatises specifically dedicated to economics and economy, their works are interesting source material for historians, but not much else.

Both Biel and Oresme, for example, reprise Aristotle's view on money as a useful and neutral means of exchange and payment that facilitates the exchange of goods.[36] In addition they both argue that a coin should be of a certain weight and be made of a precious metal, the quantity and quality of which should be guaranteed by the stamp of the competent authorities, who are allowed to change the material (*materia*), form (*forma*), value (*valor*) and name (*nomen*) of the *moneta* if, for example, the original material has become scarce. Oresme and Biel also discuss mintage right, the ownership of coinage –it belongs to the people – and the prerogative of the ruler to mint coins, and his duty to not abuse these rights.

Biel's argument that the nominal value of the money should correspond to the value of the unminted metal – including the fabrication and labor costs ('saltem deductis expensis et labore') – shows once more that his view on money is outdated.[37] It was in fact already outdated in his days, as credit and bills of exchange were already in wide use among Italian bankers from the early fourteenth century onwards, and money as a means of payment therefore no longer represented a real value.

It would obviously be unfair to accuse Oresme and Biel of failing to cast light on issues like the predictability of the market and market processes, the increasing dependence of the economy on the financial sector or the pros and cons of the Anglo-Saxon or Rhineland models of corporate governance. These issues simply did not exist yet when they were alive. Even the nation state that saw an orderly national economy as very important are not yet emerged.

interesting material for economists, we have chosen to address *quaestio* 9 of *distinctio* 15 on counterfeiting to demonstrate the continuity between Oresme's and Biel's thought; cf. also: K. Menger, *Principles of Economics* (Auburn-Alabama: Ludwig von Mises Institute, 2007 [reprint]. Translation of: *Grundsätze der Volkswirtschaftslehre* (Wien, 1871), 316–317.

35 This separate treatise was entitled : *Integerrimi profundissimique viri Magistri Gabrielis Biel ex Spira: Sacratissimarum litterarum licenciati: florentissimi gymnasij Tubingensis dum in humanis esset ordinarij lectoris resolutissimi Tractatus de potestate et utilitate monetarum* Oppenheim: Köbel, 1516. See also: H. Mäkeler, 'Nicolas Oresme und Gabriel Biel. Zur Geldtheorie im späten Mittelalter', in: *Scripta Mercaturae. Zeitschrift für Wirtschafts und Sozialgeschichte* 37 (2003), 56–94.

36 Nicole Oresme, *De Origine et Natura Iure et Mutacionibus Monetarum*, 4–5; cf. 17; Gabriel Biel, *Collectorium* IV, *Quaestio* 9, *Notabile* 1. Ed. Rückert, IV/2, 176.

37 Gabriel Biel, *Collectorium* IV, *Quaestio* 9, *Notabile* 3. Ed. Rückert, IV/2, 177.

Nevertheless, the handful of theological treatises dedicated specifically to economic issues is interesting rather than relevant, due to the restricted view on economics that they reflect: economics is concerned only with the trustworthiness of coins and the (quantity of) the metal they are made of.[38] But economics is about more than just money, or the enlightened self-interest of the ruler. It is also about collaboration, trust and serving mutual interests. The failure of the theologians mentioned here to address these issues in their treatises on trade and money seems to render their work irrelevant. Theological reflection on the new situation of the market in the first half of the 16th century was more to the point. Thus Calvin was later to emphasize in respect of his merchant hometown of Geneva that making investments is a justified way of making money.[39] The word 'seems' used when averring the irrelevance of medieval economists has been chosen with good reason. Our discussion of *bounded morality* will demonstrate that Oresme's and Biel's treatises are of more lasting value than our exposé thus far has suggested.

## 4 The Epistemological Assumptions of Economic and Theological Research

A final objection an economics faculty could have against setting up a theology department is to do with the epistemological assumptions underlying theological research. According to the Tilburg economist Eric van Damme there are three types of economics. The discipline can be seen as a system of knowledge

38 Cf. for a description of trade and the monetary system at this time: F. Braudel, *Beschaving, economie en kapitalisme (15de-18de eeuw)*. Amsterdam: Uitgeverij Contact, 1989. 2 Vols. [transl.]. Vol. 1: *De structuur van het dagelijks bestaan*, 433–470; vol 2: *Het spel van de handel*, 376–406.

39 John Calvin, *Commentarius in Mosis reliquos quator libros*. Pars I, II (in: John Calvin, *Commentaries on the last four books of Moses, arranged in the form of a Harmony*. Vol 3 (Edinburgh: Calvin Translation Society, 1855), 120–121: 'Certainly no one, I think, will deny that usury ought to be paid to the creditor in addition to the principal, to compensate his loss. If any rich and monied man, wishing to buy a piece of land, should borrow some part of the sum required of another, may not he who lends the money receive some part of the revenues of the farm until the principal shall be repaid? Many such cases daily occur in which, as far as equity is concerned, usury is no worse than purchase. Nor will that subtle argument of Aristotle avail, that usury is unnatural, because money is barren and does not beget money .... usury is not now unlawful, except in so far as it contravenes equity and brotherly union. Let each one, then, place himself before God's judgment-seat, and not do to his neighbor what he would not have done to himself, from whence a sure and infallible decision may be come to.'

about behavior on the markets –the first type –or as an analytical method or technique –the third type – that is, as 'an engine for the discovery of concrete truth' (Keynes); 'a technique of thinking' (Marshall).[40] The second type is the most widely accepted one and it could be used to stress the different epistemological assumptions that underlie theological and economic research. In this second type, economics is seen as a behavioral science that studies the efficient and functional, that is, 'economic' behavior of people in situations in which they have to make optimal use of scarce resources. In this view, economics is about the way people act, rather than about the way people should act.

Lionel Robbins' *Essay on the Nature and Significance of Economic Science* played a seminal role in the emergence of economics. Through his analytical approach and ample use of models, and his wariness of claims as to the correspondence between his models and reality, Robbins contributed to the emergence of the model of the *homo economicus*, the underlying model and starting point for analyses on the understanding that the phenomenon of the human being must be simplified for the sake of analysis.[41] His work was the prelude to a torrent of debates. The decades of scientific discussion that followed it culminated in the acceptance by most economists of the distinction between positive and normative science.[42] As a result, ethics disappeared from economics. The positivism of the mathematical economist Vilfredo Pareto also contributed to the severing of the ties that had existed between psychology and sociology, law and hedonism.

Pareto in particular helped pave the way for a schism within economic science. The Pareto criterion contends that overall wealth increases if the increase of wealth of the winners is sufficient to compensate the losers.[43] This was a noble principle that would ensure that no one on earth would lose out.

---

40 E. van Damme, 'Waarom doceren wij ouderwetse economie?', 162–165; quotes 164.

41 L. Robbins, *An essay on the nature and significance of economic science*. [second edition, revised and extended]. (London: McMillan &Co, 1945), 172: 'And thus in the last analysis Economics does depend, if not for its existence, at least for its significance, on an ultimate valuation – the affirmation that rationality and ability to choose with knowledge is desirable. If irrationality, if the surrender to the blind force of external stimuli and uneo-ordinated impulse at every moment is a good to be preferred above all others, then it is true the raison d'etre of Economics disappears'.

42 In Van Damme, 'Waarom doceren wij ouderwetse economie?', 162–167. See also V. Pareto, *Manual of Political Economy. A Critical and Variorum Edition*. Ed. A. Montesano, A. Zanni, L. Bruni, J. S. Chipman, M. McLure (Oxford: Oxford University Press, 2014 [1906–1909]), 9–20, 192–219, 232–272, especially 13–14, where Pareto explicitly argues for the severing of ties between normative and non-normative disciplines.

43 V.K. Mathur, 'How Well Do We Know Pareto Optimality?', in: *The Journal of Economic Education* 22 (1991), 172–178; W.B.T. Mock, 'Pareto Optimality', in: D.K. Chatterjee (ed.), *Encyclopedia of Global Justice* (Dordrecht: Springer, 2011), 808–809.

The mathematization of the allocation of resources that the Pareto criterion implies –and by extension the mathematization of economics – meant that Adam Smith's interpersonal comparison of utility was discarded. It also laid the foundation for the development of the model of the *homo economicus*. Economists later came to regret the jettisoning of Smith's principle, just as they came to regret the consequences of severing ties with other academic disciplines. However helpful and enlightening theoretical models were for the understanding of market processes, external effects that affected the economy as a part of perceived reality –that is, not as a science – practically ceased to be taken into account. This is a drawback inherent to any simplified version of reality.

Economists began to ignore the psychological mechanism that if one person gets richer without diminishing another person's wealth, this other person may still experience a growing sense of discomfort. The narrowing from a broad to a restricted definition of well-being in economics can be ascribed to Pareto's influence. The shift towards the Pareto criterion as a benchmark meant, for example, that shareholder value became such a dominant consideration that the issue of social inequality practically vanished from economists' field of vision. The term 'narrowing' is therefore very apt.[44] Incidentally, some economists predicted that this tendency towards abstraction would lead to the decline of their discipline.[45]

The emancipation of economics became manifest in the way it developed its theories and put them to the test, that is, by:

> 'observation, interpretation, modeling, analysis, testing, drawing conclusions and subsequent integration into mathematical models underlying a theory in which the assumptions were specified in greater detail'.[46]

The theoretical models that were developed in this manner led – so economists themselves argued – to a concept of the *homo economicus* as the starting point of a form of reasoning, a construct who has consistent preferences, is

44 Cf. J. Schumpeter, *History of Economic Analysis*, passim.

45 S. Eijffinger, 'De val van de economie en de economie van het verval', in: *Nexus* 64, 41–48.

46 Van Damme, 'Waarom doceren wij ouderwetse economie?', 166 (original: 'observeren, interpreteren, modelleren, analyseren, toetsen, concluderen en integreren uiteindelijk leidden tot wiskundige modellen die ten grondslag lagen aan een theorie, waarin de veronderstellingen gepreciseerd werden'). Cf. T. Sedláček, *Economics of Good and Evil. The Quest for Economic Meaning from Gilgamesh to Wall Street* (Oxford: Oxford University Press 2011) 321, 344–345 who also contends that mathematics are indispensable to grasp reality in the neoclassical form of economics, but that the consequence was that economic language became mathematical.

ever mindful of his own interests and acts purposefully in situations of limited supply, with unlimited cognitive abilities at his disposal. This clearly meant a simplification of human beings as actual people. It is self-evident that no such human being exists. But

> 'Economics evolved into abstract rational choice theory, the science of maximization under limiting conditions.'[47]

The radically different epistemological criteria which economics and theology applied could hardly be illustrated more concisely. In a way, the stage for this gaping chasm was set by Plato, who in his *Politeia* (379a) coined the term 'theology' to refer to the search for that which was true, good and immutable in mythological stories. Aristotle also contributed. He regarded 'theology' as the highest of the theoretical branches of knowledge because it was concerned with the divine as the first and actual principle, without linking it explicitly to his beliefs on money as a means of exchange and payment, as a unit of account and unit for measuring the value of goods and produce.

Long before the birth of economic science, developments within theology had laid the foundation for the later incompatibility of economics and theology. This incompatibility resulted first of all from theology's subject of research. According to the norms to which economics would later consider itself to be bound, 'God' can only be seen as a dubious category, as God as a research subject cannot be observed or measured in the same way that an empirically verifiable subject or object can. Christians profess that the Lord is risen.[48] But a risen subject is hardly an ideal starting point for the development and testing of a theory.

These misgivings about the subject of research can in fact be traced back to the epistemological norm for scientific knowledge that has been the heritage of the logical empiricism or logical positivism of the Vienna Circle.

---

47 Van Damme, 'Waarom doceren wij ouderwetse economie?', 164 (Original: 'Economie werd abstracte, rationele keuzetheorie, de wetenschap van het maximaliseren onder randvoorwaarden').

48 Cf. B. Casper, K. Hemmerle, P. Hünermann, *Theologie als Wissenschaft. Methodische Zugänge*. Freiburg im Breisgau: Herder, 1970; W. Pannenberg, *Wissenschaftstheorie und Theologie*. Frankfurt am Main: Suhrkamp, 1987 [reprint]; J. Ratzinger, *Theologische Prinzipienlehre. Bausteine zur Fundamentaltheologie*. München: Wewel, 1982; W. Kern, H.J. Pottmeyer, M. Seckler (eds), *Handbuch der Fundamentaltheologie*. Vol. 4: *Traktat theologische Erkenntnislehre*. Tübingen: Francke, 2000. See for the situation of theology as an academic discipline in the Netherlands: *Klaar om te wenden. De academische bestudering van religie in Nederland: een verkenning*. Amsterdam: KNAW, 2015.

First of all, the scholars who belonged to this circle assumed on the basis of the positivist premises devised by Galileo Galilei (1564–1642), René Descartes (1596–1650) and later David Hume (1711–1777) in particular, only statements that could be verified by observation were meaningful, and that objective conclusions could be drawn from the observation of human beings about the essence of humankind or human nature. Only analytical and synthetical *a posteriori* propositions constitute scientific knowledge. Because value judgments are subjective, they should not be admitted in any way in scientific discourse, and they must therefore also be excluded from economics. As a result, the neo-classical view of economics became that of a positive, non-normative science, free of any inclination towards value judgments.[49] Thus, it was hoped, it would be possible to avoid subjective influences in scientific practice, although that is a well-nigh impossible endeavor, as there will always be concealed value judgments and beliefs in how things such as 'efficiency in the allocation of scarce resources' are formulated, or even how the subjects of research are selected. The preference for 'efficiency' as a criterion instead of, for example, 'the common good' (two criteria that are not mutually exclusive) is the result of an underlying judgment. Even the choice of a deductive method, which requires that conclusions must follow inevitably from assumptions, instead of an inductive one, in which observations lead to generalizations, is not necessarily objective. The philosopher Karl Popper (1902–1994) has shown that induction could not lead to firm general conclusions. He fundamentally criticized this criterion of verification by observing that the statement 'all swans are white' can never be fully verified. In addition, it has been recognized that each 'neutral' observation is in fact premised upon hypotheses that not only steer the observations, but also determine the conclusions.[50] Nevertheless, statements about God have continued to be seen as emotional, religious, and therefore illusory, because concepts like 'God' are unverifiable and therefore devoid of cognitive significance. In this perspective, theology equaled ideology.

Secondly, based on the scientific norms accepted within economics, objections could be raised against the *objectum materiale*, which as we have just seen, had come to include unverifiable claims about the research object. Christian theologians invariably base their reflections on humankind as a phenomenon or on the ideals of the Kingdom of God here on earth on the Scriptures

49 M. Boumans, J. Davis, *Economic Methodology: Understanding Economics as a Science* (London: Palgrave Macmillan, 2010), 169.

50 Cf. for ambiguity in *sense-datum theories*: W. Sellars, *Empiricism and the Philosophy of Mind* (London: Routledge & Kegan Paul, 1963), 127- 196, especially 127- 134; 149–161 (first held in 1956 as London Lecture of Philosophy).

–either directly or indirectly through study of the work of their predecessors. Even if Bible books are subjected to historical-critical research, Holy Writ is still the *norma normans non normata*: the norm of norms which itself is not subject to any norm. The fact that the *objectum materiale* of all of Christian theology is interpreted as normative does not square with the concept of economics as a science that strictly limits itself to describing and explaining how people act, rather than how they should act.

And thirdly, there was the fact that economists found unacceptable the ranking of the different sources of knowledge that had shaped theological practice over the ages. One of Catholic theology's most authoritative works on the hierarchical ordering of the various sources of knowledge about God was *De locis theologicis libri duodecim* (1563), by the Dominican Melchior Cano. In his ranking, the books of Holy Scripture occupy the most authoritative position (*locus*), while reason, philosophy and history come second in a way that is unfathomable to us. The low esteem in which reason was held meant the historicity of pericopes or the modifications authors made to emphasize certain aspects of his theology were not questioned. As a result of Cano's rigorous ranking, reason and authority came to be seen as irreconcilable opposites during the Early modern period, although this must certainly not be taken to mean that the authorities in Protestant and Catholic theology at the time did not make use of their reasoning faculties. They turned post-Enlightenment theology into a *scientia practica* which, rather than prescribing Christian beliefs, reflected upon the practice of believing and the purpose of that practice. (Johann Salomo Semler). Schleiermacher, meanwhile, interpreted theology as a kind of business and social administration science for the benefit of church leadership.

Even the efforts just mentioned cannot ostensibly alter the judgement that theology, due to its research object ('God'), its *objectum materiale* (the Scripture) and the ranking of its sources of knowledge, must be declared unfit as a partner for interdisciplinary research with economists.

It is worth mentioning, however, that economists themselves criticized any one research method that became excessively dominant. We have seen this above in our discussion of Pareto. The neoclassical, deductive approach that worked on the basis of the model of the *homo economicus* was an effort to extend the scope of economics to all domains of life by trying through deduction to formulate hypotheses intended to capture reality by using simplifying assumptions, and to evaluate them in the light of the experimental outcomes.[51]

51 J.J. Graafland, *Economics, Ethics and the Market. Introduction and Applications* (London-New York: Routledge 2007), 134.

However, other economists observed that choosing a model as the basis for an account of reality could not possibly do justice to the changeability and capricious nature of reality.[52] It led them to write economic histories in which they used the inductive method to study economic source material, enabling comparison between findings and ultimately generalizations and conclusions that were sensitive to the complexity of reality.[53]

Another objection raised was that modern economics all too easily assumed that the 'factual behavior' of human beings equaled 'rational behavior', the latter interpreted as behavior that was both consistent and aimed at the maximization of self-interest. Closer study of the sources from which this scientific discipline sprung, however, showed that Adam Smith did not exclusively favor an anthropology in which the pursuit of self-interest is regarded as the constitutive element.[54] One aspect of Smith's work that has been lost in modern economic interpretations was that with the pursuit of self-interest was only one factor, alongside 'mutual sympathy' and other virtues, that he identified as conducive to the proper distribution of labor and as indispensable for successful transactions.[55] Partly due to free trade, which was on the rise in his time, Adam Smith saw that freedom and love of self can become fertile ground for charity. The most quoted sentence from Adam Smith's work is about a baker, a brewer and a butcher: 'It is not from the benevolence of the butcher, the brewer, or the baker that we expect our dinner, but from their regard to their own self-interest'. This line from *The Wealth of Nations* has often been interpreted as justifying self-interest as the only motive in economics. But this famous sentence is immediately followed by an even more important statement: 'We address ourselves not to their humanity but to their self-love, and never talk to them of our own necessities, but of their advantages'.[56] One person's self-love stimulates another's empathy and charity. In this way, self-love mobilizes the moderating forces of charity. Smith realized that selflove and charity are not opposites but arise from love as such. Charity is founded on love of self: love your neighbor as yourself(Mark. 12:31) Although Smith's *The Wealth of Nations* is often quoted to justify the pursuit of self-interest as the only relevant trigger in the economy, the same book also explicitly points out

52 Graafland, *Economics, Ethics and the Market*, 143.

53 Th. Piketty, *Capital et idéologie*. Paris: Seuil, 2019.

54 M. Blaug, 'The fundamental theorems of modern welfare economics, historically contemplated', in: *History of Political Economy* 39 (2007), no. 2, 185–207.

55 Cf. K. Haakonsen, ' Introduction', in: Adam Smith, *The Theory of Moral Sentiments*. Ed. K. Haakonsen (Cambridge: Cambridge University Press), viii–xxxi.

56 Adam Smith, *The Wealth of Nations*, 1.27.

the corollary of the golden rule of ethics: always do to others what you would have them do to you (Matthew 7:12).

These criticisms that economists have directed at the underlying assumptions of their discipline do not change the fact, and make it even simpler to understand, that Schumpeter, following in the footsteps of his teachers from the Vienna Circle, ignores theology in his *History of Economic Analysis*. The book contains a section in which he discusses the benefits of interdisciplinary collaboration between economics and other disciplines like philosophy, sociology, logic, the humanities, psychology and social psychology and biology: this can help to develop a good method for economics (logic, mathematics) or to analyze social phenomena like societies, groups and leadership. He states in passing in this section that economic propositions should not be influenced by theorems from philosophy or personal religious convictions.[57] He does acknowledge that economic analysis must take religion into account as a determining factor of behavior.[58] But Schumpeter has little or nothing to say about theology.

## 5 Developments in Theology

Even though the theologian's research subject (God) is immeasurable and unverifiable, even though she holds the *objectum materiale* (Scripture) of her discipline in high esteem, and even though the traditional ranking of the sources of theological knowledge still holds, theology as an academic discipline is ready for collaborative research with economists.[59] This section will

57 Schumpeter, *History of Economic Analysis*, 25–38, especially 26, 30–31.

58 Schumpeter, *History of Economic Analysis*, 31, 780.

59 A number of subdisciplines are currently distinguished within the discipline of Christian theology. Biblical studies, Biblical theology, patristics, patrology and historical theology study Scripture, the works of the Church Fathers and theologians up to the Enlightenment. Systematic theology, fundamental theology, dogmatics and ethics use more or less the same sources to analyze the content of the Christian faith and the corresponding way of life. There is also practical theology as a 'critical science of action', which studies practices that can be observed in faith communities. Liturgical studies stands at the intersection between these various disciplines, as does the *theologia ascetica et mystica*, which is currently called 'spirituality'. In the 20th century, intercultural theology was added as a discipline that studies the relations between Christian theology and practice in the context of different cultures, religions and societies, and which is particularly interested in intercultural and interreligious coexistence. The line dividing it from religious studies is very thin. See literature in footnote 48 and A.J. Denaux, *De plaats van theologie in universiteit, kerk en samenleving. Afscheidsrede, uitgesproken door Adelbert Denaux, bij*

begin to substantiate this hypothesis, which we will address in greater detail in the next chapter.

First of all, and somewhat in the spirit of Schleiermacher, theologians themselves have suggested that research at theological faculties could voluntarily limit itself to studies using tools and methods from the social sciences to empirically test theological theories to see how they relate to the practice of church life.[60] The aim of this ongoing exercise is to reach a better understanding of the practice of faith and the church or, to put it more broadly, of the practice in those institutions in our society – school, care facilities, certain governmental institutions – in which meaning is a recurring topic of thought and discussion.

Biblical scholars and systematic theologians responded in a different way. Their premise was that God is the object of active faith. Theological research meant research of the way in which people have *thought and spoken* about God. They often added a disclaimer to their conclusions to the effect that thinking and speaking about God does not do justice to his Mystery, the more so because John the Evangelist not only wrote that no-one had ever actually seen God, and the first letter to Timothy, generally regarded as Deutero-Pauline, described God as unapproachable light.[61]

The recognition that God can not be grasped in word or thought – and that the word 'light' therefore, based as it is upon sensory perception, already leads to incorrect associations – yielded yet another insight.

This was that the words of prophets, evangelists and apostles in Scripture could never adequately express God's being and his inscrutable works, the normativity of the Bible notwithstanding. The way they speak of God's envy, justice and mercy is more inadequate than adequate as a description of God's being and his inscrutable works; a flaw of which they themselves seem to have been aware, judging from, for example, Isaiah's words about God's

---

*zijn afscheid als decaan van de Tilburg School of Catholic Theology, op 14 december 2012* (Tilburg: Tilburg University Press, 2012), 10–21.

60 See A. Dinter, H.-G. Heimbrock, K. Söderblom (eds), *Einführung in die Empirische Theologie: gelebte Religion erforschen.* Göttingen: Vandenhoeck & Ruprecht, 2007 (*Empirical theology* 38). Empirical theology is involved in discussions on truth and method, on the relationship between deduction and induction, and on the relationship between data and theory. See H. Schilderman, 'Truth and method in empirical theology', in: L.J. Francis, M. Robbins, J. Astley, *Empirical Theology in Texts and Tables. Qualitative, Quantative and Comparative Perspectives* (Leiden: Brill, 2009), 27–41 (*Empirical studies in theology* 17); Chr. Hermans, 'Epistemological reflections on the connection between ideas and data in empirical research into religion', in: *ibidem*, 73–99.

61 Sura 112; Exodus 3: 13–14; 33: 18–23; John 1: 18; 1 Timothy 6: 16.

hiddenness, or Paul's reminder that God is an unknown God.[62] Throughout the ages the theologians who denied that thinking and language are adequate – 'negative theologians' –were in good company. Like Paul, Augustine compared humankind on earth to a child that can only tolerate milk early in its development.[63] By characterizing the way human beings talk and think about God as liquid food for infants rather than solid food for grown-ups, these two authors underlined the insufficiency of human language and thought. In this way, theology tried on the one hand to respect the mystery of God, while on the other hand[64]– in the awareness that God is the subject of human knowledge through a mysterious revelation – speaking openly about God so as to ensure that this mystery would not remain secret to the point of complete obscurity, that is, that no one would be aware of Gods existence any longer. Whereof one cannot speak, thereof one must *not* remain silent. Later in this book we will return to the arguments developed in negative theology when we introduce both negative and affective theology as preludes to a deeper insight into *bounded rationality*.

What these comments on Scripture as the *objectum materiale* of research of God demonstrate is that theological work deserves to be called research, because it meets the criteria for qualitative research. Unlike quantitative research, qualitative research does not aim to test theories, but to gain insight into the meaning people attach to events they experience personally or collectively.

Thirdly and finally, there is one prime example of the fact that the ranking of sources of knowledge as presented in Melchior Cano's *De locis theologicis* did not lead to the despising of reason as a cognitive faculty. Reason was an important textual-critical research tool in the work of someone who incidentally preceded Cano's rise to authority: Erasmus. His aversion to the 'petty little summata' of scholastic theologians – which he regarded as signs of decline – was the foundation for his critical editions of the New Testament and works of Church Fathers like Jerome and Augustine, research outcomes that paradoxically confirmed Cano's ranking, because as we have seen, Scripture was regarded as the highest source of knowledge of God. Instead of viewing the Church Fathers as instances of authority (*auctoritates*) that provided the

62 Acts 17: 23.

63 1 Corinthians 3: 2; Augustine, *sermo* 117. Cf. P. van Geest, *The Incomprehensibility of God. Augustine as a Negative Theologian* (Leuven-Dudley: Peeters, 2010), ix–x, 175–190 (*Late Antique History and Religion* 4).

64 For this element, see C. van der Kooi, *As in a Mirror. John Calvin and Karl Barth on Knowing God*, 291–299, especially 293, 299.

building blocks for a theological edifice to be built by the theologians,[65] Erasmus saw them as springs (*fontes*) from which readers might drink to derive inspiration for the social, ecclesiastical and personal reform that he had in mind.[66]

Incidentally, the dialectic between a scholastic and a text-critical approach to texts is never far away in theology. During the 1950s, the edifices of neo-scholasticism were quite radically criticized by the leading lights of *Nouvelle Théologie* like Henri de Lubac SJ and Yves Congar OP, who advocated a return to the integral reading of the early Christian sources with due regard for each author's intentions. In doing so they discovered, among other things, that the wording of dogmas changed with cultural and historical circumstances, and that truths were therefore expressed differently in different times and circumstances.[67] It was a conclusion that had escaped Neo-Scholastic theologians. Not surprisingly, around this time theology began to manifest itself as an interdisciplinary field of study. Biblical scholars –theologians well-versed in philological methods – assessed the completeness, authenticity, context of origin ('milieu') and redactional layers of early Christian texts.[68] Dogmatic theologians studied the works of the Church Fathers as a form of faith testimony within the Christian community.[69] Both groups needed each other, and they still do. Dogmatic theologians realized that they could not neglect the findings of Biblical scholarship, as this would mean they were building an ideological and ahistorical structure on quicksand. The Biblical scholars, meanwhile, became aware that a strictly philological approach runs the risk of neglecting the faith of the Christian community of interpretation, communication and reception spanning two millennia. This interaction between dogmatic theology and Biblical scholarship led to the discovery that Scripture and the constitutive texts of the tradition contained an anthropology that the world had been waiting for, and so, possibly, has economics.

65 Erasmus, *Hieronymi Vita in S. Hieronymi Stridonensis Opera Omnia* (Frankfurt am Main-Leipzig, 1684), vol. 1, fol. BB 5r. Cf. *Collected Works of Erasmus* (Toronto, 1991), vol. 61 *Patristic Scholarship. The edition of St. Jerome*. Ed. J.F. Brady – J.C. Olin (Toronto, 1992), vol. 1, 196.

66 Cf. Erasmus, *Exhortation à la lecture de l'Évangile*. Ed. A. Vanautgaerden. 2 Vols. (Turnhout: Brepols, 2005). Vol. 1: *Le texte Latin*. Edition, annotation et introduction J.-F. Cottier. Traduction J.-F. Cottier - A. Vanautgaerden (Turnhout: Brepols, 2005), 104–108.

67 Cf. H. de Lubac, *Augustinisme et Théologie moderne* (Paris, 1965), passim (*Théologie. Études publiées sous la direction de la faculté de théologie S.J. de Lyon-Fourvière* 63).

68 Cf. P. van Geest, 'Patristics among the tulips. Interdisciplinarity as a chance for theology and patristics', in: *Gregorianum* 95 (2014), 73–94.

69 Cf. A-G. Hamman, *Études patristiques. Méthodologie, liturgie, histoire, théologie* (Paris: Beauchesne, 1991). (*Théologie historique* 85).

To put it differently: the qualitative research that theologians have conducted into the views of humankind as they evolved in Scripture and tradition could form the basis for a dialogue with economists. After all, the economists, through quantitative research, created a concept of the human being as *homo economicus*. It is a model that economists themselves now describe as insufficient to satisfactorily explain the broad range of economic behaviors that can be observed, because human beings as a phenomenon are neither consistent in their preferences nor capable only to pursuing their own good. But as has been argued above, economists have accepted that using a model as the instrument to analyze reality cannot account for the changeability and capriciousness of reality. Actual behavior is not always rational behavior, as history shows. Their new perspectives on human behavior are sensitive to the fact that human beings should be seen as social, relational or even loving creatures who have a fundamental desire to belong to a group, who are characterized by intersubjective values and convictions with corresponding rules of conduct that are accepted in order to gain access to a group as a valued member. [70] The Rotterdam and Tilburg economist Lans Bovenberg has even stressed that the view of humankind traditionally held by economists – the rational *homo economicus* with stable preferences – needs to be replaced in economics, in the boardroom and in the teaching of economics by a broader, relational anthropology. People are not driven exclusively by financial appreciation, but also by their desire to be known, valued and trusted and to be meaningful to others. Bovenberg has argued that traditional economists often prefer the interchangeability of transactions to the firmness of relationships. Interchangeability indeed helps to contain market power, external effects and credit and liquidity risks. In relationships, on the other hand, partners are tied to each other for the longer term. The relative durability of the relationships allows for exchange over longer periods time, with mutual obligations and responsibilities. One party may today sacrifice something, but will regard this sacrifice in the long-term perspective of the future rewards that the relationship may yield. Instead of asking each other for some form of direct compensa-

70 Concisely formulated in: D. Kahneman, 'A psychological perspective on economics', in: *American Economic Review* 93 (2003), no.2, 162–168; L. Bruni, R. Sugden, 'The road not taken: how psychology was removed from economics, and how it might be brought back', in: *Economic Journal* 117 (2007), 146–173; A. Damasio, *Descartes' error: emotion, reason and the human brain*. London: Penguin, 1994. Literature on the economy and charity can be found for instance in: R. Dur, 'De economie van de liefde', in: *ESB Gedrag* 99 (2014), 780–782. See also: N. Ellemers, *Morality and the Regulation of Social Behavior. Groups as Moral Anchors*. New York: Routledge, 2017.

tion, the partners implicitly give each other credit.[71] In the so-called 'relational economy', therefore, participants seek relationships in which they are tied to each other for the long run, that is, relationships that are less likely to be the result of transactions and competition. In a broader, relational view of human beings, the exchange between flexibility and tie-in changes, partly because the relational model attaches great value to reciprocity. This reciprocity entails the willingness of people to be of service to others as long as they can be sure that their own interests will not be forgotten by the other party. It is closely linked to the moral value of justice and to the golden rule of ethics: 'Do unto others as you would they should do unto you.'[72]

In conclusion: we have seen in our first chapter how economists can help theologians to gain a sharper focus on the texts they are studying. A number of economists have distilled from The story of the good Samaritan (Lk 10: 25–39) incentives to enrich the 'market theory as a morally neutral zone' with a 'grammar of trust' for 'economic and business relationships'. This 'economic exegesis' complements the theological one, which stressed that precisely the person who ranked below the temple priest and the Levite in the social hierarchy of the time was the one to practice a higher and more valuable virtue than the others. But will theologians in turn be able to help economists in their quest for ways to deepen and broaden their perspective on humankind?

---

71 See footnote 23 and 24.

72 P. Seabright, *The Company of Strangers. A Natural History of Economic Life*. Princeton: Princeton University Press, 2010; E. Fehr, S. Gächter, 'Fairness and Retaliation: The Economics of Reciprocity', in: *Journal of Economic Perspectives* 14 (2000) no. 3, 159–182.

CHAPTER 4

# Towards a Mutual Rapprochement between Economics and Theology: A First Sketch

## 1 Introduction: Theological Economics or Economic Theology?

As we attempted to show in the introduction to this book and in the last part of the previous chapter, there are signs of a rapprochement between theologians and economists. This rapprochement is not happening because economists are interested, for example, to know more about the fiscal aspects of Paul's collection for the Jerusalem community.[1] Nor is it motivated by the desire to sponsor a Christian folklore workshop for the study of authors who show how social and economic structures are founded in God and his unfathomable order.

This mutual scholarly rapprochement between theologians and economists is characterized instead by maximum collaboration when it comes to substance, but with respect for each other's research methodology. Theology have always looked at their sources with a view to the times they live in, to interpret economic developments in the light of what they regarded as Biblical or Christian. Thus in the 1960s Marxist theologians and liberation theologians (1) regarded Scripture as a source for critiques of economic developments or capitalism and for their own views on society.[2] And when Biblical scholars became interested in contemporary mainstream economics, (2) this led to a steady flow of publications that (a) interpreted economic developments in the light of values that can be gleaned from certain passages in Scripture. In addition, (b) the societies of the Hebrew Scriptures were interpreted on the basis of current market models, and (c) the inequalities in these societies were highlighted. Moreover, (3), topics in contemporary economics such as scarcity or interest, or the background of the word *oikonomia* were examined on the basis

1 See for this J. S. Kloppenborg, 'Fiscal Aspects of Paul's Collection for Jerusalem', in: *Early Christianity* 2 (2017), vol.8, 153–198. An excellent study in this area is: J. Cornillon, *Tout en commun ? La vie économique de Jésus et des premières générations chrétiennes*. Paris: Cerf Patrimoines, 2020.

2 See P. Oslington, 'Economics and Biblical Studies', in: C. Matthews (ed.), *Oxford Bibliographies in Biblical Studies*. New York: Oxford University Press, https://www.oxfordbibliographies.com/view/document/obo-9780195393361/obo-9780195393361-0053.xml. 2015

 | DOI:10.1163/9789004501706_005

of theological sources.[3] Conversely, (4) theological notions such as the theodicy were explored as a frame of reference to facilitate the analysis of economic suffering and evil. This use of Scriptural and theological notions to acquire a more profound insight into economic developments. The responses have been twofold. Economists have often asked to what extent the publications by theologians necessarily introduce theism or religious belief into economic discourse. Other economists have welcomed the broadening of their frame of reference without, however, adopting theological research methodologies themselves.

This has not prevented (5) economists from using Scripture and exegetical studies as basis for studies that employ contemporary economic models and techniques like rational choice theory and game theory.[4] And many publications (6) have attempted and continue to attempt to clarify or even bridge the methodological, epistemological gap between economics and theology.[5] One research subject has been the question to what extent economics and theology can both contribute to normative social theory.[6] George Stigler, Nobel Laureate in Economic Sciences, described economics in 1988 as an 'imperial science': 'The very nature of economic logic invites a sweepingly wider application of economic analysis to social phenomena'. He argued for a much wider

---

3 See P. Oslington, P.S. Williams, M. Hirschfeld, 'Introduction', 3, for references to studies on scarcity, the theodicy and interest. See also: G. Richter, *Oikonomia. Der Gebrauch des Wortes Oikonomia im Neuen Testament, bei den Kirchenvätern und in der theologischen Literatur bis ins 20. Jahrhundert*. Berlin: de Gruyter, 2013 [reprint].

4 Cf for instance L. Bruni, *The Economy of Salvation. Ethical and Anthropological Foundations of Market Relations in the First Two Books of the Bible*. Cham: Springer, 2019.

5 See for instance: J. Ballor, 'Theology and Economics: A Match Made in Heaven?', in: *Journal of Interdisciplinary Studies* 26 (2014), no. 1/2, 115–134; C. Beed, Cl. Beed, 'Economics and Theology', in: *Journal of Interdisciplinary Economics* 21 (2009), no. 2, 143–161; G. Brennan, A.M.C. Waterman, 'Christian Theology and Economics: Convergence and Clashes', in: I. Harper, S. Gregg (eds), *Christian Theology and Market Economics* (Cheltenham: Edward Elgar, 2008), 77–93; L. Bruni, P. Oslington, S. Zamagni, 'Economics and theology special issue: introduction', in: *International Review of Economics* 63 (2016), no. 1, 1–5; A. van den Hoogen, 'The Relationship between Economics and Theology', in: *Jahrbuch Fur Kontextuellen Theologien* 4 (1996), 39–57; A.M.C. Waterman, 'The Beginning of 'Boundaries': The Sudden Separation of Economics from Christian Theology', in: G. Erreygers (ed), *Economics and Interdisciplinary Research* (London: Routledge; Block, 2001), 41–63. Hartrop, A., 'Why is Engagement between Christian Theologians and Economists Difficult?', in: J. Kidwell, S. Doherty, (eds), *Theology and Economics: A Christian Vision of the Common Good* (New York: Palgrave & McMillan, 2015), 11- 26 (difficulties because of different, terminology, concepts, assumed emphasis on self- interest and rationality in economy; different modes of analysis, goals, priorities, questions).

6 H.G. Brennan, A.M.C. Waterman, 'Introduction', in: H.G. Brennan, A.M.C. Waterman (eds), *Economics and Religion: Are They Distinct?* (Boston: Kluwer, 1994), 3–15; J. Dean, A.M.C. Waterman (eds.), *Religion and Economics: Normative Social Theory*. Dordrecht: Kluwer Academic Publishers, 1999.

application of economic instruments of analysis to interpret developments in society that are beyond economists' traditional field of interest, even describing this prospect as 'as exciting as any development in the history of economics, or, for that matter, in the history of science'.[7] Although economists have followed Stigler's example and recommended their methods for adoption in other disciplines, attempts were also made to realize a new interdisciplinary study: 'economics-theology', precisely to emphasize the links between virtue ethics and the market. This did require a certain belief in the mutual indispensability of the two disciplines. Theologians had to realize that 'piety is no substitute for technique' (Etienne Gilson). Economists can also help to temper the sometimes utopian expectations that theologians and church activists are prone to foster. On the other hand, 'Economics needs theology because man does not live on GDP per capita alone'.[8]

It comes as no surprise, then, that more recent years have seen the emergence of the research field of economic theology. This (7) studied the explicit or implicit theological assumptions underlying modern economics or economic thought.[9] And studies in the field of (8) the theology of economics have boldly attempted to engage in theological reflection on economic developments and actions.[10] If we assume that (9) spirituality is a subdiscipline of theology, the study of issues, approaches and models in the field of spirituality in business, economics and society must also be mentioned.[11] In addition, there have been numerous attempts to interest church people in economic issues.[12] Finally, the genre of books that discuss the interplay between theology and economics

7 G. Stigler, *Memoirs of an Unregulated Economist* (New York: Basic Books, 1988), 193, 203.

8 J. Ballor, 'Theology and Economics: A Match Made in Heaven?', in: *Journal of Interdisciplinary Studies* 26 (2014), no. 1/2, 117, 123–124. https://www.academia.edu/10094190/_Theology_and_Economics_A_Match_Made_in_Heaven_?email_work_card=view-paper

9 Cf. A. Morriss, 'Understanding Economics through Theology: Reflections on Robert Nelson's Economics as Religion', in: *Case Western Reserve Law Review* 56 (2006), no. 3. R.H. Nelson, *Reaching for Heaven on Earth. The Theological Meaning of Economics.* Savage: Rowman & Littlefield, 1991; id., *Economics as Religion from Samuelson to Chicago and Beyond.* Pennsylvania: Pennsylvania State University Press, 2001; id. 'What Is Economic Theology', in: *Princeton Seminary Bulletin* 25 (2004), no. 1: 58– 79; Ph. Goodchild, *Credit and Faith.* Lanham: Rowman & Littlefield, 2019; id. *Economic Theology: Credit and Faith* II. Lanham: Rowman & Littlefield, 2020. See footnote 19.

10 M. Novak, *Toward a Theology of the Corporation.* Washington: AEI, 1981; id. *The Spirit of Democratic Capitalism.* New York: Simon & Schuster, 1982.

11 L. Bouckaert, L. Zsolnai (eds), *The Handbook of Spirituality and Business.* London: Palgrave McMillan, 2011, part two (comprehensive pluralistic view covering all the major religious and spiritual traditions and spiritually inspired economics).

12 M.D. Meeks, *God the Economist: The Doctrine of God and Political Economy* (Minneapolis: Fortress, 1989), esp. xii. 33, 41–45.

also include works that call to action rather than engage in detached scientific analysis. Without resorting to overly complicated hermeneutical interpretation, they sometimes present a series of quotes from Scripture that imply that God prefers a type of financing that is remarkably similar to what can be found in socialist manifestos.[13]

A number of high-quality scholarly contributions have appeared in Dutch that aimed to develop a research field in which theologians and economists can advance together. In *Door het oog van de naald. Over markt, geluk en solidariteit* ('The Eye of a Needle. On market, happiness and solidarity') Graafland tests the earliest free market mechanisms that have been empirically researched and compares them with existing historical and current theories. Ultimately, he addresses the mechanisms and theories in relation to ethical principles and values, like justice, derived from the Old and the New Testament. This interdisciplinary approach permits Graafland to answer the question to what extent market processes as such contribute to a more equal distribution of goods in the 'surprisingly productive capitalist system' (verbazingwekkend produktieve kapitalistische systeem) and the question whether market processes contribute to the development of virtues and a virtuous life. Just like McCloskey in her masterly trilogy *The Bourgeois Virtues*, Graafland's answers in the affirmative. If market mechanisms are shaped by the pursuit of a kind of love that seeks to serve, the market can even contribute to human happiness.[14] In *De homo economicus. Een familiegeschiedenis* ('The homo economicus, a family history') Joost Hengstmengsel states, for example, that the anthropology that economists have adhered to, which in turn underpins the calculation models that are applied in politics by government bodies and banks, was shaped by specific developments in their field. Whereas economics began as a scientific discipline focused on the acquisition of fortune (1800–1850) and wealth (1850–1930), as Robbins has observed, it later became a science that focused on scarcity (1930-present).[15] This led to the appreciation of the human being as *homo rationalis*, who in the current economy performs information-based risk analyses in order to maximize utility.[16] The genealogy of his close relative the *homo economicus*, a being bent on self-interest, thus shows that the ability of

13 See for instance C. Hovind, *Godonomics. How to Save Our Country – and Protect Your Wallet – Through Biblical Principals of Finance* (Colorado Springs: Mutnomah Books, 2013), passim.

14 J.J. Graafland, *Door het oog van de naald. Over markt, geluk en solidariteit*, 384–388.

15 Cf. Robbins, *Essay on the Nature and Significance of Economic Science*, 21, 45. He has defined economics as 'the science which studies human behaviour as a relationship between given ends and scarce means which have alternative uses'.

16 Hengstmengel, *De homo economicus. Een familiegeschiedenis*, 9.

human beings to test economic actions against the virtues of temperance and justice is declining. The ability that ancient philosophers, Church Fathers and medieval theologians had regarded as a norm to judge human actions became lost, as did the ambition, which once accompanied 'the advent of Christianity', to regard 'the theological virtue of charity' as the crucial factor in economic considerations.[17]

Finally, a number of handbooks published in the field of theological economy are important for the study of the relationship between theology and economics, most recently two works edited by Paul Oslington and Stefan Schwarzkopf respectively. In an earlier article, on the basis of theological claims that God created the world and Christ has redeemed humanity, Oslington argued that the primacy of theology over economics should be maintained. Economics to him is 'subject to theology in that it is positioned, put into perspective and criticized by theology', the more so because economic and religious claims imply 'basic belief' and can therefore not be subjected to the falsification criterion. He also assumes the presence of a certain 'hostility to theology held by secular culture'.[18] Whether his assumptions can serve as a starting point for a dialogue between European economists and theologians, a precondition for interdisciplinary collaboration, remains to be seen. But Oslington's excellent *Handbook of Christianity and Economics* contains contributions which reveal the common ground between economics and theology in the works of Adam Smith, or even Marx and Keynes. In Weber's spirit, the book offers clear insight into the attitude towards the economy that evolved within Anglicanism, the Orthodox churches, Anabaptism, Pentecostal churches and Protestant (Reformed) churches. The interaction between Christianity and capitalism is, also in the description of the different stages in the relationship between theology and economics, one of the connecting threads of contributions that suggest that the idea that theology is the mother of all sciences is not meant to imply that economics should be treated as a kind of auxiliary subject.[19]

Schwarzkopf's *The Routledge Handbook of Economic Theology* is based on the premise that economics and business administration have undergone a

17 Hengstmengel, *De homo economicus. Een familiegeschiedenis*, 155–156. In her *The Vices of Economists* (1997; *De zondeval der economen*) Mc Closkey referred to three sins: a sacrosanct belief in statistical significance (Lawrence Klein), in paper proof (Paul Samuelson) and in a society that can be remade by human design (Jan Tinbergen). She also concluded that virtue was neglected.

18 P. Oslington, 'A theological economics', in: *International Journal of Social Economics* 27 (2000), 32–44.

19 P. Oslington (ed.), *Handbook of Christianity and Economics*. New York: Oxford University Press, 2014.

theological turn of their own after secularism. Schwarzkopf's version of 'economic theology' conceptualizes the theological dimension of everything related to the economy and economics:[20]

> 'It is the study of the forms of interaction between theological imaginaries on the one hand, and economic thought and economic– managerial practices on the other, both past and present. It identifies explicit and implicit theologies inherent in economic concepts, institutions and practices as well as the role of economic terminology within theological thought, both past and present'.[21]

On this basis, the contributors study the way in which the development of theories in economy is indebted to that in the history of theology, or the way in which the sacral is activated in profane realms of 'management, production, consumption, finance and entrepreneurship in the contemporary world'. Thus, the theological notion of justification by grace is seen as a source of inspiration for a way of speaking about the economy in which the good life is not seen as booty in a victorious trade war, but as a gift. Starting from this definition, economic concepts like money, debit and credit, property, prosperity, governance, markets, profit, poverty as they appear in Jewish, Islamic and Christian views of humankind, the world and God are interpreted as incentives for the renewal of personal relationships, while the exchange of goods and services is seen as potentially beneficial to the community (D. Stephen Long, W. Cavanaugh, D. Bell, L. Bruni, S. Zamagni). Many contributions in Schwarzkopf's book show that economists are critical of the concept of *homo economicus* when it comes to explaining actual economic behavior.[22] There is a growing realization, at least among theological economists, that human beings should first and foremost be seen as social, relational or even loving beings.[23]

---

20 S. Schwarzkopf (ed.), *The Routledge Handbook of Economic Theology*. New York: Routledge, 2020.

21 S. Schwarzkopf, 'An Introduction to Economic Theology', in: id. (ed.), *The Routledge Handbook of Economic Theology* (New York: Routledge, 2020), 1–15, quotation 4 (brief historiography: 11–12).

22 See for instance the contribution by D. Bell, 'Justification and Salvation', in: S. Schwarzkopf (ed.), *The Routledge Handbook of Economic Theology* (New York: Routledge, 2020), 64–71.

23 Concisely formulated in: D. Kahneman, 'A psychological perspective on economics', in: *American Economic Review* 93 (2003), no.2, 162–168; L. Bruni, R. Sugden, 'The road not taken: how psychology was removed from economics, and how it might be brought back', in: *Economic Journal* 117(2007), 146–173. Literature on the economy and charity can be found for instance in: R. Dur, 'De economie van de liefde', in: *ESB Gedrag* 99 (2014), 780–782.

However different they may seem in nature and in their approach, these publications are incontrovertible evidence that there is a mutual interest in each other's field of study in the work of economists and theologians. We will now offer three different arguments to support this mutual rapprochement.

## 2 Criticism of the *homo economicus*, a Prelude to Interdisciplinarity

As has been mentioned regularly, the concept of the *homo economicus* was – and is –the cornerstone of many economic models. We will now explore this concept in greater depth. The *homo economicus* is a model, a man-made construct that is part of an economic analysis in which human beings are seen as actors who, armed with consistent preferences and unlimited cognitive capacity, consistently act to further their self-interest and achieve their goals therefore eschew bonds with others.[24] The *homo economicus* has only two goals in mind: maximizing financial gain and quantitative production growth.[25] This rational human being was and is seen as an individual whose actions are not determined by others and for whom collaboration is not a worthwhile goal in itself, as the material outcome is their only relevant consideration.

The *homo economicus* did not materialize out of the blue. An early forebear can be identified for instance in the work of Niccolò Machiavelli, specifically in his book *Il principe* (The Prince), written towards the end of Machiavelli's diplomatic career, which contains a very realistic portrayal of human beings, who are obviously corrupt, domineering and greedy, particularly leaders. [26] In their effort to gain power, prevent violence and keep their followers in check, leaders or anyone striving to become one should act opportunistically and look strictly at their self-interest only.[27]

The hypothesis that the traits of Machiavelli's prince make him a possible ancestor of the *homo economicus* is further supported by his tendency ascribed to him to pursue external goals such as wealth, power and status in his own

24 L. Bovenberg, 'Finance: A Relational Perspective', in: C. van Beuningen, K. Buitendijk (eds), *Finance and the Common Good* (Amsterdam: Amsterdam University Press, 2019), 79–97, especially 79, for literature; id., 'Economics as a discipline of hope', in: P. Nullens, C. van den Heuvel (eds.), *Driven by Hope: Economics and Theology in Dialogue* (Leuven: Peeters Publishers, 2018), 21–40 (*Christian Perspectives on Leadership and Social Ethics* 6).

25 R. Haan, *Vergeten vragen. Humanisme in economisch-theologisch perspectief* (Vught: Uitgeverij Skandalon, 2016), 36.

26 P.J. Galie, C. Bopst, 'Machiavelli & modern business: Realist thought in contemporary corporate leadership manuals', in: *Journal of Business Ethics* 65 (2006), no. 3, 235–250.

27 Galie, Bopst, 'Machiavelli & modern business', 205–206.

interest. Like the model of the *homo economicus*, that of *il principe* lacks the moral principle that his rational pursuit could be harmful to others.[28] In a sense Machiavelli's prince is a trailblazer for the type of human Adam Smith described in his *Inquiry into the Nature and Causes of the Wealth of Nations* (1776). Smith wrote that 'economic man' distinguishes himself precisely because he insulates himself from the kind of principles give rise to consideration, charity and love of the common good. Instead, this human being is characterized by the pursuit of self-interest, without any regard for the interests of others. It is true that Smith, in his *Theory of Moral Science*, presents a more variegated outlook on humanity. Like Mandeville, he assumes that individual idiosyncrasies may indeed lead to an increase of wealth for all, provided the state creates the right conditions. Yet Smith's *Inquiry into the Nature and Causes of the Wealth of Nations* paved the way for John Stuart Mill (1806–1873), who resolutely isolated the pursuit of self-interest from other possible motives for human behavior. Thus these two men created a 'model' of the human being which omitted certain facets and aspects of being human.

The run-up to the advent of *homo economicus* may have been long, and the model may have become influential, but ongoing developments in economics that are based on observation of actual human beings are shedding new light on a number of presuppositions that economists have long held.[29] After publication of Herbert Simon's 'A behavioral model of rational choice', behavioral economists increasingly began to critique rationality as a constant in the

28 See Berlin's acute analysis of Machiavelli's ideas; I. Berlin, *Against the current: Essays in the history of ideas*. Ed. H. Hardy (New York: Viking Press, 1980), 25–79.

29 E. van Damme, 'Waarom doceren wij ouderwetse economie?', in: A. L. Bovenberg, F. Haan (eds), *Preadviezen van de Koninklijke Vereniging voor de Staathuishoudkunde 2016: Economieonderwijs* (Amsterdam: Koninklijke Vereniging voor de Staatshuishoudkunde, 2016), 161- 171. Van Damme himself observes that his view is similar to D. Rodrik's in his *Economics Rules: The Rights and Wrongs of the Dismal Science*. New York: Norton, 2015. See also id., 'Verwevenheid van recht en economie', in: M. Groenhuijsen, E. Hondius, A. Soeteman (eds.), *Recht in Geding* (Den Haag: Boom Juridische uitgeverij, 2014), id., 'Liefde, geluk en economische wetenschap', in: *Economisch Statistische Berichten* 101 (2016), 57–61; L. Bruni, 'Economics and Vulnerability: Relationships, Incentives, Meritocracy', in: P. Rona, L. Zsolnai (eds), *Economics as Moral Science* (New York: Springer International Publishing, 2017), 107–128; O. Goodenough, M. Gruter Cheney, 'Is Free Enterprise Value in Action?', in: P. Zak (ed), *Moral Markets. The Critical Role of Values in the Economy* (Princeton-Oxford: Princeton University Press, 2008), xxiii–xxx; R. Solomon, 'Free Enterprise, Sympathy and Virtue', in: *ibidem*, 16–41; P. Zak, 'Value and Values: Moral Economics', in: *ibidem*, 259–279; L. Bruni, R. Sugden, 'Reclaiming virtue ethics for economics', in: *Journal of Economic Perspectives* 27 (2013), no. 4, 141–164; and, in more popularizing fashion: L. Bovenberg, 'Markteconomie is ondergeschikt aan menselijke relaties', in: P.J. Dijkman a.o. (eds), *Menselijke waardigheid* (Amsterdam: Boom, 2011), 97–104 (*CD Verkenningen* 2011–4).

choices that people make, as if they are always able, on the basis of the knowledge available to them, to make the right choice, without experiencing any conflict between their feelings and their reason, and as if they have unequivocal and stable preferences.[30] Many economists began to realize the *homo economicus* as an agreed concept or model obfuscates many aspects of the human reality for the sake of analysis. As a result the *homo economicus* as 'a methodological tool rather than as an assumption about how people actually make decisions' no longer fulfilled the expectations scientific economists have of a model.[31] They increasingly argued that the concept of the *homo economics* should be replaced by a more realistic model of human behavior that accounts for the fact that people are influenced by their surroundings, set goals for themselves, and derive their identity not just from the outcomes they produce, but also from the group that they want to serve to become happy. The limitations of rationality were also addressed, and as a consequence, so were the limitations of the rational choice model, although it was never totally rejected.[32] Economists became aware once more of what Adam Smith had already described in *The Theory of Moral Sentiments*. People are not exclusively or even particularly rational. Apart from the fact that people are inclined towards mutual sympathy and strive for harmony, they also experience envy, an emotion that is lasting proof that people are not as rational as the model of the *homo economicus* implies.[33] This is where theologians can help economics out.

## 3 The Drive for Insight into Motives as a Second Prelude

In a sense Herbert Simon's observation described above can itself be traced back to earlier comments by Lionel Robbins. Until the beginning of the last

---

30 H. Simon, 'A Behavioral Model of Rational Choice', in: *The Quarterly Journal of Economics* 69 (1955), Issue 1, 99–118.

31 Cf. G. Gigerenzer, 'Moral Satisficing: Rethinking Moral Behavior as Bounded Rationality', in: *Topics in Cognitive Science* 2 (2010) 528–554 (quotation: 531); see also: V. Pareto, *Manual of Political Economy. A Critical and Variorum Edition*. Ed. A. Montesano, A. Zanni, L. Bruni, J. S. Chipman, M. McLure (Oxford: Oxford University Press, 2014 [1906–1909]), 8.

32 This development was summarized for a wider public in: A.J. Biemond, H. Commandeur, P. van Geest, '*Homo dignus*. Erkenning van de intrinsieke waardigheid van de mens in de organisatie', in: *Management en Organisatie* 72–6 (2018), 26–39. See also R.L. Ackoff, 'From data to wisdom', in: *Journal of Applied Systems Analysis* 16(1989), 3–9; H. Opdebeeck, 'Rediscovering a Personalist Economy', in: P. Rona, L. Zsolnai (eds), *Economics as Moral Science* (New York: Springer International Publishing, 2017), 69–79.

33 Cf. Adam Smith, *The Theory of Moral Sentiments*, Part I, Section III, Chap. II ('Of the origin of ambition') and III ('Of the corruption of our moral sentiments').

century, the economy was seen as a dynamic involving the pursuit of affluence and wealth, and economics as a science that studied the way in which this could be done as efficiently as possible. It was no coincidence that Adam Smith's *The Wealth of Nations* was called precisely that. Since the publication of Robbins's *An Essay on the Nature and Significance of Economic Science* (1932) however, the economy began to be described more in terms of scarcity, whereas economics began to study human *behavior* in terms of choices between scarce resources. As scarcity was no longer seen as an invitation to hoarding, but instead as a reason for collaboration, to the figure of the *homo economicus* was added that of the *homo cooperans*.[34] This meant taking leave of the assumption that one person's gain inescapably meant another person's loss, as if the economy were a zero-sum game. Robbins' view was supported by facts. After the Industrial Revolution, financiers and entrepreneurs became increasingly willing to invest up front in anticipation of future growth and wait for possible revenues, accepting the so-called credit risk. It was this trust in collaboration and its rewards, and hence also in reciprocity, that enabled the enormous increase in the standard of living over the past two centuries. Commitment and faith in cooperation triggered the creative power that this development required.

Paradoxically, this realization can similarly be traced back to Smith's ideas. In an era in which nation states were emerging and mercantilism began to shape trade, he and his friend David Hume develop a healthy aversion to the mercantilist *jealousy of trade*. Their basic idea was that this type of mutual envy between trading nations caused counterproductive competition, and that the states involved could instead transform relative shortages into prosperity and wealth. Because the greater the diversity between partners, the larger the potential added value of cooperation towards economic growth.

In short: notwithstanding the importance of *homo economicus*, the founder of economics as a scientific disciple, and in his wake other economists, began to see the human being as a creature of feeling and as 'pronum ad malum', that is, prone to evil, as theologians like Augustine, Thomas Aquinas, Martin Luther and John Calvin had long before pointed out.

Since then economists have begun to study forms of deception, scapegoat and exclusion mechanisms and people's willingness to incur costs in order to impair others.[35] In the spirit of the Jesuit, theologian and economist Oswald von Nell-Breuning, they aim to relate the interaction between a person's under-

34 T. de Moor, *Homo Cooperans. Instituties voor collectieve actie en de solidaire samenleving*. Utrecht: Universiteit Utrecht, 2013 [inaugural address].

35 L. Bovenberg, 'Finance: A Relational Perspective', *passim*.

standing of their own motives and their overview of economic developments. Unlike Friedman, who in *Free to choose* praised the market price mechanism as an organizing, practical and efficient control mechanism, Von Nell-Breuning remained alive to the complexity of the motives that shape the human reality and hence human economic behavior. Like the scholastic economists before him, and drawing particular inspiration from the spirituality of his order – the Jesuit order has developed numerous methods of introspection and 'the discernment of spirits' – he stressed the importance of awareness and understanding of individual motives as a way to prevent people from using the idea of an impersonal market as an excuse for their economic behavior.

In *Zur Kritik des wirtschaftlichen Liberalismus*, Von Nell-Breuning warned his readers against the idealized concepts of liberalism as a framework within which the *homo economicus* was postulated as a rational subject. He stressed that people do not act logically in ways that follow the laws of the market, all the less so because monopolization often occurs, particularly in highly developed economies.[36] Even in old age, Von Nell-Breuning, as *ghost writer* to Pope Pius XI and as a university professor, helped shape Catholic social doctrine, stressing that economic and ethical theories should take into account the influence of circumstances and the motives of workers within capitalism, which he actually cherished rather than despised.[37]

In the spirit of Von Nell-Breuning, Philip Hans Franses, at the time Dean of the Erasmus School of Economics, writes, in his foreword to the aptly entitled book *Canon van de economie* (Canon of the economy):

> 'The financial crisis of 2008 and the adversity that followed it laid bare the overconfidence and blind spots of economists: many (not all) of them long blindly trusted the advantages of financial innovation, of self-regulating markets and a common currency. Economists have since been jolted awake, but for how long?'[38]

---

36 O. von Nell-Breuning, 'Zur Kritik des wirtschaftlichen Liberalismus', in: id., *Wirtschaft und Gesellschaft heute*. Vol. 1. *Grundfragen* (Freiburg i. Br.: Herder, 1956), 103–122.

37 O. von Nell-Breuning, *Unsere Verantwortung. Für eine solidarische Gesellschaft* (Freiburg im Breisgau: Herder, 1987), 23.

38 Ph. H. Franses, 'Een woord vooraf', in: S. Phlippen, G. Werner (eds), *Canon van de economie* (Rotterdam: ESE, 2015), 8–11, especially 9: 'De financiële crisis uit 2008 en de tegenspoed erna hadden de overmoed en blinde vlekken van economen blootgelegd; vele (nee, niet alle) hadden zich lange tijd blindgestaard op de voordelen van financiële innovatie, van zelfregulerende markten en van een gemeenschappelijke munt. Inmiddels zijn economen wakker geschud, maar voor hoe lang?'.

Von Nell-Breuning was not alone in his plea for new economic and ethical theories that would take workers' motives into account. Among his allies was the Nobel Laureate Amartya Sen, who argued that modern interpretations of Smith's work neglected the key role of sympathy and ethical considerations in a well-functioning society.[39] Sen then advocated widening the purely technical approach in economics by allowing room for ethical principles, because in his view an approach that is simultaneously ethical and technical will lead to increased efficiency of trade relations. By looking further than just the legitimate pursuit of self-interest, and including human motivation and its ethical evaluation (that is, the *agency* aspect), economic analysis can be improved. Taking into account that ethically responsible behavior has an impact on developments in the economy means it could be used for more precise predictions.[40] According to the classical economic assumptions, individuals maximize their own well-being by fulfilling their own preferences, regardless of the preferences of others.[41] Agents thus go no further than maximizing their self-interest.[42] But Sen believes economic models should be built in which the choices people make to maximize their utility also include their empathy and sympathy for other actors and their mutual connectedness, which would allow the efficiency of the economy to be tested more conclusively.[43] Sen regards assessing behavior and choices against one criterion only, specifically rational selfishness, as problematic.[44] Like the ancient philosophers and theologians before him, Sen thinks economic transactions should be seen in connection with the practice of virtues. He has rekindled their ambition to present virtuous motives and virtues as benchmarks for assessing the morality and utility of certain economic developments or actions. Sen's endeavor is as effective an overture to theology by a modern economist as is likely to be found.

---

39 A. Sen, *On ethics and economics* (*The Royer Lectures*). (Oxford: Blackwell 1987), 28.

40 Sen, *On ethics and economics*, 40 – 41.

41 Cf. J. Reiss, *Philosophy of economics: A contemporary introduction* (London-New York: Routledge, 2013), 213 - 214.

42 A. Sen, *Development as freedom* (Oxford: Oxford Paperbacks, 2001), 118.

43 Sen, *On ethics and economics*, 14. Cf. G. Akerlof, 'Loyalty filters', in: *The American economic review* 73 (1983), no. 1, 54 – 63.

44 A. Sen, 'Rational fools: A critique of the behavioral foundations of economic theory', in: *Philosophy & Public Affairs* 6 (1977), no. 2, 317 - 344.

## 4 The Complementarity of the Economic and Theological Views on Nature and Exhaustibility

The mutual understanding that is a basic requirement for interdisciplinary collaboration can also be fostered by a systematic search for common ground in the views economists and theologians have, for example, on scarcity, nature and the interplay between virtue and market.

In his social encyclical *Laudato si'* (2015), Pope Francis pointed out to a very wide audience that economic and ecological developments are closely intertwined, and moreover that they touch upon moral issues. He stated in no uncertain terms that climate change, water scarcity and decreasing biodiversity will affect the poor in particular. Water shortages directly translate into crop failures for them. The pope also criticized as intolerable the fact that these climate changes are caused by people in rich countries' insatiable need to consume. Ecology and social justice are therefore directly related.[45] This theme has only very recently made its appearance in scientific discourse, for example by Spencer Banzhaf. He has stressed that if scarcity is connected to the finiteness of everything in creation instead of being seen as a deficiency, theologians and economists could contribute to the development of an 'economics *of* the environment', instead of taking cover behind the proposition that most economists think in terms of 'economics *versus* the environment'.[46]

According to the Tilburg professor Aart de Zeeuw, most economists who reflect on the optimal allocation of limited resources have trouble integrating ecological principles into the basic assumptions of their discipline. They are still insufficiently aware that the prosperity, health and well-being of future generations will be much more closely linked to the availability of natural resources than has up to recently been realized. Unsurprisingly, when environmental issues came into focus during the seventies of the last century, they were largely ignored by economists.[47]

Banzhaf is therefore perhaps a little too optimistic when he points out that human beings are not merely seen as 'restless consumers' in the *environmental*

---

45 Cf. Francis, *Laudato si'* 24, 30, 49, 165, 169, 225. Cf. also Francis, *Evangelii Gaudium* 71 and his message for the 2015 International Day of Peace: *No longer slaves, but brothers and sisters'*. http://www.vatican.va/content/francesco/en/messages/peace/documents/papa-francesco_20141208_messaggio-xlviii-giornata-mondiale-pace-2015.html

46 S. Banzhaf, 'Economics and Theological Ethics: An Environmental Economist Replies to his Queen', in: *Journal of Economics, Theology and Religion* (JETR), 1, no. 2, in press.

47 A. de Zeeuw, *Integrating Economics and the Environment. Valedictory Adress delivered by Aart de Zeeuw as Professor of Environmental Economics at Tilburg University on 22 september 2017* (Tilburg: Tilburg University, 2017), 8–21.

*economy*, but also as part of nature and of natural surroundings that are no longer reduced to the status of a consumer good that can be exploited at will.[48] In response to the objection voiced by some theologians that the market rests upon an 'ontology of violence' (J. Milbank), or presupposes the unscrupulous exercise of power 'rather than to be subservient to God', Banzhaf points out that Adam Smith already noted that tradespeople must always respect the interests of the other party, and that economists like McCloskey, Bruni and Sugden believe virtues like wisdom, justice, courage, self-restraint and trust can thrive in economic relations.[49] The environmental economist Banzhaf searched his discipline for insights that had been neglected by theologians in their writing about economic developments, but that could nevertheless benefit from theological reflection. Theologians have written extensively about the finiteness of life, about nature as a gift and about humankind as part of a universal nature that should be regarded in the same way that fellow human beings should be respected. The invitation to engage in dialogue on the common ground between theology and economics has thus come from an economist.

In sum: it seems evident that meetings of the mind between theologians and economists can be fruitful. But there is one question that must still be answered: what should interdisciplinary collaboration between theology and economics look like. How structurally scientific could it really be? Would not the incompatibility between these two disciplines, which arises from the difference in their object of knowledge and methodology, thwart any attempt by economists and theologians to engage academically? In the next chapter, we will propose a scientifically sound approach that overcomes this incompatibility.

48 For the theological criticism, see W. Cavanaugh, *Being Consumed: Economics and Christian Desire* (Grand Rapids: Eerdmans, 2008), 90; D. Bell, *The Economy of Desire: Christianity and Capitalism in a Postmodern World*. Ada, MI: Baker Academic, 2012; N. Wirzba, *The Paradise of God: Renewing Religion in an Ecological Age* (Oxford: Oxford University Press, 2003), viii–ix: 'The desperate, frantic, and anxious character of much of our lives, as well as the languishing of many of the earth's habitats, suggests that we have not yet learned what it is to be creation; A properly human life depends upon the acceptance of our own poverty, … the acceptance of our being one part of an interdependent order'. For Banzhaf's reply, see 'Economics and Theological Ethics', in press.

49 J. Milbank, *Theology and Social Theory*, 278–326. See for Banzhaf's reply, 'Economics and Theological Ethics', in press. See for the positions defended by Bruni, Sugden and McCloskey p. 57, 61 of this book.

CHAPTER 5

# The Indispensability of Theology for Enriching Economic Concepts

## 1 Introduction

As we already noted, theological texts that addressed economic issues seem to have lost much of their relevance after the Enlightenment, while the epistemological assumptions underlying theological research appear to be incompatible with those upon which economic research is based. Mutual integration of the key principles of economics and theology seems impossible, due to great differences in objects of knowledge, methodology and epistemology, even if, as has been seen, there are indeed areas in which economists and theologians can mutually enrich each other's disciplines through their insights into human reality and motivation, and the finiteness of natural resources.

Economists have recently begun to reflect on notions like 'gratuity', 'trust' and 'inner motives and intentions', concepts that theology has been thinking about for centuries. In doing so, economists are accepting the invitation that Daniel Kahneman extended towards the end of his best-selling book *Thinking, fast and slow,* to develop 'a richer language' for reflection upon economic processes. The identification of errors of judgment is a diagnostic task that requires a precise vocabulary.[1] Heeding Kahneman's exhortation, we aim to show in this chapter that theology can contribute to, and even be indispensable to, the development of a language that is more sensitive to human complexity and that could help lay the foundations for broadening the analytical framework economists use. The advantage of interdisciplinary research by economists and theologians at the level of conceptual definition is that differences in objects of knowledge, methodology and epistemology can be circumvented.

Though it is not entirely new, this interdisciplinary approach is not very common either. Kahneman's suggestion is addressed in only one contribution in *The Routledge Handbook of Economic Theology*. The author of this piece, C. Sløk, notes that in debt is a pecuniary issue in modern economics, without any moral connotation. By adding the theological, moral connotation of 'failure' to the economic concept, Sløk strengthens the awareness that market relations

1 D. Kahneman, *Thinking fast and slow* (London: Penguin, 2011), 8.

 | DOI:10.1163/9789004501706_006

and the economic balance of power should also be interpreted in terms of moral debt and injustice, and not just in terms of outstanding debt.[2]

Our aim here is to demonstrate that mutual 'Begriffsklärung' (clarification of terms and concepts) can be a way to foster interdisciplinary research between economists and theologians, and that 'theology' can help to develop a language that is more sensitive to the complexity of human beings as economic actors, and we will do this through a discussion of these ideas in the work of the economists Luigino Bruni, Alessandra Smerilli, Bart Nooteboom and Samuel Bowles. In recent works, they have interpreted the gratuity, trust and morality that are concealed within motives as virtues that are essential for social and economic innovations. Bowles in particular has presented proof that substantiates the claim that the *homo economicus* is too limited as a model for economic reflection, as it leads to the development of motives that lie at the root of the demise of the economic principle of reciprocity and of social cohesion.

## 2 The Economy and Community Building. Luigino Bruni and Alessandra Smerilli on Gratuity and Augustine's Doctrine of Grace

The underlying thread that runs through the many works of Luigino Bruni, presently professor at the *Libera Università Maria Santissima Assunta* (LUMSA) in Rome, is the conviction that economics has increasingly limited itself over the past two centuries to answering the question how people can mutually benefit each other when engaging in transactions while keeping their relationship as noncommittal as possible.[3] Bruni argues that turning citizens into individuals without a community impedes the innovative and civilizing power of the capitalist market economy. Whether he writes about economic processes in the Bible books of Exodus, Job, Ecclesiastes, or Matthew, or about the interaction between market developments and market ethics, time and again he points out that economic relationships should be determined not only by profit seeking, but also by the pursuit of altruism, solidarity and a sense of community if human beings are to have orderly and contented lives.[4]

---

2 C. Sløk, 'Guilt', in: *The Routledge Handbook of Economic Theology*, 72–80.

3 L. Bruni, *Civil Happiness: Economics and Human Flourishing in Historical Perspective*. (London: Routledge, 2006), 34–117.

4 Cf. for instance L. Bruni, S. Zamagni, L. Becchetti, *Dall'homo oeconomicus all'homo reciprocans*. Bologna: Il Mulino, 2010; L. Bruni, *Gli imperi di sabbia. Logiche del mercato e beatitudini evangeliche*. Bologna: Edizioni Dehoniana, 2016; id., *La sventura di un uomo giusto. Una rilettura del libro di Giobbe*. Bologna: Edizioni Dehoniana, 2016; id., *Reciprocity, altruism and civil society*. London: Routledge, 2008; id. *The Genesis and the Ethos of the market*. Basingstoke: Palgrave Macmillan, Houndmills, 2012.

The latter also applies to 'gratuity'.[5] In his book *L'altra metà dell'economia. Gratuità e mercati* (2014) Bruni and his co-author Alessandra Smerilli view gratuity as the capacity – or even the urge – of human beings to act from selflessness rather than from the desire to maximize their own interests. Bruni argues that, if the calculated pursuit of material riches, efficiency and profit is not accompanied by a willingness to serve a community, people won't be able to achieve fulfilment.[6] Without this willingness, this gratuity, Bruni does not think it is possible for economic innovations to be truly fruitful; innovation which are necessary to increase profit, open up new markets and make new products, and that take shape in the development of new commercial and organizational formulas and new technologies.[7] But if gratuity is to be consolidated into a *habitus*, it will be necessary to transcend the dichotomy between the market and the non-market.[8] Just as the great monastic orders after the fall of Rome in 410 shaped Europe by implementing irrigation methods, founding libraries that could transmit the works of writers like Plato, Seneca and Aristotle, or later founding banks for the poor ('monti di pietà') that issued out micro credit, modern entrepreneurs who really want innovation to be successful should apply themselves to relieving needs such as poverty, paradoxically as part of their very pursuit of profit and continuity.[9]

In Bruni's and Smerilli's view, gratuity is also intrinsically linked to charisma, a gift of grace. In the spirit of St. Paul he regards charisma as a talent that has been given to an individual and that comes to full fruition when it is employed for the benefit of the community and the well-being of all.[10] Unlike Max Weber, he does not think that the rejuvenating, transformational or even revolutionary power of personal charisma throughout history i lost when the charisma is institutionalized after the demise of the charismatic leader.[11] Quite the reverse: he believes individual charismas can be safeguarded, consolidated

5 L. Bruni, A. Smerilli, *L'altra metà dell'economia. Gratuità e mercati*. Roma: Città Nuova, 2014. The Dutch edition was used here: *De ongekende kant van de economie. Gratuïteit en markt.* (Nieuwkuijk: Uitgeverij De nieuwe stad, 2014), because it presents a number of ideas more precisely than the original text. Cf. also: L. Bruni, *Il prezzo della gratuità.* Roma: Città Nuova, 2006; L. Bruni, A. Smerilli, *Benedetta Economia*. Roma: Città Nuova, 2008; L. Bruni, *Il mercato e il dono. Gli spiriti del capitalismo.* Milano: Università Bocconi, 2015.

6 Bruni, *De ongekende kant van de economie*, 13

7 Bruni, *De ongekende kant van de economie*, 13, 22, 23, 57 (he relies here on Schumpeter).

8 Bruni, *De ongekende kant van de economie*, 60–63.

9 Bruni, *De ongekende kant van de economie*, 23–27.

10 Bruni, *De ongekende kant van de economie*, 32, 37.

11 Bruni, *De ongekende kant van de economie*, 34, 37, 50–55.

and intensified in hierarchically ordered organizations that propagate the charisma, 'generalize' it and, in doing so, keep innovating it.[12]

In order to create a society in which charisma fosters gratuity, Bruni and Smerilli argue, it is important to attend to the anthropology that underlies the view we have of society. If we see the human being as a calculating and greedy creature, the incentives that will motivate human beings to perform are bonuses. If the aim is a society in which human relationships have intrinsic value and gratuity has become a feature of social interactions, this requires a different view of humankind and different incentives based on it.[13] These incentives should foster situations in which decisions are made collectively rather than individually, where a sense of community and identification with a group or awareness of mutual dependence rather than greed are rewarded, and in which people are honored who set greater store by the common good than by their own personal welfare.[14] Bruni thinks this will bring about a civil economy marked not just by the pursuit of efficiency, profit and calculating interactions, but by a willingness and drive to act gratuitously. In this lies human happiness, as ultimately human beings are an *esse ad*: beings that find fulfillment in relationships, rather than in maximization of self-interest.

It is tempting to point to examples from church history to criticize the way Bruni uses Weber's thesis on charisma. The history of monastic communities in the late-medieval Modern Devotion reform movement, for example, shows that the institutionalization of communities through canonical embedding in an order or congregation soon led to arrogance that was due to the material security and social status that came with it.[15] But precisely because of the many associations with the word 'grace' that Bruni himself mentions – and that are concealed in the Italian words 'grazia' and 'gratuità' – we will now further explore the notion of 'gratuity', based upon the first of the disputes about grace that there have been over the centuries.

The foundation for this epochal theological controversy regarding divine grace was laid in one of the most frequently discussed works in theological history: Augustine's *De diuersis quaestionibus ad Simplicianum*. We will return to this controversy in chapter 6.4, at somewhat greater length, because the works that Augustine wrote in the context of this controversy are a rich source for a

12 Bruni, *De ongekende kant van de economie*, 39, 55, 63–65, 70–73, 88.

13 Bruni, *De ongekende kant van de economie*, 99, 127.

14 Bruni, *De ongekende kant van de economie*, 128, 146, 149.

15 See, for just one example from church history: P. van Geest, 'Gabriel Biel, Brother of the Common Life and *alter Augustinus*? Aim and Meaning of his *Tractatus de communi vita clericorum*', in: *Augustiniana* 58(2008), 305–357.

profound understanding of *bounded willpower*, and concomitantly for a fundamental critique of meritocracy as a political and economic. *Ad Simplicianum* was written in response to eight questions posed by Augustine's friend Simplicianus. All of them are on the relationship between free will and grace, God's foreknowledge of the way his creatures will live their lives and ultimately predestination: the conviction that the fate of human beings is preordained and they are woefully incapable of changing their fate by their belief in God or their deeds.[16]

In the *Expositio quarundam propositionum ex epistula ad Romanos* (393/4) Augustine still assumed that people themselves are responsible for the development of their belief and their good works.[17] In *Ad Simplicianum* 1.2.7, however, he wrote that the human will and good works can only be good through grace, and not through human effort. In other words: both chronologically and causally, God's grace precedes any human undertaking.[18] This Augustinian turn met with incomprehension as the emphasis on grace and on God's power was felt to downplay human autonomy, freedom and individual responsibility.[19] Partly for these reasons Kurt Flasch has qualified Augustine's doctrine of grace as was articulated in in *Ad Simplicianum* 1.2 as a tremendous shadow over Europe.[20]

Notwithstanding Flasch's negative assessment, the word 'gratuity' as an economically charged term could be enriched by interpreting it in the light of Augustine's altered conviction regarding the primordiality or effect of grace. What Augustine tried to express by using 'gratia' –apparently both a theological and a psychological principle – is that people are fundamentally if not completely dependent on the benevolence, friendship and love of others and, in

---

16 Augustine, *Ad Simplicianum* 1.1: 'Quaestio prima: Lex ad quid data'; *Ad Simplicianum* 2.1: 'Quaestio secunda: Argumentum Epistolae ad Romanos.... Gratia fidei precedit bona opera'.

17 Augustine, *Expositio quarundam propositionem ex epistola ad Romanos* 37.52; 54–56; *Ad Simplicianum* 1.2.7; *Ad Simplicianum* 1.2.10.

18 Cf. *Ad Simplicianum* 1.2.1–1.2.2; *Ad Simplicianum* 1.2.20.

19 Cf. J. Rist, 'Augustine on Free Will and Predestination', in: *Journal of Theological Studies* 20(1969), 420–447, especially 437–440, where he says that the marionet-like status of fallen humankind is manifested in the doctrine of original sin. Cf. also: id., *Augustine. Ancient Thought Baptized* (Cambridge: Cambridge University Press, 1994), 133 ('virtual puppets').

20 Cf. K. Flasch, *Logik des Schreckens. Augustine von Hippo. De diversis quaestionibus ad Simplicianum* I 2 (Mainz: Dieterich, 1990), 15: 'Mit unserem Text [De diuersis quaestionibus ad Simplicianum I 2, pvg] haben sich gewaltige Schatten über Europa gelegt', see also: 7–18, 30 and passim. See also D. Ogliari, *Gratia et certamen. The relationship between grace and free will in the discussion of Augustine with the so-called semipelagians* (Leuven: Peeters, 2003), 106, 183, 411, 419 (*Bibliotheca Ephemeridum Theologicarum Lovaniensium* 169); J. Delumeau, *Le péché et la peur: La culpabilisation en Occident, 13e-18e siècles* (Paris: Fayard, 1983), 331–338 and passim.

the theology of grace, on the power that the inscrutable God gives them. After rereading Paul's letters, he concluded that people are unable to do anything good on their own –love their neighbor, for example –but can only do this if they have received this love for free, that is, *gratis*, themselves first. No one can pass on what they have not first received themselves. Paradoxically, even in the disputes on grace, Augustine underscores the freedom of the will and its consequence, that people can indeed be responsible for what they strive to attain and do. This freedom, however, has been given. In Augustine's view mortal beings should therefore not first become aware of their freedom and individuality, but should first realize thoroughly that there is nothing that has not been given to them.[21] People become what they become thanks to the talent that they have received. And whatever they attain in terms of social standing depends on what others in the public domain have granted them. Augustine does not stress this awareness of radical dependence on others in order to instill fear in people. On the contrary. His aim is for people to realize that the dependence on 'gratia', the benevolence of others and sometimes, indistinguishably, the concurrent grace of God, impels people to modesty and humility that are caused by an awareness of dependence ('humilitas').[22] The latter is a virtue that he believes induces people as relational beings to see each other as fellow-dependents, rather than as autonomous individuals who follow the law of the jungle and establish a pecking order in which they exploit others to consolidate their own positions.

As it happens, 'gratuità' is etymologically derived from 'gratis' and 'gratia'. It is justified therefore to include this layer of meaning, this implied meaning of the word 'gratia', when we consider the meaning of 'gratuità' with Bruni.[23] If we do this in the light of the explanation of the historical origin of the word, we can enrich its meaning in a way that contributes to Bruni's and Smerilli's reflection on economic processes in their book.

This outlook on life left its mark on Augustine himself and his interaction with others, as his famous statement shows: 'For you I am a bishop; but with you I am a Christian.'[24] The structure of this sentence suggests that to him being a member of a community is more important than being addressed as a high church or secular official, who was economically responsible for an enterprise called a diocese and moreover endowed with judicial power. Very loosely translated the sentence reads: 'for you I am chairman of the board, with you I am

21 Augustine, *Ad Simplicianum* 1.2.8; 1.2.9.

22 Augustine, *Contra secundam Iuliani responsionem imperfectum opus*, I, 131; *Epistula* 73.10.

23 Bruni, *De ongekende kant van de economie*, 153–155.

24 Augustine, *sermo* 340.1: 'Vobis enim sum episcopus, vobiscum sum Christianus'.

a partner and employee of this organization.' This statement has far-reaching consequences. The person who says this underscores their desire to be part of a group and makes it impossible to accept some bonus that his co-workers oppose.

## 3 The Economy, Probabilities and Uncertainty. Bart Nooteboom on Trust and the Theological Notion of *pistis*

Some may find Bruni and Smerilli suspicious because he has been spotted in theological circles in Rome, and even visiting the pope. But economists untainted by such accusations are also challenging theology. The academic career of Bart Nooteboom, professor emeritus of business administration and innovation at the universities of Groningen, Rotterdam and Tilburg, has been marked by a constant interest in 'trust' in economic interactions. In 2002 he published his award-winning book *Trust, Forms, foundations, functions, failures and figures*, and he returned to this subject in his recently published *Vertrouwen. Opening naar een veranderende wereld* (Trust. Gateway to a Changing World), which is partly based on a number of crucial earlier publications.[25]

In this latest book, Nooteboom critically observes that, to calculate costs and revenues, economists invariably try to translate uncertainties into probabilities. It leads him to the conclusion that they are unable to deal with trust.[26] Just as Bruni sees 'gratuity' as a prerequisite for innovations that help safeguard survival in the economy, Nooteboom regards 'trust' in objects, people, organizations or larger systems as indispensable.[27] Trust in systems is lost when a bank collects profits in times of prosperity but saddles society with the bill in times of adversity and losses, confident that the system can not afford to let banks go bust.[28] Trust in organizations is not stimulated when bank directors place the blame on their quantitative analysts (quants) and other whiz kids who developed models whose implications they, let alone their management, were unable to oversee.[29] Trust in people declines because our behavior is not just characterized by openness or the ability to acknowledge our own imperfection, but also by risk aversion that stems from calculated distrust.[30] Trust in people or organizations increases, however, when both the competence and

25 B. Nooteboom, *Trust, Forms, foundations, functions, failures and figures*. Cheltenham: Edward Elgar, 2002; id., *Vertrouwen. Opening naar een veranderende wereld*. Utrecht: Klement, 2017.

26 Nooteboom, *Vertrouwen*, 18–20.

27 Nooteboom, *Vertrouwen*, 20.

28 Nooteboom, *Vertrouwen*, 22.

29 Nooteboom, *Vertrouwen*, 24.

30 Nooteboom, *Vertrouwen*, 28–29.

the pure intentions of actors are established by experience. Although there will always be an irrational emotional side to trust, the ability and willingness to trust are based on knowledge, experience and reflection.[31]

Nooteboom learns from the philosopher Levinas that rather than submitting to the other and safeguarding his rights, opposition is the essential first step towards trust. He learns from Nietzsche that striving for transcendence to reach a higher self implies a self-centralization that does not inspire trust either.[32] In Nooteboom's work, Aristotle's virtue ethics forms the basis for a correction of contemporary virtue ethics because temperance, justice, courage and reason –later known as the cardinal virtues – and faith, hope and love –the later theological virtues –are seen as prerequisites for the strengthening of trust.[33] Nooteboom argues that contemporary ethics, which uses the utility function as an intellectual device to explain personal economic behavior, sees the pursuit of self-interest as a virtue because it leads to the greatest possible prosperity. This does not foster mutual trust between people, particularly because this ethic will condone phenomena like the take-over compulsion and the urge to control, as long as they are conducive to economic growth.[34] A rediscovery of Aristotle is therefore in order,[35] as fostering trust is an economic necessity. Nooteboom shows with great precision that the realization of the limits of one's own rationality, and hence of the existence of an irrational component in decision making, fosters awareness of dependence on others. Nooteboom points to investment as a concrete example where this mechanism is at work. On the other hand, the realization of one's limitedness or finiteness also leads to feelings of insecurity due to uncertainty on how negotiate competition and cooperation.[36] In organizations or during mergers it can even culminate in suspicion due to the complexity that is experienced.[37] Nooteboom has answered these objections thus:

> 'to an economist who says that in order to survive in markets you can not afford trust my reply would be that in order to be able to deal with radical uncertainty you can not do without trust.'[38]

31 Nooteboom, *Vertrouwen*, 36–39, 118–119.

32 Nooteboom, *Vertrouwen*, 57–61.

33 Nooteboom, *Vertrouwen*, 13, 108, 110–116.

34 Nooteboom, *Vertrouwen*, 109, 157.

35 Nooteboom, *Vertrouwen*, 109, 157, 160, 165–166, 171, 190.

36 Nooteboom, *Vertrouwen*, 159–160; 165; 171; 190.

37 Nooteboom, *Vertrouwen*, 178–179.

38 Nooteboom, *Vertrouwen*, 171. (Original: 'als een econoom zegt dat je om te overleven in markten geen vertrouwen kunt permitteren zeg ik dat je om moet kunnen gaan met radicale onzekerheid en dat daarvoor vertrouwen nodig is').

At this point in his exposé Nooteboom argues like Bruni that the 'new economy' should be based on a model of humankind in which people are not seen as creatures chiefly intent on the gratification of their material needs. Instead an anthropology is needed in which altruism and *philia*, that is, selfless friendship, are taken into account as an intrinsic value, goal and reward.

At this point it is tempting to draw parallels between Nooteboom's portrayal of the systemic tragedy and the way Pope John Paul II does this in his encyclical *Sollicitudo rei socialis* when he speaks about the 'structures of sin' of which people become part despite themselves as soon as they perform economic acts.[39] At this point Kahneman's call for the development of a 'richer language' for reflection on economic processes prompts us to embark on yet another brief etymological exploration.

In classical literature, 'pistis' refers to faith in people and in gods, as well as the belief or credibility attached or ascribed to something or someone. Demosthenes extends it to refer to 'economic credit'. The verb 'pisteuo' in fact means 'to have faith in a person' and also means meeting commitments or observing agreements. Influenced by the skeptics and philosophers who denied the existence of the gods, 'pistis' began to take on the meaning not just of 'trust', but also of 'faith' and became a term used to express the conviction that the gods do exist. The Stoics used 'pistis' to express their belief in the divine world order, of which human beings as autonomously and morally acting subjects were the center.

In the Hebrew languages, the root 'ãman (derivatives of which were translated as 'pistis' in the Septuagint) means 'reliable', 'faithfulness'. This qualification was attached to people like messengers or prophets and to God,[40] whereas 'faithful to' and 'faith in' are almost synonymous, particularly in later Judaism, just as in Antiquity.[41] In the synoptic gospels 'pistis' can refer to the faith sick persons or the people in their surroundings have in Jesus.[42] In Paul's letters 'pistis' is a very crucial notion.[43] He employs the term no fewer than 142 times, with conjugations of 'pisteuo' appearing 54 times and the adjective 'pistos' 33 times. The precise meaning of the word is the subject of vigorous debate among scholars of the New Testament, and particularly of the Pauline writings. Biblical scholars still have trouble separating 'pistis' from the interpretation

39 Nooteboom, *Vertrouwen*, 238; John Paul II, *Sollicitudo Rei Socialis* 36.

40 Deuteronomy 7: 9.

41 Cf. Proverbs 30: 8.

42 Mark 2: 5; 5: 34–36; Matthew 8: 10.

43 S. Agteres, 'Pistis and Fides as Civic and Divine Virtues: A Pauline Concept through Greco-Roman Eyes', in: C. Breytenbach (ed.), *Paul's Graeco-Roman Context* (Leuven: Peeters, 2015), 541–559. (*Bibliotheca Ephemeridum Theologicarum Lovaniensium* 277).

that Luther gave to this word when he decided to translate it as 'faith' (*Glaube*, in Luther's native German). But philological research over the past decades has shown that the word does indeed have significantly different shades of meaning in its widely varying contexts.

Drawing on his great familiarity with the letters of Paul Augustine after 414 arrived at a synthesis of his interpretation of 'pistis' that brought 'faith' and 'trust' within touching distance of each other. In his new interpretation, faith and trust are inherent to entering a relationship, a claim he substantiates by discerning three gradations that are ideally intrinsically connected. In *sermo Dolbeau* 19 'credere illi' (to believe him) refers to the belief that what a person (Christ) says is true. 'Credere illum' entails the confidence that what the other person professes to be –the chosen or the anointed one –is also true. And finally, 'credere in illum' for Augustine entails 'diligere', loving. This places the other fully center stage, with self-interest relegated to a wholly subordinate position because, as Augustine indicates in *sermo Dolbeau* 19, the other in question, that is, Christ, has demonstrated that he is capable of leading people to salvation.[44] It is a path – the preposition 'in' and the accusative indicates direction and dynamism – that ideally leads to full knowledge of each other: 'without mirror and not in riddles'. Nor does Augustine value despair as the opposite of hope and trust. In *sermo* 22 he states that Judas did not go to hell for betraying the Lord – as that was already foreseen in God's plan – but because he cut himself off from love in his despair and no longer had faith in anyone or anything. And, in Augustine's view, that equals hell.[45] All through his working life he thought the gravest sin was to be heedful only of God's justice and to ignore God's mercy. He regarded sins against hope as worse than any other sins he has committed in his life because someone who despairs or is afraid acts as if a sentence has already been passed. And to Augustine this is an insult both to God's justice and his mercy.[46]

---

44 Augustine, *Sermo Dolbeau* 19.5: 'Et quoniam paulo ante distinximus aliud esse credere illi, credere illum et credere in illum - credere illi est credere vera esse illa quae loquitur, credere illum est credere quod ipse sit Christus, credere in illum diligere illum -, iam discute tua ista: credere quae loquitur vera esse, credere ipsum esse Christum, diligere Christum. Credere vera esse quae loquitur, multi et mali possunt. Credunt enim esse vera et nolunt facere ea: ad operandum pigri sunt. Credere autem ipsum esse Christum, hoc et daemones potuerunt … Ecce quam verum dictum est: *Hoc est opus Dei, ut credatis in eum quem ille misit* (Rom 13: 10), hoc est ut diligendo eatis in eum, id est incorporemini ei'. Cf. *Sermo Dolbeau* 19.6.

45 Augustine, *sermo* 22.6; *In Johannis euangelium tractatus* 41.8: 'Non enim est sine causa et terruit, et spem dedit: terruit, ne peccatum amaremus; spem dedit, ne de peccati solutione diffideremus'.

46 Augustine, *sermo* 20. 1, *sermo* 351.5.12 and passim.

As has been seen, Nooteboom convincingly argues in his latest book that living the Aristotelian virtues not only gives rise to a critique of utilitarianism but also, and in particular, leads to economic interactions based on trust. It can be deduced from Scripture and from patristic sources that trust is fostered not just by leading a virtuous life, but also through and within relationships. As a matter of fact, the capacity to establish relationships is precisely the human characteristic that the concept of the *homo economicus* failed to take into account. As we noted above, this concept sees human beings as individuals with consistent preferences who act only out of self-interest and in doing so become fearful of committing themselves. Study of the sources just mentioned suggests that such a model of the human fails to do justice to the actual reality of human beings.

Having reached a certain age, Augustine distinguishes three gradations of trust: as a subjective feeling (1), a belief in the truth (2) and honesty of acts, insights or statements (3). Loosely interpreted, someone can still speak the truth during an economic transaction in which they employ clever sales tricks and closing techniques. The 'credere illi' by the buyer –trusting that the seller speaks the truth –is then justified. If the broader aim beyond the transaction itself is to enter into a genuine relationship with the customer, however, a more existential form of trust will arise, which Augustine expresses through the word pair 'credere illum'. It involves trust in a person as such, not just in what the other says based on their knowledge and competence. Aside from the fact that a study summarized in *Harvard Business Review* shows that (my summary, PvG) it is not 'credere illi' but 'credere illum' that safeguards the continuity of an enterprise; these different degrees of trust lead to a sense of security and belonging, even in relationships shaped by economic transactions.[47] Lastly, it can be deduced from Augustine's threefold division that it is love when people in a personal relationship based on genuine trust are prepared to sacrifice their self-interest for the benefit of the other, for no other reason than the personal fulfillment it brings them. Then they are close to 'credere illum'.

Although Augustine does not elucidate how 'dilectio' or 'caritas' could determine economic interactions, the way he brings together the three gradations of trust suggests that he chooses to see them as part of one dynamism. Elsewhere he shows an awareness that love can take on two different forms. In its ideal form, it is selfless, *gratis*, and therefore the most healing and pure force that can move a human being. There is also a self-interested love, however.

47 https://hbr.org/2014/10/the-value-of-keeping-the-right-customers

Augustine characterizes this love more in terms of desire (*concupiscentia*).[48] It expresses itself for example in efforts to help each other on each other's individual quest for wisdom.[49]

In his younger days, Augustine, taking inspiration from Cicero, already spoke of the 'mutua benevolentia', the reciprocity that is the mark of any good relationship.[50] Over the years, however, he was influenced by Paul's notion, closely related to Augustine's relational interpretation of 'pistis', that is, that Christians see themselves as flawed and sinful in the light of the One in whom they trust. In Augustine's thinking, this realization was not a goal in itself. The realization that one is flawed paves the way for the aspiration not to disappoint others, including God, in Augustine's case, and thus to speak the truth and also to be authentic and loving.

We can therefore conclude from Scripture and from works from the Christian tradition that trust not only relates to the cultivation of virtues, but also assumes that human beings should first and foremost be seen as an *esse ad* –a being-to – that is, as relational beings. Incidentally this deeply contradicts the Aristotelian theory of categories, in which substance is the first and most important category. Scripture and tradition can make us realize that trust as key note or root can have different but cohesive gradations, like the intensity of the various types of relationships . And this is just one of the things they can reveal to us.

## 4 The *homo economicus* as a Threat to Social Cohesion. Samuel Bowles on 'Outcrowding' of Morally Responsible Behavior and Augustine on *timor servilis* and *amor castus*

One of the constants in the work of Samuel Bowles, professor emeritus at the University of Massachusetts at Amherst, is the way markets and other economic institutions influence people's preferences or the patterns of interaction

48 Augustine, *epistula* 155.1.1; *Enarratio in Psalmum* 55.17; cf. I. Hadot, 'Amicitia', in: C. Mayer (ed.), *Augustinuslexikon* (Basel-Berlin: Schwabe Verlag, 1986-.....), vol. 1, col. 287–293, especially 291; D. Dideberg, 'Caritas', in: C. Mayer (ed.), *Augustinuslexikon* (Basel-Berlin: Schwabe Verlag, 1986-.....), vol. 1, col. 730–743; id. `Amor', in: C. Mayer (ed.), *Augustinuslexikon* (Basel-Berlin: Schwabe Verlag, 1986-.....), vol. 1, col. 294–300.

49 Augustine, *Soliloquia* I, 13, 22.

50 T. van Bavel, 'The influence of Cicero's Ideal of Friendship on Augustine', in: J. den Boeft (ed), *Augustiniana Trajectina* (Paris, 1987), 59–72. Cf. also R. Canning, *The Unity of Love for God and Neighbour in St. Augustine* (Louvain: Peeters, 1993), 49–65; 114–115.

that shape a particular society. To show that it is a mistake for economists to ignore exogenous motives receive, he adds proof upon proof of the impact economic institutions have on social interactions, and hence on the evolution of social norms. The greater the anonymity in which transactions take place, the less the other party is experienced as human. Bowles argues that this does not lead to a market entirely without norms: the norm that agreements should be respected, for example, survives. At the same time, however, this emphasis on transaction instead of relationship prevents virtues like generosity and altruism from gaining a foothold in economic traffic.[51]

Thus, in his book *The Moral Economy. Why Good Incentives Are No Substitute for Good Citizens*, Bowles contends that it is wrong to take the concept of the *homo economicus* as the point of departure for reflections on human motives, if only because mutual cooperation or interaction are more likely driven by extrinsic, often financial incentives than by intrinsic motivation.[52] Bowles discusses a now famous experiment by Uri Gneezy and Aldo Rustichini at great length. As a key part of the experiment, conducted at a daycare center in Haifa, Israel, parents who were late for the evening pick-up of their child or children were fined. As it turned out many parents gradually began to see their fine as a straightforward payment for their tardiness and began to postpone their pick-up times even further. The findings lead Bowles to observe that, as soon as people really begin to embody the calculating *homo economicus*, the 'outcrowding' of ethical motives will ensue, as well as erosion of the moral sense, a decay of the economic principle of reciprocity and the decline of a 'robust civic culture' shaped by cooperative and generous citizens.[53]

Bowles uses the Haifa experiment to show that there can be a *debitum* that is not purely financial but has moral overtones. Bowles takes modern economists to task for their inability to prevent situations like that in Haifa, a failure caused by their choice to keep *incentives* and *morals* separate. He decries this

---

51 S. Bowles, 'Endogenous Preferences: The Cultural Consequences of Markets and other Economic Institutions', in: *Journal of Economic Literature* 36 (March 1998), 75–111, especially 75–77, 80, 89 ('other regarding behavior'), 97–101, 105; Bowles, 'Endogenous Preferences', 101: 'A broader concept of market failure is thus required, one encompassing the effects of economic policies and institutions on preferences and for this reason more adequate for the consideration of an appropriate mix of markets, communities, families, and states in economic governance'.

52 S. Bowles, *The moral economy. Why Good Incentives Are No Substitute for Good Citizens*. New Haven - London: Yale University Press, 2016.

53 Bowles, *The moral economy*, 145. See also: U. Gneezy, A. Rustichini, 'A fine is a price', in: *Journal of Legal Studies* 29(2000), 1–17. See for the opposite view, however: J.J. Graafland, 'Do Markets Crowd Out Virtues?', in: *Journal of Business Ethics* 91(2009), 1–19.

'separability assumption', as it means that 'motives such as altruism, reciprocity, intrinsic pleasure in helping others, aversion to inequity, ethical commitments and other motives that induce people to help others' are not nurtured.[54] In addition, Bowles observes, the separation is also incompatible with the pursuit of 'natural liberty' described by Adam Smith. This natural liberty should never come at the expense of others: in the case of the Haifa experiment, the women providing daytime care.[55] Bowles therefore argues for the enacting of laws that, while allowing people freedom to pursue their personal goals, stimulate them to take into account the possible consequences for their fellow beings. As Bowles himself puts it:

> 'In economic language, this can be done if each actor internalizes the entire costs and benefits of an action, including the effects on others, rather than taking account merely of one's private benefits and costs, that is, those that affect one's own profit or loss, pleasure or pain'.[56]

At the same time Bowles observes that, thanks to the civilization process in developed countries, citizens enjoy protection against personal injury of unlawful loss of property. On the other hand, he also observes that countries have no punitive sanctions against misbehavior like the utter lack of respect shown by the parents in Haifa –their 'malfeasance' –or their opportunism.[57] Bowles advocates a rule of law that protects citizens against 'cataclysmic loss' but also encourages if not forces them to behave socially appropriately, cooperatively, and therefore respectfully.[58] In the spirit of Deirdre McCloskey's trilogy *Bourgeois Virtues, Bourgeois Dignity* and *Bourgeois Equality* and of papal social encyclicals from *Rerum Novarum* to *Laudato si'*, Bowles convincingly argues that modern capitalism is anything but immoral, and in fact remains successful to the extent to which biblically founded virtues like 'temperance', 'courage' 'wisdom' and 'justice' are present in the motives of those who shape it. Bowles summarizes this dynamic as follows: 'Markets may have assisted "the

54 Bowles, *The moral economy*, 44–45; 'separability assumption', 21–25.

55 Bowles, *The moral economy*, 20, '[Smith] His famous line, "Every man ... is left perfectly free to pursue his own interest in his own way," was conditioned in that very sentence by the proviso: "as long as he does not violate the laws of justice," meaning that "every member of the society [is to be protected] from the injustice or oppression of every other member of it'.

56 Bowles, *The moral economy*, 26.

57 Bowles, *The moral economy*, 144.

58 Bowles, *The moral economy*, 145.

civilizing process".' And along the way, trust in the own family or group gradually began to extend to trust in society.[59]

In *Moral economy*, Bowles does more than just criticize parents in Haifa who were bent on their own self-interest and disregarded the interests of the employees to whom they had entrusted their children. He is mainly out to show that the availability of a simple means of buying off a moral obligation inevitably leads to loss of respect for the well-being of others and to corrosion of people's moral compasses.

Having read Bowles's book, I am tempted to further reflect on the problem he raises and revisit the history of the commercialization of indulgences in the Catholic Church. As a matter of fact, indulgences did not grant absolution from sin – that required genuine remorse and absolution in confession– but cancellation of the corresponding punishments in the hereafter.[60] Indulgences became a booming business when Albert of Brandenburg was

59 Bowles, *The moral economy*, 145, 149–150; cf. 145–150. Cf. D. McCloskey: *The Bourgeois virtues. Ethics in an Age of Commerce*. Chicago: The University of Chicago Press, 2007; id., *The Bourgeois Dignity. Why Economics Can't Explain the Modern World*. Chicago: The University of Chicago Press, 2011, and id., *Bourgeois Equality. How Ideas, not Capital or Institutions, Enriched the World*.Chicago: The University of Chicago Press, 2016. See also: A.Hirschman, *The Passion and the Interests* (Princeton, New Jersey: Princeton University Press, 1977), 9–66. In all social encyclicals, the successive popes also contended that the free market economy offers human beings the means to realize a creative and responsible commitment and solidarity (Cf. for instance John Paul II, *Centesimus Annus* 34, 42, Benedict XVI, *Caritas in Veritate* 65, and passim). But they have also acknowledged that capitalism will not automatically bring all people the prosperity desired (*Centesimus Annus* 42). This presupposes a free economy with a certain degree of equality between all parties. (*Centesimus Annus* 48). An appeal must therefore be made to people's social conscience (*Caritas in Veritate* 35–36, 65, 68) and guarantees must be put in place for the weakest members of society according to the principle of solidarity (*Centesimus Annus* 15; *Caritas in Veritate* 65). See P. van Geest, 'Armoede en menselijke waardigheid. Het Magisterium van de katholieke kerk over de wisselwerking tussen beide- Poverty and human dignity: The magisterium of the Catholic Church on the interaction between the two', in: *Tydskrif vir Geesteswetenskappe/Journal of Humanities* 60(2020), nr. 3, 646–658. L. Ladaria, P. Turkson, *Oeconomicae et pecuniariae quaestiones* (Roma: Libreria Editrice Vaticana, 2018), section 2–16 says that capitalism is not intrinsically evil or morally unjustified, but becomes evil if it is isolated from the economic goal of furthering the dignity of every human being, or if the economic order is no longer based on the golden rule.

60 E. Amort, [*Historia indulgentiarum*] *De origine, progressu, valore, ac fructu indulgentiarum, necnon de dispositionibus ad eas lucrandas requisitis, accurata notitia, historia, dogmatica, polemica, critica* (Venetiis: apud Joannem Baptistam Recurti, 1733), 355–410: accurately explains that forgiveness of sins was necessary before an indulgence could be granted. Cf. for a brief history of indulgences: A. Angenendt, *Geschichte der Religiosität im Mittelalter*. 3. Auflage. (Darmstadt: Wissenschaftliche Buchgesellschaft, 2005), 652–657. See also: *Handbuch der Ablässe* (Rom: Libreria Editrice Vaticana, 2008), 17–24; 27–81.

ordained bishop of Mainz, a privilege for which he had to pay Pope Leo x a substantial sum of money. To enable Albert to pay off the loan given to him by banker Jakob Fugger, the pope gave him permission to sell indulgences to the people of his diocese. The Dominican and doctor of theology Johannes Tetzel became Albrecht's indulgence minister and head of sales. Tetzel's sermons are textbook cases of the way repentance was emphasized as a prerequisite for absolution from sin to underscore the importance of the available indulgences, and so increase sales. Even a cursory impression suggests that further study of the rhetorical and commercial strategies employed in sermons like Tetzel's could greatly increase our awareness of the dangers of corrosion of the moral compass and blunting of the moral conscience caused by an unduly rigid separation of *incentives* and *morals*. Incidentally, Luther's criticism of Tetzel's practices, in his *Eynn Sermon von dem Ablasz vnnd Gnade*, focused on another aspect. In this treatise he denounced the image of God as a bookkeeper that underlies the trade in indulgences, and also the trivialization of God's unfathomable benevolence and grace. The trade in indulgences was one of the root causes of the outbreak of the Reformation. On the other hand, its revenues also helped finance the construction of Saint Peter's Basilica in Rome, with free admission for all, including Protestants. Even this cloud had a silver lining.

Back to business. The objections that Bowles raises against modern economists closely resemble the objections a church historian could make against the salesman Tetzel's practices: they both employ strategies using external triggers that could prevent people from acting on motives that are intrinsically good. In Tetzel's case, his emphasis on the liberation from temporary punishments in life after death can hinder reflection on one's own imperfection in words and thoughts and deeds. In the case of modern economists, Bowles refers to an arrangement that causes people to lose sight of, and lose touch with, a way of life marked by the pursuit of reciprocity, altruism or pleasure in helping others. Buying off moral responsibility and the concomitant erosion of ethical awareness is the unintended but inevitable outcome of a strategy that has gained widespread adoption in many fields.

In the early days of Christianity, long before the arrival of Tetzel and Bowles's modern economists, a kind of kill-or-cure remedy against the atrophy of moral, altruistic sensitivity was developed that bears a remarkable similarity to the mechanisms that play a key role in the theories of moral development expounded by the Swiss developmental psychologist Jean Piaget and others. The Apostle Paul, who was both an entrepreneur (he was a tent maker) and a scribe, argues that it is not wrong to focus people's minds on the message by instilling fear of God's punishment on the Day of Judgement.

In his letters Paul regularly gives variations on the psalmist's theme that the fear of God is the beginning of wisdom.[61] At the same time he implies that people whose only motivation to do right and refrain from evil is fear of punishment should be considered immature. In various places throughout his works, Calvin summarizes this fundamental idea in Paul's thinking by saying that love is 'the purpose of the law'.[62] But it was Augustine, Calvin's source, whom he affectionately called 'Augustinus totus noster', who presented, the most systematic treatment of the interplay between the *timor servilis* (the 'servile' fear that 'attests to immaturity') and *amor castus* ('pure love'), in his commentary to the psalms, the *Enarrationes in Psalmos*.[63]

We will discuss Augustine's thoughts on this as an invitation to reflect further on the question whether real fear of repercussions can indeed serve as an external trigger to counter the 'outcrowding' of ethical considerations and morally responsible behavior towards one's neighbor that Bowles so loathes. The next question that presents itself is how this real fear then relates to the benevolence, friendship and love that ideally characterize relationships, including economic ones, or even have a positive influence on them. For now, we will leave aside the question whether the fear of God is a *real* fear, if it is accepted that God exists and people therefore have ensure they do not displease God, or an *imaginary* fear like that people have of non-existent monsters lurking under their beds. For Augustine, God's existence was a given. It would take us too far afield here to discuss his 'proofs of God's existence' to make fear of God as realistic as possible.

Augustine divides the *timor servilis* into four consecutive instances. The first form of fear he discerns concerns people who know that their acts are wrong, who fear adversity on earth, or live in fear of punishment on earth or

61 Cf. Psalm 110 (111): 10; Galaten 2: 16; Romeinen 3: 21–3.

62 Cf. for instance: John Calvin, *Commentarius in Mosis reliquos quator libros*. Pars I, II, where he contends that love is the end of the Law. Cf. for the manner in which Calvin attempts to instill fear: 8. Calvin ascribes to Moses the words that if people were free to rob and plunder, a more terrible judgement is to be expected, because God hears the cries of the poor (25, 28; cf. 32 and passim): 'usury is not now unlawful, except in so far as it contravenes equity and brotherly union. Let each one, then, place himself before God's judgment-seat, and not do to his neighbor what he would not have done to himself, from whence a sure and infallible decision may be come to' (translation taken from: John Calvin, *Commentaries on the last four books of Moses, arranged in the form of a Harmony*. Vol 3 (Edinburgh: Calvin Translation Society, 1855), 121.

63 *Joannis Calvini opera quae supersunt omnia* (Brunsvigae: C.A. Schwetschke, 1863), Ed. E. Cunitz, J.-W. Baum, E.W.E. Reuss. 59 parts in 58 vols. Vol. 8, 266. See also J. M. Lange van Ravenswaay, *Augustine totus noster. Das Augustinverständnis bei Johannes Calvin*. Göttingen: Vandenhoeck & Ruprecht, 1990 (*Forschungen zur Kirchen- und Dogmengeschichte* 45).

in life after death.[64] Then there is the fear caused by threats uttered by others that keep us from doing the right things. Thirdly there is the fear of the consequences of a bad deed one has committed.[65] And finally there is fear of divine judgment. ('It is a servile fear, the fear of burning in hell with the devil').[66] It is the fear of those who are not frightened of worldly suffering, but worry about their final destiny. Although they too are governed by *timor*, their form of fear can still become *timor castus*,[67] sometimes called *timor Domini castus*, if the fear of punishment disappears.[68] In Augustine's view this latter form of *timor servilis* is the purest and even best (and most eternal),[69] because it is free of servile fear, a sign of immaturity.[70] Nurtured by and born from love,[71] *timor castus* is therefore not characterized by the fear, for example, of being caught by the taxman after committing fraud, but entails the fear of forever being denied the love of the loved one whose countenance we can no longer behold.[72] *Timor castus* corresponds to and is sometimes synonymous with *amor castus*, and it also entails longing for God's proximity, a longing that is stronger than the desire to enjoy prosperity on earth.[73] Augustine also relates *timor castus* to love

64 Augustine, *Enarratio in Psalmum* 55.17 (not acting rightly); *Enarratio in Psalmum* 127.7 (not wanting to be affected by illness); *Enarratio in Psalmum* 18, *sermo* 1. 10; *Enarratio in Psalmum* 18, *sermo* 2. 10 (fear of punishment).

65 Augustine, *Enarratio in Psalmum* 127.7.

66 Augustine, *Sermo* 161, 9: 'servilis timor est, quo times cum diabolo ardere'.

67 Augustine, *Enarratio in Psalmum* 127.7; 127.8.

68 Augustine, *Enarratio in Psalmum* 18, *sermo* 1.10; *Enarratio in Psalmum* 18, *sermo* 2.10.

69 Augustine, *Enarratio in Psalmum* 18. *sermo* 2.10 (timor Domini castus); *Enarratio in Psalmum* 127.7; *Enarratio in Psalmum* 18, *sermo* 1.10; *Enarratio in Psalmum* 150.1. (eternal).

70 Augustine, *Enarratio in Psalmum* 149.15; *Enarratio in Psalmum* 150.1: 'Quae operatio septenaria per Isaiam prophetam ita commemoratur: *Requiescet super eum Spiritus Dei; Spiritus sapientiae et intellectus, Spiritus consilii et fortitudinis, Spiritus scientiae et pietatis, Spiritus timoris Domini.* Ipse debet intellegi timor Domini castus, permanens in saeculum saeculi. Servilem autem timorem consummata caritas foras mittit; et nos liberos facit, ne servilia opera faciamus, quae sabbato prohibentur'.

71 Augustine, *Enarratio in Psalmum* 127.7 (nourished by love); *Enarratio in Psalmum* 127.8 (born from love).

72 Augustine, *Enarratio in Psalmum* 127.8 (deprived of closeness beloved); *Enarratio in Psalmum* 77. 12.

73 Augustine, *Enarratio in Psalmum* 127. 8–9. For the relation between *timor servilis* and *timor castus* in other works, see: P. van Geest, '*Ante omnia igitur opus est Dei timore converti* (*doctr. chr.* 2.7.9). Augustine's Evaluation of Fear', in: A. Dupont, G. Partoens, M. Lamberigts (eds), *Tractatio scripturarum. Philological, Exegetical, Rhetorical and Theological Studies on Augustine's Sermons* (Louvain: Peeters, 2012), 443–464 (*Instrvmenta Patristica et Medievalia. Research on the Inheritance of Early and Medieval Christianity* 65- *Ministerium Sermonis* II).

of justice: he calls the fear of punishment an iron chain, but in this context characterizes the motive of love of justice as a gold chain.[74]

Augustine thus keeps emphasizing that fear of ever-lasting death and love for what God has promised, like *timor castus* and *amor castus*, are nearly indistinguishable.[75] Fear of God and his justice ideally goes hand in hand with love of God for his mercifulness.[76] In the same vein Augustine portrays fear and longing not as opposites, but as complementary, and occasionally as simultaneous and therefore similar. On the one hand, he indicates that he himself is constrained by fear of the Judgment and the return of Christ. On the other, he immediately adds that this testifies to inconsistency, as Christians who live righteously develop a longing for the coming of Christ. It's impossible to love someone whose arrival one dreads.[77]

His strategy in the *Enarrationes* thus clearly shows that Augustine regards fear as an incentive to introspection and a safeguard against pride. For Augustine fear is necessary, even indispensable, but at the same time it is 'only' an *ancilla* of hope, joy, love and longing.

Jean Piaget (†1980) established that young children accept and internalize rules for conduct out of fear of punishment. At a later stage, children rebel against these rules before eventually reappraising and readopting the old rules, but not without taking into account their own personal experiences. Augustine's *sermo* 156, a reply to the Pelagians, shows that he could be called an early precursor to this Swiss developmental psychologist. Augustine writes there that human beings discover their own flaws through the Law. They see the Law as a code that commands, threatens, and at the same time promises, and that helps them to gain a better insight into themselves and thus temper their arrogance by inducing fear of punishment. Only when a person lives under grace does the motivation that guides their actions change. Once they are sure of having been mercifully accepted after the coming of Christ, human beings will no longer act out of fear of punishment, but out of love of justice. Whereas *timor* is the spiritual state of the slave, *amor* is that of the friend. The two are not separate. Augustine even discerns an evolutionary process that links them

74 Augustine, *Enarratio in Psalmum* 149. 15.

75 Augustine, *Enarratio in Psalmum* 64. 16: 'Quod supra homines est time, et homines te non terrebunt. Mortem sempiternam time, et praesentem non curabis. … Ama ergo, et time: ama quod promittit Deus, time quod minatur Deus; nec corrumperis ex eo quod promittit, nec terreberis ex eo quod minatur homo'.

76 Augustine, *Enarratio in Psalmum* 70, *sermo* 1.1: 'Multum enim movet Dei amor et timor: timor Dei, quia iustus est; amor, quia misericors est'.

77 Augustine, *Enarratio in Psalmum* 147.1.

together.[78] In this process, fear is the servant of love, rather than the other way round.

The late *sermo* 156 once again shows that Augustine regards fear as belonging to an early stage of development.[79] Whenever he describes fear, he depicts it as beneficial to the extent that it inspires people to honest self-assessment. The realization that one cannot fully satisfy the law, and that one is flawed, causes a fear that ideally leads to humility, a basic attitude that implies better contact with others and at the same time a good relationship with God. Fear is wholesome as long as it does not lead to defeatism, and as long as it functions as the precursor to love in the first stage of individual human development.[80] This means it is a beneficial force, provided a person's development continues.

## 5 Taking Stock

Samuel Bowles, whom we've just discussed, once asked himself why economists could be so beholden to the model of the *homo economicus* for so long. He regards the lack of interdisciplinary collaboration that he observes among his fellow economists –and not just among them – as the main reason for the persistent tendency to keep postponing work on a new model of humankind that is better able than the *homo economicus* model to analyze the economic reality. As Bowles himself phrases it:

> '... economics pay a heavy price for its self-imposed isolation from the other behavioral sciences. At its simplest, the conception underlying contemporary disciplinary boundaries is one of society marked by an implausible degree of specialization among institutions: families and religious institutions shape culture, governments govern, and economic institutions allocate resources. These disciplinary boundaries have favored the development of parochial, incompatible, and inadequate models of human behavior in the various disciplines, ranging from the

78 Cf. Augustine, *Contra duas epistulas Pelagianorum* 1.22. Cf. evenwel voor de richting waar Augustine naar toe wil: *De gratia Christi et de peccato originali libri duo* 25.29: 'non sub lege terrente, convincente, puniente, sed sub gratia delectante, sanante, liberante'.

79 Augustine, *sermo* 156, 13.14: 'Timor servus est, caritas libera est; et ut sic dicamus, timor est servus caritatis'.

80 The salutary nature of fear, as long as it is kept in check and connected with *amor* can also be deduced from the hermeneutical and mystagogical way that Augustine sets out in *De doctrina christiana* 2.7,9–11 or for instance in *sermo* 347 (*De timore Dei*).

> oversocialized homo sociologicus to the undersocialized homo economicus. Recognition of the cultural effects of markets (and other economic institutions) may foster a more unified approach to the behavioral sciences, a benefit of which might be the more successful resolution of outstanding puzzles in economics'.[81]

We hope to have shown that, in addition to rapprochement between behavioral scientists and Bowles's confrères, a structural meeting of the minds between economists and theologians is justified, because theology and economics as scientific disciplines are compatible. In addition, leading economists such as Bruni and Nooteboom themselves have, as part of their ambition to broaden the perspective of their colleagues, begun to consider notions that theologians have long reflected on, like 'gratuity' and 'trust', in a way that should invite others to do the same. Their fruitful interpretation of these terms – which are also relevant to economics –has inspired us to interpret them in the light of several tropes in Scriptural and patristic sources. We did this to substantiate the thesis that theology has a meaningful contribution to make to the development of a richer language for reflection on economic processes, one that is alert to the complexity of human beings as economic and relational beings. Bowles's own criticism that the caesura between ethical motives and external triggers leads to a decreasing awareness of these motives, and hence of the economic principle of reciprocity, has turned out to be grist to the mill of historical theologians. This criticism was the prelude to a reflection on the possible use of Augustine's view on the relationship between fear and love to eliminate the consequences of external triggers and heighten the awareness that reciprocity, altruism, benevolence towards and love for the other lead to happiness.

However, as we have seen in the introduction, it is possible that the economists we have discussed so far are exceptions to the rule that theology is of interest to economists, as they are alone among their colleague in thinking about economic notions that could be enriched through recourse to theological sources. In our next chapter we will therefore take a critical, theologically inspired look at the notions of *bounded morality, bounded rationality* and *bounded willpower*, on the assumption that our comments will be able to contribute to the design of a relational economy.

81 S. Bowles, 'Endogenous Preferences: The Cultural Consequences of Markets and other Economic Institutions', in: *Journal of Economic Literature* 36 (March 1998), 75–111, esp. 102–105.

CHAPTER 6

# Economic Notions Seen in the Light of the History of Theology

## 1 Introduction

It may well be possible that the economists discussed in the previous chapter are the proverbial exceptions to the rule that theology is of interest to economists because of the theologians' age-long tradition of reflection upon notions like mercy and unselfishness, trust, motives and intentions. In this sixth chapter we will try to counter this objection by discussing crucial economic notions like *bounded morality, bounded rationality* and *bounded willpower*. For many scientists these notions have become the starting point for research in a new branch of economic science called behavioral economics. It is in fact clear from the outset that behavioral economics is much more alive to the imperfection of individuals than traditional economics, as the latter takes the ability of rational human beings to assess or deal with matters optimally for granted. But human brain capacity is limited, as is human morality. In this chapter we will therefore try to show that the involvement of theologians in reflection on the notions of *bounded rationality, bounded morality* and *bounded willpower* is both useful and necessary and can help to respond to Daniel Kahneman's call for the development of a more refined language that does greater justice to human complexity and that will broaden the analytical framework of economics. The model of the *homo economicus* will be questioned as a preliminary step towards the design of a more relational economy, for example (as exemplified by Bovenberg's work), one which takes relationships into account and does not treat the economy as mere sequences of anonymous transactions.

## 2 Negative and Affective Theology as a Prelude to a Deeper Insight into *Bounded Rationality*

In his ground-breaking work *The General Theory of Employment, Interest and Money* (1936) John Maynard Keynes wrote that the economy is not just driven by people whose actions are determined by rational considerations alone. He drew attention to the *animal spirits* of human beings: forces that are seen as a disturbance in the economy, as they can just as easily paralyze people as

 | DOI:10.1163/9789004501706_007

incite them. In Keynes's view the government should play a role similar to that of parents who give their children the opportunity to discover the irrational forces that often determine their behavior, but also know where to draw the line to keep their offspring from succumbing to their *animal spirits*. Following Keynes's line of thinking, in their book *Animal Spirits: How Human Psychology Drives the Economy, and Why it Matters for Global Capitalism*, Akerlof and Shiller argue that the government should put as few obstacles as possible in the way of initiatives by entrepreneurs, but should not leave capitalist economies to their own devices either. If the latter were to happen, chances are that there will be excesses that the authors trace back to *animal spirits*, which in turn are nurtured by changes in trust, temptations, envy, rancor, illusions and ever-changing stories about the economy.[1] Akerlof's and Shiller's presentation of irrationality as a causal factor did not meet with general approval. But they clearly deplored that nearly all *animal spirits* that Keynes had named in *The General Theory* as root causes of the Great Depression had been obscured from view by later economists.

There was yet another path along which it became clear to the world that people are neither perfect nor always rational. In our introduction we mentioned in passing that the economist and psychologist Herbert Simon in 1955 was the first to fundamentally question the concept of the *homo economicus*. As we have seen, this model assumed that people are equipped with correct and complete knowledge, reach perfect conclusions and have a clear and complete view of the consequences. What Simon proved was that the information a person relies on to come to his assessment is more often than not incomplete, as lack of time and routine limit the ability to take the right decisions, and that people's ability to comprehensively process and correctly evaluate information is much more limited than the concept of the *homo economicus* allowed for. Simon concluded that human beings are endowed with a *bounded rationality*. This notion combines the limited availability of information, human cognitive limitations and the limited time available to come to a decision, thus confronting humanity with the realization that a truly optimal solution for problems

1 G.A. Akerlof, R. Shiller, *Animal Spirits: How Human Psychology Drives the Economy, and Why it Matters for Global Capitalism* (Princeton-New Jersey: Princeton University Press, 2009), passim; see also the sequel: G.A. Akerlof, R. Shiller, *Phishing for Phools: The Economics of Manipulation & Deception*.Princeton-New Jersey: Princeton University Press, 2015. This book focuses on 'phishing equilibria' in which every chance for exceptional profit is taken, even if this entails conscious manipulation, deception and fraud. They argue that the failure of free markets is due to 'phishing' by markets and to 'phools' who are purposefully deceived.

will never be found.[2] Simon coined the term 'satisficing' for this, an inseparable compound verb created by splicing together 'satisfy' and 'suffice'.[3] He used it to refer to the decision strategy or cognitive heuristic that is meant to select the most satisfying and sufficient of all available options. In his view mathematical calculations were indispensable for finding this most satisfying and sufficient solution to a problem. With reference to management studies, he observed that the decision theory they use was marred by the absence of a clear choice between the possibility on the one hand that an optimal solution may be found, albeit for a theoretically simplified world, and the possibility on the other of finding a sufficient and satisfying solution for a more realistic world.[4]

We know the subsequent course of events: following in the footsteps of Herbert Simon, psychologists like Amos Tversky and particularly Daniel Kahneman –and many others with them –have refined the view on the cognitive limitations of people, their inconsistency when making decisions and particularly the thoughtlessness of their decisions in uncertain conditions. The results of Kahneman's experiments also showed that people's assessments and choices do not just rely on their reason, but are also strongly influenced by intuitions and emotions or anticipated emotions (for instance, aversion to expected loss, disappointment, guilt or regret).[5] Relying on our intuition, it transpires, is not without its perils. Whereas intuition can be very fruitful when, for example, experts with boundless hours of relevant practice rely on it, Kahneman's research shows that intuitive decision making can lead to systematic assessment errors. According to Kahneman there are two distinct systems at work within each of us.[6] What he calls system 1 represents a fast, intuitive mode of thinking, while system 2 is characterized by a slower, more reflective mode of thinking, in which more conscious attention is given to a particular

2 H.A. Simon, *Models of bounded rationality*. Cambridge, MA: MIT Press, 1982; id., 'Rationality as process and as product of thought', in: *American Economic Review* 68 (1978), no. 2, 1–16. An indispensable reference book is: R. Viale (ed.), *Routledge Handbook of Bounded Rationality*, Routledge, 2020.

3 H. A. Simon, 'Rational Choice and the Structure of the Environment', in: *Psychological Review* 63 (1956), no. 2, 129–138; 129: 'Evidently, organisms adapt well enough to 'satisfice'; they do not, in general, 'optimize'; 136: 'A 'satisficing' path, a path that will permit satisfaction at some specified level of all its needs'.

4 H. A. Simon, 'Rational Decision Making in Business Organizations', in: *The American Economic Review* 69 (1979), no. 4, 493–513.

5 For the role of emotions in economic behavior and in rational decision making, see: J. Elster, 'Emotions and economic theory', in: *Journal of Economic Literature* 36 (1998), 47–74; S. Rick, G. Loewenstein, 'The role of emotion in economic behavior', in: M. Lewis, J.M. Haviland-Jones, L. Feldman Barret (eds), *Handbook of emotions* (New York: Guilford Press, 2008), 138–156.

6 D. Kahneman, *Thinking, Fast and Slow*. New York: Farrar, Straus and Giroux, 2011.

choice or problem. For most of our decisions we rely on the automatic pilot of system 1, which requires little energy and attention. However, the automatic, ingrained patterns are not always suited for new, complex environments. Time and again it is evident that people are only partly able to control the unconscious, automatic, associative routine and often emotionally charged cognitive processes of system 1 by activating system 2, which allows people to reach conclusions in a controlled, analytical, conscious and rule-bound way.[7]

At this point in our discussion, it is useful to dwell on the way 'negative theology' could contribute to a deeper realization that human reason is limited and unable to reach optimal conclusions and decisions.

Negative or apophatic theology is an almost intuitive way of thinking that was first outlined in the fifth century by the Christian and neo-platonic philosopher Pseudo-Dionysius the Aeropagite in his book on mystical theology *Perì mustikès theologías*. He makes a distinction between an approach of God 'towards language' (*kataphatikè*) and an approach 'away from language' (*apophatikè*). In the cataphatic approach, it is assumed that human beings can obtain very limited knowledge of God by observing things in creation or interpreting historical events and using these observations and interpretations as the basis and justification for portraying God as 'strict' or 'merciful'. The apophatic approach proposes what could be called a serious *disclaimer* of its cataphatic counterpart. Pseudo-Dionysius emphasized that God was unknowable to mortals in time and space. He argued that statements like God 'is' are impossible. In other words: God does not 'exist', because human beings can only associate 'being' and 'existing' with being in time and space. God's 'being' is incomparably different from being in time and space, and thus the substantivized forms 'being' and 'existence' are inappropriate for a description of God.[8] More than other thinkers, Pseudo-Dionysius thus inflected his statements about God 'apophatically', that is, through negations. In doing so he did not deny God, but aimed to show that the language in which people speak about God, and the imagery they use, are inadequate to truly understand God. God can certainly be called 'merciful', but not without immediately denying that God is merciful in the way people are when they treat others according to the characteristics that have come to be attached to this virtue. But then the

7 See D. Kahneman, 'A perspective on judgment and choice: Mapping bounded rationality', in: *American Psychologist*, 58 (2003), no. 9, 697–720, especially 698–699, which also explains his views of the systems. See also: D. Kahneman, *Thinking, Fast and Slow*. New York: Farrar, Straus and Giroux, 2011.

8 Cf. for this view see for instance John Eriugena, *Periphyseon* II, 597D -598A (*Corpus Christianorum Continuatio Mediaevalis* 162), 99.

denial itself has to be denied, too. After all, Dionysius said, turning statements about God into their opposite does not mean that the resulting description of God is now adequate. In this sense his apophatic way of speaking about God was characterized by the desire to let the mystery of God work in people in a way that preserves the mystery as much as possible. This set a tone in the history of theology.[9] Augustine regularly addresses the tension that exists between language and thinking about God and the reality – *dictio, cogitatio* and *esse* – of God.[10] AndCalvin states that God has not revealed to humankind what God is (*quid sit*), but only what God is like to humankind (*qualis sit*). 'Something more real' lies hidden behind this revelation; and this 'real' aspect of God is impenetrable to human cognition.[11]

It goes without saying that the negative theologian's understanding of the inadequacy of human reason is achieved differently that which underlies an economist's or psychologist's criticism of the model of the *homo economicus*. But there are similarities: both approaches call into question an image, a model, a concept of the research subject. Economists do this based on their observation of the human phenomenon, the theologian from the observation that thinking about God cannot be grasped in language and that human reason is unable to grasp God 'himself'. Negative theology has enormous potential to evoke awareness of the inadequacy of human reasoning, not in relation to taking decisions but for articulating Mystery. For those seeking a confrontation with the depth and scope of the implications of this awareness of inadequacy – the accompanying feeling of powerlessness, but also of resignation and liberation – the apophatic passages in the work of Church Fathers are a wonderful source and very recognizable.

Back to business. All his life Herbert Simon stuck to his conviction that, in order to solve a problem in a way that is as satisfactory and sufficient as possible, prior mathematical calculations offer the greatest benefit. However, when he was confronted in the early 1960s with the idea that mathematical calculations and machines would at some point become able to take into account emotions like pain, pleasure and desire, he wrote an article on emotional

---

9 V. Lossky, 'Les éléments de théologie négative', dans la pensée de saint Augustin', in: *Augustine Magister (Congrès International Augustinien, Paris, 21–24 Septembre 1954)*. Paris, 1954. 2 vols. vol. 1, 575–581; G. P. Rocca, *Speaking the Incomprehensible God: Thomas Aquinas on the Interplay of Positive and Negative Theology* (Washington D.C, 2004); further literature in P. van Geest, *The Incomprehensibility of God*, 8–15.

10 Cf. R.J. Teske, 'Properties of God and the Predicaments in *De Trinitate* V', in: *The Modern Schoolman* 59 (1981–1982), 1–19.

11 Cf. C. van der Kooi, *Als in een spiegel. God kennen volgens Calvijn en Barth* (Kampen: Kok, 2002), 119–120.

cognition.[12] His contribution was overlooked at first. The attention it ultimately did receive prepared the way for wider recognition of the idea that feeling and intuition should be taken into account in research of the causes of man's *bounded rationality*, as has been argued above

In order to show how Simon's later work can help to see how theology can contribute to developing a richer language that would broaden the economic analytical framework and foster reflection on the implications of *bounded rationality*, we will now discuss Augustine's view on feeling and love. As it turns out, he regarded love as a way towards knowledge that leads people to a more profound insight than reason alone can furnish.

In his *Confessiones* and *De ciuitate Dei*, Augustine discerns four 'perturbationes' (passions): fear ('metus'), disordered, unordered desire ('cupiditas'), happiness ('laetitia') and sadness ('tristitia').[13] He emphasizes that actions that arise exclusively from these emotional states –from what neurologists would later identify as the lower layers of the brain –are not good, because they generally create havoc and obscure the view on the *lex aeterna*, Gods law and order. This also applies to passions that are remembered. His 'hidden stores' or 'grand spaces', as Augustine calls his memory, contain not only images of lilies or violets, or numbers, arguments, ideas and rules of grammar and logic, but also memories of emotions like sadness and happiness, pain and pleasure or happiness at the disappearance of pain subsided, or grief when all reasons to be cheerful had gone.[14]

Again, only when the 'perturbationes' are reined in by 'ratio' can they become fruitful. In this case, 'metus', for example, morphs into 'cautio'.[15] In other words, our passions, filtered by reason, can lead us to virtue. In *De ciuitate Dei* Augustine writes that emotions can not be eliminated, but must be controlled by the will: if it is people's desire to do the good thing, their fear will be good too, as it will be dominated by the spirit of that desire.[16] Cicero argued

---

12 H. A. Simon, 'Motivational and Emotional Controls of Cognition', in: *Psychological Review* 74 (1967), no. 1, 29–39.

13 Augustine, *De ciuitate Dei* 14.8.1–9.6. Cf. E. Bermon, 'La théorie des passions chez saint Augustin', in: B. Besnier, P.F. Moreau, L. Renault (eds), *Les passions antiques et médiévales* (Paris: Presses Universitaires de France, 2003), 173–197, especially 178–190 (*Théories et critiques des passions* 1).

14 Augustine, *Confessiones* 10.12–18 (passions: 21–22).

15 Augustine, *De ciuitate Dei* 14.8.1; M. Fiedrowicz, "Ciues sanctae ciuitatis Dei omnes affectiones rectas habent" De ciuitate Dei 14,9): Terapia delle passioni e preghiera in S. Agostino', in: *L'etica cristiana nei secoli III e IV: eredità e confronti* (Roma: Institutum patristicum augustinianum, 1996), 431–440, especially 437 (*Studia Ephemeridis Augustinianum* 53).

16 Fiedrowicz, "Ciues sanctae ciuitatis Dei omnes affectiones rectas habent", 431–440.

that our morals are shaped by our mind, because the mind of a wise man, the perfect Stoic, is no longer a slave to his desires.[17] Augustine does not adopt the stoic viewpoint that all 'perturbationes' should be banned so as to allow reason to rule.[18] In his later writings he sees victory over the 'pathè', the *apatheia*,[19] as an anomaly, as it is foolish to say that the wise man should not feel commiseration because commiserating equals suffering.[20]

What is striking about Augustine's vision on passion and emotion, is that he ascribes a power to all 'perturbationes' that, provided that they are purified through reason, frees reason from some of its limitations whenever choices have to be made that involve the well-being of others. The combination of disordered or unordered feeling and reason not only leads to virtue, but is also the antidote to a reasoned self-centralization that prevents people from truly engaging with others.

This view on passion and emotion is related to Augustine's reflections on love. He does not consider love to be a 'perturbatio', and when he speaks about love in his *In epistolam Johannis ad Parthos* he adds another crucial aspect to his reflection on the added value of the interaction of feeling and reason.

This is not the place to give a detailed description of all instances of meaning of the word love in Augustine's works. In its highest form love is God himself.[21] But it is also an inner power and longing in human beings,[22] although it is not always clear from the context whether Augustine uses love to refer to this inner power or to God's gift of grace.[23] A more richly layered and fascinating concept than love cannot be found in Augustine's writings. In his *In epistolam Johannis ad Parthos*, Augustine interprets love as a form of knowledge that, even more so than reason, allows people to fathom God, reality and their fellow-human beings.

If we look more closely at this last point: Augustine describes hating one's neighbour as staying in darkness. He sees the opposite of hatred, love, as

17 Cicero, *De finibus* 3, 75–76.

18 Cf. M. Spanneut, 'Le stoïcisme et saint Augustin', in: P. Courcelle (ed.), *Forma futuri. Studi in onore del Cardinale Michele Pellegrino* (Torino: Bottega d'Erasmo, 1975), 896–914, especially 909 - 914. S. Byers, 'Augustine's debt to Stoicism in the Confessions', in: J. Sellars (ed), *The Routledge Handbook of the Stoic Tradition* (New York: Routledge, 2016), 56–69.

19 M. Spanneut, 'L'impact de l'apatheia stoïcienne sur la pensée chrétienne jusqu'à Saint Augustin', in: A. Gonzáles Blanco (ed.), *Cristianismo y aculturación en tiempos del Imperio Romano* (Murcia: Universidad de Murcia, 1992), 39–52 (= *Antigüedad y cristianismo* 7).

20 Augustine, *sermo* 348.2.3; cf. *De moribus ecclesiae catholicae et de moribus Manichaeorum* 27. 53–54.

21 Augustine, *In epistulam Iohannis ad Parthos* 1.11; 8.5–8.7.

22 Augustine, *In epistulam Iohannis ad Parthos* 6.8; 6.10; 6.12; cf. on desire: *In epistulam Iohannis ad Parthos* 4. 6; 9.9.

23 Augustine, *In epistulam Iohannis ad Parthos* 6.8 (reference to Romans 5: 5).

staying in a Light which gives optimal understanding of oneself, one's neighbor and even of the dynamics that shape the world.[24] Therefore, according to Augustine, it is possible to grasp the essence of another person to the extent to which one is able to love this person. It is a conviction that Augustine had acquired long beforehand, well before his inauguration as bishop in 395 – when he wrote in *De diversis quaestionibus* that a thing (or a person) is known to the extent to which it is loved: 'res tantum cognoscitur, quantum amatur'.[25]

The road that led him to this realization was long and winding. As we mentioned earlier, in his younger years, Augustine saw friendships as an effective means of attaining personal and individual wisdom.[26] Friendships were for a purpose: they were friendships of convenience. Later, however, he came to realize that friendship involves a mutual love based on equality. At the same time, he recognized that true friendship is *gratis*, altruistic, and that this altruism creates room for getting to know the other better.[27] It is no surprise, then, that he describes the *via amoris* in *In epistolam Johannis ad Parthos* as a path to knowledge that shows traces of this view on friendship.

*Amor ipse notitia*: love is itself knowledge of the thing or person one wishes to love. That is how Pope Gregory the Great recapitulated Augustine's *via amoris*.[28]

It would be difficult to find a more succinct summary of why it is wrong to treat employees in Machiavellian fashion.[29] The Machiavellian approach chooses to distrust, check, control and, if necessary, manipulate persons in order to maintain power. The Augustinian approach treats persons on the basis of benevolence, empathy, friendship and love. Employees still serve economic reality in this approach. But they realize they are lucky, because luck is inherent in the way in which the virtues just mentioned determine their employer's interaction with them. Someone who is consistently treated with benevolence, friendliness and empathy will at some point realize that they have encountered happiness.

24 Augustine, *In epistulam Iohannis ad Parthos*1.10–13 (reference to 1 John 2: 11); cf. *In epistulam Iohannis ad Parthos* 5.10 (verwijzing naar naar 1 John 3:15). cf. *In epistulam Iohannis ad Parthos* 9.11.

25 Augustine, *De diversis quaestionibus* 83, quaestio 71, 5.

26 Augustine, *Soliloquia* I, 13, 22.

27 Augustine, *epistula* 155.1.1; *Enarratio in Psalmum* 55.17.

28 Gregorius Magnus, *In homilia in euangelia* II, 27, 4, in: *Patrologia Latina* 76, 1207.

29 Cf. J.J. Dahling, B.G. Whitaker, P.E. Levy, 'The Development and Validation of a New Machiavellianism Scale', in: *Journal of Management* (2009) 35, no. 2, 219–257.

## 3 Theological Anthropology as a Source of Insight into *Bounded Morality*

As we have seen earlier on, Adam Smith already observed in his book *The Theory of Moral Sentiments* that people can be affected not only by the pursuit of 'mutual sympathy', but also by envy, a vice that could be seen as the ultimate proof that people are not always rational beings. As we have argued above, economists advocating a relational understanding of the economy have the founding father of their discipline on their side when they claim that a relational view of humankind implies belief in the goodness of human beings, but is also coupled with an awareness that humankind embodies vices such as various forms of deception, exclusion mechanisms or even the willingness to incur expenses in order to damage others.

In order to show that people's ability to come to ethically justified choices is limited, *bounded morality* is often discussed in conjunction with *bounded rationality*. People fail to make use of this ability when they make a moral choice intuitively, for example, without evaluating it in the light of their own ethical standards.[30]

Human reason on occasion makes its own contribution to *bounded morality* by justifying immoral choices. In *The (Honest) Truth about Dishonesty. How we Lie to Everyone – Especially Ourselves*, the American psychologist Dan Ariely has shown that people's cognitive attitude and training are crucial determinants of their self-assessment. The more cognitively inclined they are, the more able they are to justify any foul play they commit in order to get the most out of a particular situation. The more creatively they are able to use their cognition, the greater their ability to justify their behavior. In this context Ariely introduced the term *fudge factor*. His theory neatly underpins the thesis that people can gradually become less moral in an increasingly unconscious way.[31]

*Bounded morality* is also evident when people are pressurized into morally irresponsible behavior by their entourage. This interpretation of *bounded morality* rests upon the observation that good and bad deeds are not always the outcome of individual effort or balanced deliberation, but are sometimes

30 See J. Haidt, 'The emotional dog and its rational tail: a social intuitionist approach to moral judgment', in: *Psychological review* 108(2001), 814–834; for an overview of literature on intuitive ethical decision making. See: G. R. Weaver, S.J. Reynolds, M.E. Brown, 'Moral intuition: Connecting current knowledge to future organizational research and practice', in: *Journal of Management* 40(2014), no. 1, 100–129.

31 D. Ariely, *The honest truth about dishonesty: how we lie to everyone – especially ourselves*. Durham, NC: Duke University Press, 2012.

a byproduct of the way people's social environment influences their choices.[32] Long before the term was coined, Augustine gave a telling example of this type of *bounded morality*. In his *Confessiones* he recalls a childhood episode in which he and his mates decided to help themselves to someone else's pears.[33] His recollection leads him to reflect upon the duality in his will: on the one hand he knew that stealing was illegal and he therefore did not want to do it, but on the other hand this did not stop him from stealing the pears and he even reveled in the theft. However, in this story Augustine also specifically mentions the way his environment influenced the moral choice he made.

The indispensability of theology for economics can be strikingly illustrated by looking at the instruments that Christians have developed over the ages to face up to the consequences of their *bounded rationality*. Familiarity with these instruments helps us to better understand the depth and scope of these consequences –known as 'sins' in theological jargon – and draft better questionnaires for research of *bounded morality*.

A closer look at the works mentioned above by Nicole Oresme and Gabriel can similarly help to formulate questions for the development of an improved *bounded morality* scale. Earlier we criticized their works for the limited view on the economy that they contained. But the old theological treatises on economic questions have lost none of their power and value as sources for the questionnaires we have in mind. Now we must turn to the Christian instruments we have just mentioned.

Still young, Christianity developed a first instrument as early as 150 AD. In *The Shepherd of Hermas* the author, Hermas, a married freed slave and brother of bishop Pius I of Rome, writes that reading Scripture helps one to realize one's own imperfection and longing for forgiveness of sins. He says that it induces remorse for morally irresponsible deeds. He describes this state of mind as the admission of guilt and hence as a first step towards the restoration of the disturbed relationship with the other.[34] Recognizing before the other that one's own morality is limited in fact expresses appreciation and respect for the other, which ideally spring from love.

Augustine follows the way pointed out in *The Shepherd of Hermas*. Towards the end of his life, around 428, he compiled an anthology of all the commandments and prohibitions in the Old and New Testament in order to, as he himself phrases it, hold up a mirror to people and help them acquire detailed

---

32 G. Gigerenzer, 'Moral Satisficing: Rethinking Moral Behavior as Bounded Rationality', in: *Topics in Cognitive Science* 2 (2010), 528–554, especially 529- 533; 549.

33 Augustine, *Confessiones* 2. 9–26.

34 The Shepherd of Hermas, *Mandata* 4.2 (penance implies knowledge of self).

insight into the limited morality of their motives and actions.[35] He titled the work: *Speculum* (Mirror). In his *Enarratio in psalmum* 103, written around 412, he had already compared Scripture to a mirror that allows us to see what we are, what we should have been or, more hopefully, what we could become. His selection of text fragments betrays Augustine's intention to confront his readers as harshly as possible. In fact, he includes nearly all prohibitions of idolatry, murder, adultery and theft and all commandments regarding strangers, respect for the rights of the poor or fair administration of justice that can be found in the Pentateuch or the letters of Paul.[36] It is evident also from what Augustine leaves out that his aim was to effect a confrontation. Outdated laws, passages that require complicated hermeneutic translation, miracle stories, histories, prophecies, parables and pericopes that require allegorical interpretation are all ignored. Neither does his *Enarratio* contain the passages used elsewhere in his work to settle theological disputes to his advantage. These too would distract too much from his purpose.[37] Long before Ariely coined the phrase, Augustine in his *Speculum* launched a well-aimed attack on the *fudge factor*. The more refined the mirror of commandments and interdictions, the less space is left for the *fudge factor* that prevents people from facing their own failures.

Over the ensuing centuries, other mirrors of form of confession written along similar lines appeared. In fact, Augustine can be considered the founder of this genre. The *Moralia in Job* by Pope Gregory the Great was redacted by Adalbert of Metz, who entitled it *Speculum*, arguing that it would impel its readers to effect thorough self-evaluation. Arnoul de Bohéries wrote the *Speculum monachorum* ('Mirror for Monks'), Étienne de Sallay a *Speculum novitii* ('Mirror for Novices'), and a Speculum prelatorum ('Mirror for Prelates') was published in 1270.

The *Speculum ecclesiae* ('Mirror of the Church') and Godfrey of Viterbo's *Speculum regum* ('Mirror for Kings', 1103–1105) use a different confrontational strategy. They present a summary of calamities in world history and the church

35 Augustine, *Speculum*, Praefatio.

36 For the prohibition of idolatry see: Deuteronomy 5; 6; 7; 12; 13; 17; Leviticus 19; 20; 26; Exodus 20; 22; 34; Joshua 22, of murder: Ex. 20; 21, of adultery: Ex. 20; Lev. 20: Deut. 5; 22; 27, of theft: Ex. 21; 22; 23; Deut. 5; 22; 27; Lev. 19, on the commandments on respect for parents: Ex. 20; 21; Lev. 19; 20; Deut. 5; 27, on the just treatment of foreigners: Ex. 22; Lev. 19; Deut. 24, the respecting of the rights of the poor: Ex. 23; Lev. 19; Deut. 24 or on the just administration of justice Deut. 6; 19; 25.

37 Cf. P. van Geest, 'Sed ea quae obscura sunt praetermitto' (*Speculum* 108). Augustine' selection of Scriptural quotations as proof of his desire to effect a confrontation', in: *Rivista Augustinianum* 57 (2017), 493–513.

to impress upon royalty and the clergy that the conflicts between good and evil forces in the world are mirrored by an inner struggle that they themselves will have face. The medieval summaries of history and salvation history –with creation, the story of Noah, the lives of Mary and Christ, the Ascension and Last Judgment, hell and heaven as highlights – are likewise confrontational exhortations to self-knowledge and self-improvement. Self-evaluation therefore takes place in the context of the time and eternity. In these mirrors, it transpires that the overview of the different stages of history and salvation history and insight into the observer's own 'I' are two sides of the same medal.

In addition to the Bible as a mirror, Christendom acquired a second instrument to help Christians realize that people are deficient as moral actors. Towards the end of the second century, the Church Father Irenaeus spoke in his *Adversus Haereses* of the –apparently clearly established – practice of public penance and prior individual examination of conscience which this required. [38] He observes that there are Christians who do not dare to confess to their own imperfection publicly out of shame. This reticence is unacceptable to Irenaeus. Reconciliation with the community, with Christ and his church requires sincere remorse and a public confession of guilt. He expresses his admiration for Christians who are courageous enough to follow up negative self-evaluation with a public, mostly once-only, confession.

The question arises here why the early church deemed it necessary for sinners and apostates to confess their sins in front of the entire church community before the bishop would grant them sacramental forgiveness.[39] It would seem that the management of an organization that forces dysfunctional employees to publicly submit to the critical eye of the entire organization or their assembled colleagues would make it impossible for them to ever feel safe again turns them into damaged goods.

The early church, however, took the exact opposite view. In its idealized perspective, the church community was regarded as a safe place where people could show their vulnerability. The safer the community, the sincerer the confession and the more existential the experience of liberation from sin were felt to be. The experimentally verified consequences of *bounded morality* were interpreted in the early church as forces that led to inner renewal and more authentic restoration of relationships within the community, especially if they were confessed in public. At the same time, public confession served as a

38 Irenaeus, *Adversus Haereses* 1.13.7.

39 See for instance 2 Corinthians 2, James 5:16, *Didache* 4:14, 14:1, Cyprianus, *epistula* 9.2.

mirror held up to the community.[40] If the community acted harshly towards the repentant sinner, its members had to engage in collective soul-searching.

More than 200 years after Irenaeus, Augustine was still condemning such heartlessness. In an incident that touched Augustine deeply, an apostate who made his confession with the aim to be readmitted to the Catholic Church, but was subsequently excommunicated because of his admission. In a sermon delivered in 410–411 he recounts that he was sickened by this.[41] In the years that followed, his reaction made the sermons in which he denounced the reprehensible behavior of orthodox Christians even more penetrating. [42]

Finally, a third instrument was developed. In the Irish-Scottish and Anglo-Saxon monastic life of the sixth and seventh century private confession began to be practiced more widely. This type of confession was part of spiritual counseling and hence took place more frequently than the public confession of yore. People confessed their to a priest who subsequently granted forgiveness (absolution), but not without imposing a suitable penance. Although this practice was initially defined in terms of illness and recovery, from the ninth century onwards it was cast in the legal terms in the so-called penitentials, the *libri poenitentiales*. These tomes listed all the sins that could be confessed –a massive and growing collection. In addition, the penitentials contained guidelines and instructions for the confessor when determining the penalty. As a side effect it allowed people to 'calculate' in advance if the sin they were thinking of perpetrating was worth the punishment. 'Outcrowding' of either morally sound or unsound behavior using instruments introduced with good intentions has been a recurring phenomenon throughout church history, even if it was only given that name much later by economists like Samuel Bowles, as we have seen.[43] But Martin Luther – whose excommunication in 1517 by Pope Leo X became the starting shot for the Reformation – saw personal confession as a useful tool, as he believed in the therapeutic effect of acknowledging one's sins.

---

40 Cf. N. Marshall, *The penitential discipline of the primitive church for the first four hundred years after Christ: together with its declension from the fifth century, downwards to its present state* (Oxford: Parker, 1844); H. Brewer, 'Die kirchliche Privatbusse im christlichen Altertum', in: *Zeitschrift für katholische Theologie* 45(1921), 1–42.

41 'Dico caritati vestra, torta sunt ex hoc viscera nostra', in: Augustine, *Sermo Casinensi* 1, 33, in: *Sancti Augustini Sermones post Maurinos repertos*. Ed. G. Morin (Roma, 1930), 401–412 (*Miscellanea Agostiniana* 1), quotation: 410–411.

42 Augustine, *In epistolam Johannis ad Parthos, Tractatus III*, 9, in: P. Agaësse (intr., ed., trans.), *Commentaire de la première épître de S. Jean* (Paris, 1961), 202.

43 P. H. D. Lang, 'Private Confession and Absolution in the Lutheran Church: A Doctrinal, Historical, and Critical Study', in: *Concordia Theological Quarterly* 56 (1992), no. 4, 241–261.

It would lie outside the scope of this book to attempt an exhaustive overview of all the mirrors, confessionals and manuals for confessors that were produced throughout the ages.[44] The brief summary given here, however, already suggests that the books in question are not only of interest as source material for social history or the history of mentalities, but also to behavioral economists, as the sins they list –leaving aside the punishments –help obtain deeper insight into the many aspects and nuances of *bounded morality*.[45] They are proof that instruments were devised within Christendom, more than anywhere else, to chart the causes and consequences of *bounded morality*.

As a brief aside: at the level of underlying theological content, Catholics and Protestants shared the realization that morality is bounded, but that this weakness could be turned into an advantage if three criteria were met. These criteria are summed up in unison by both the council fathers of Trent –the council convened by Pope Paul III to formulate a response to the Reformation –and the authors of the *Heidelberg Catechism*, Caspar Olevianus and Zacharias Ursinus. In the protocols of the fourteenth session of Trent, titled *Doctrina de sacramento poenitentiae* (1551), the council fathers stated that genuine remorse ('contritio'), acknowledgement in confession ('confessio') and restoration of the damage done ('satisfactio') were preconditions for absolution from sins committed.[46] Olevianus and Ursinus turned this tripartition into the structuring principle of their *Catechism*. They too stated that Christians needed to be remorseful for their sins, had to acknowledge them and had to restore the damage inflicted.[47] The obligation to fulfill these conditions turned the weakness that *bounded morality* entailed into a force that served to restore relations marred by sin.

---

44 See: *Medieval Handbooks of Penance: A Translation of the Principal Libri Poenitentiales.* Translated by John Thomas McNeill, Helena M. Gamer. New York: Columbia University Press, 1990. The traditional manuals of moral theology used to be very influential because they were prescribed reading in theological colleges; they are dated, but can still be used as sources for the Catholic view of moral issues: J. Aertnys, *Theologia Moralis*. Doornik, 1967–68, eighteenth edition; E. Génicot, *Institutiones theologiae moralis*. Leuven, 1964, seventeenth edition.

45 See for the continental tripartite penitential books that continued in the Irish, Anglo-Saxon and Frankish tradition: R. Meens, *Het tripartite boeteboek. Overlevering en betekenis van vroegmiddeleeuwse biechtvoorschriften (met editie en vertaling van vier tripartita)* Utrecht: Uitgeverij Verloren, 1994 (*Middeleeuwse Studies en Bronnen* 41).

46 See: H. Denzinger, *Kompendium der Glaubensbekenntnisse und kirchlichen Lehrentscheidungen*. Verbessert, erweitert, ins Deutsche übertragen und unter Mitarbeit von Helmut Hoping herausgegeben von Peter Hünermann (Freiburg: Herder, 1991[37]), 552–556 (*canones* 1701–1715).

47 C. Olevianus, Z. Ursinus, *Catechismus oder christlicher Underricht, wie der in Kirchen und Schulen der Churfürstlichen Pfaltz getrieben wirdt* (Heidelberg: J. Mayer, 1563), 12–17.

At this point in our treatise the time has come to make good on our promise to look more closely at *De Origine et Natura Iure et Mutacionibus Monetarum* by Nicole Oresme and *Tractatus de potestate et utilitate monetarum* by Gabriel Biel. Our analysis will show that further study of their work could indeed make a significant contribution to the development of a *bounded morality* measurement scale, for example.

When Oresme in his *De Origine et Natura Iure et Mutacionibus Monetarum* speaks of the 'monstrous and perverse' pursuit of profit that leads to tampering with coins it immediately becomes clear how limited human morality is in his view. The words 'usura', 'vilis' and 'fraus' are never far off. Counterfeit coins no longer reflect God's justice and the proper natural proportions by the relative proportions of the coin's constituents and/or the appropriate mint mark.[48] Which leads to a whole train of vice and misery: envy, *dissensio*, legal procedures and scandals ensue, which the author paints in broad and vivid strokes.[49]

In the first *capitulum* Oresme also formulates the basic assumption of his thinking about the acting person. Human nature is always inclined to amass riches as long as they are easy to come by.[50] And once people have money at their disposal, they are more likely to feel the urge to commit fraud and increase injustice than the desire to do good with it.

Nor does Oresme spare the ruler, who, he writes, is uniquely able to create 'innumerabiles perplexitates, obscuritates, errores et inextricabiles difficultates' in the bookkeeping in which receipts and expenditure are recorded, for example by secretly letting his allies know that he is planning to change the nominal value of coins. Such reprehensible behavior by a ruler leads to court cases. It turns virtuous people into victims, as they are no longer able to redeem their debts. As a result of shady practices instigated by the ruler, they lose control of their own money.[51] In numerous places Oresme cynically states that fraud[52] is inherent in the ruler's privilege to alter the shape and weight of coins.[53] To him suspicion is a virtue: particularly rulers who claim that their intended changes are for the benefit of the people's wealth should

48 Nicole Oresme, *De Origine et Natura Iure et Mutacionibus Monetarum* 19, 20, 22.

49 Nicole Oresme, *De Origine et Natura Iure et Mutacionibus Monetarum* 23 ('pericula'), 25 ('monstruosum est en contra naturam'); cf. 26, 27 ('quod lucrari in mutacione monete peius est quam usura'), 29, 34, 36.

50 Nicole Oresme, *De Origine et Natura Iure et Mutacionibus Monetarum* 25.

51 Nicole Oresme, *De Origine et Natura Iure et Mutacionibus Monetarum* 35.

52 Nicole Oresme, *De Origine et Natura Iure et Mutacionibus Monetarum* 24 ('falsitatem et decepcionem'). Cf. 28, 30–31.

53 Nicole Oresme, *De Origine et Natura Iure et Mutacionibus Monetarum* 24 ('emolumentum uel lucrum').

not be trusted: 'non est credendum sibi'.[54] Moreover, coin revaluations by the ruler will often be the first of a series.[55]

Incidentally, Oresme distinguishes two types of fraudulent rulers. In addition to tyrants who impose their will on the people and whose fraud is evident, there are rulers who quietly alter the inscription, material or weight of coins to their own advantage. He condemns these even more vehemently than the tyrants.[56] He compares extortion ('exaccio') by cunning rulers to the spreading of chronic diseases which similarly are more pernicious if they are hard to detect. After all, people feel the consequences of the *grauamen* of tampering with currency less readily than the pain of increased taxes.[57]

The way Oresme charts the interlinked consequences through which *bounded morality* manifests itself and his description of the internal and external factors that exacerbate this inability to act ethically is astonishingly rich in detail. The combination of economic thinking and psychological insight that characterizes his judgment makes his work a rich source for behavioral economists.

In *quaestio* 9 of his *Collectorium* – published as *Tractatus de potestate et utilitate monetarum* by the later editor Johannes Adler – Gabriel Biel even more extensively discusses the characteristics of a *falsarius*,[58] fraud and dissimulation.[59] *Falsitas* occurs when the perception of a thing by our mind ('ab intellectu') does not correspond with reality. There can also be *falsitas* inside the mind (*in mente*) when one simply misunderstands something, in language ('in verbo'), in writing ('in scripto') when something is named incorrectly. Biel contrasts such forms of *falsitas* with the ethically reprehensible form, which receives most attention. These types of *falsitas* are the result of incorrect reports ('falsis relationibus'), lies ('mendacibus'), promises ('promissionibus'), traps ('fallacibus'), keeping silent about things ('verborum cautelis loquendo vel tacendo'), fiddling ('in opere') with certain materials ('substantia'), with measures ('mensura'), weight ('in pondere') or numbers ('numero'; cf. Sap. 11: 22 or by dissimulation ('in pharisaica simulatione'). According to Biel all of these, with the exception of *falsitas in mente*, can be easily demonstrated.[60]

---

54 Nicole Oresme, *De Origine et Natura Iure et Mutacionibus Monetarum* 24.
55 Nicole Oresme, *De Origine et Natura Iure et Mutacionibus Monetarum* 26.
56 Nicole Oresme, *De Origine et Natura Iure et Mutacionibus Monetarum* 22 ('tacite mendacium'); cf. 32.
57 Nicole Oresme, *De Origine et Natura Iure et Mutacionibus Monetarum* 32.
58 Gabriel Biel, *Collectorium* IV, *Quaestio* 9, *Notabile* 1, Ed. Rückert, IV/2, 176.
59 Ibid.
60 Ibid.

His *notabile* 4 includes a treatise in which he explains human greed and pride as motives that lead to financial fraud.

In *notabile* 5 Biel again specifies these forms of falsity *in rebus*. His specification is a prelude to a treatise on the many ways in which falsity, simulation and hypocrisy are committed. In *conclusio* 6 and 7 he concludes that anyone who, either in speech or writing, deceives his neighbor by giving an incorrect account of the material, the quantity, quality, weight or dimensions of coins, thereby commits a mortal sin and is liable for all damage caused. He stresses that it is also a violation of the commandment 'Thou shalt love thy neighbor as thyself' ('contra fraternam caritatem'). In *conclusio* 7 Biel states that a person who, hoping to receive something, feigns an attitude without which he would not get the desired item, is not only a cheat but is also obliged to return the gift thus received. In those passages where Biel intensifies the sense of sin by naming all aspects of fraudulent behavior *in extenso* he includes instructive examples of the consequences of *bounded morality*, long before the term was coined by psychologists and economists.[61]

A striking feature of the later adaptation of Biel's *Quaestio* 9 into the separate *Tractatus de utilitate en potestate monetarum* is that such passages were systematically omitted. The jurist Johannes Adler, like Biel a professor at Tübingen University, excluded *Notabilia* 1 and 5, *conclusiones* 6 and 7 and *dubium* 4 completely. As a consequence, the *Quaestio* was cut down to a technical-legal treatise in which only the problem of counterfeiting was discussed. Apparently Adler's aim was not to bring his readers to a deeper understanding of their motives and *bounded morality*. What he retained was the external aspect of the sin. His editorial work can be linked to the rising acceptance of profit-related attitudes in the later Middle Ages and the Early Modern era. Omitting Biel's discussion of greed and pride seems to express a more pro-profit attitude than keeping it. Moreover, he was a jurist whose aim was probably to stimulate discussion of the prohibited act, and therefore very likely did not see human beings primarily as creatures who, marked by the Fall, had become disorientated by the conflict between their instincts and reason, as Biel frequently did in his scholastic *Collectorium*. Adler's redacted version the economy and ethics are not treated as separate phenomena either. It concentrates on describing a moral problem: counterfeiting. On the other hand, a comparison of Biel's original *Quaestio* and Adler's redacted version shows that Biel's attempt to convince readers of his own strength benefits from a critical review of that strength. It results in a more realistic anthropology, one that takes into account

61 Gabriel Biel, *Collectorium* IV, *Quaestio* 9, Ed. Rückert, IV/2, 177–183, quotation 183.

the awareness of humankind's *bounded morality*, long before these two words became intimately connected.

To summarize: it is clear both from Scripture, the mirrors and the penitentials that served as instruments for the examination of conscience and from an analysis of theological works on economic issues, that all of these can help to understand what *bounded reality* really entails. Theological sources like these are indispensable for gaining insight into the human limitations that lie at the root of wrong ethical choices that cause harm to others. Whenever Biel speaks of lies, or Oresme of fraudulent rulers, they enrich our view of what Ariely calls the *fudge factor*, a feat that, incidentally, Augustine also accomplishes in his two treatises on lies: *De mendacio* and *Contra mendacium*.

The works just discussed are but a handful of examples from the history of theology. Countless works still await rediscovery that could greatly expand our knowledge of the root causes, consequences and immensity of the *bounded morality* of humankind.

## 4 *Bounded Willpower* Explained in the Light of the Theology of Grace

What applies to rationality and morality ultimately also applies to the human will. It too is subject to limitations. Earlier we observed that years after Augustine's pear theft, he wondered where exactly the duality in his will came from and how it could be that he was controlled by it instead of the other way around. His story could serve as the opening to any handbook on *bounded willpower*.

It should be noted that the concept of 'bounded willpower' as such hardly occurs in behavioral economics literature, as it is equated there with 'bounded self-control' and is therefore subsumed under research into self-control. Taken as synonyms, self-control and willpower refer to the ability to assign more weight to the rational considerations that precede a decision or act than to gut feelings (*visceral influences*). Interpreted in this way, *bounded willpower* thus implies a departure from acting rationally and is closely linked with *bounded rationality*. Studies that have specifically looked at *bounded willpower* describe its limitations as follows. To begin with it involves a lack of self-control or problem awareness. These two things explain why people do not always make the right decision or do the right things.[62] Secondly, throughout their lives people have only a fuzzy idea of what they really want. Thirdly, people are limited by a lack of willpower to actually execute what they have in mind. Obstacles, fears

62 S. Mullainathan, R. Thaler, 'Behavioral Economics' (October 2000). *NBER Working Paper* No. w7948. (https://ssrn.com/abstract=245733).

or lack of self-confidence can all lie at the root of this restriction. In addition, their social environment –an organization, company or family –can equally prevent people from putting their wishes into action.

The next two insights are the result of neurological research. The first of these, that is, the fourth in our summary, is that the will can be called bounded because people's 'free' exercise of their will, although they experience it as such, is in fact determined by impulses that almost literally light up and are therefore visible in certain parts of the brain.[63] The human will is controlled by physical processes, which suggests or means that freedom of the will is an illusion. The fifth observation is related to this. During pregnancy the brain of the human fetus undergoes a critical period of brain differentiation. Research has shown that our brain structure is determined by hereditary factors in utero, while environmental factors before and shortly after birth also play a critical part in determining our brain structure for the rest of our lives. This too suggests that our will is predetermined rather than free.[64]

A sixth conclusion that could be added to the recent studies was drawn long ago. Augustine, who is credited in handbooks with 'discovering' the will,[65] observes that the will ('voluntas') is inextricably linked to memory ('memoria') and thinking ('intelligentia'). These faculties are both autonomous and one. When people remember that something was unpleasant, they do not want it to return or reoccur.[66] And if after some deliberation they think something will improve their well-being, they want to have it.

The determinism that resonates in the modern neurosciences is of course far removed from the multifaceted theological doctrine of predestination. This doctrine teaches that God has predetermined who are chosen and who are rejected, regardless of whether they wished or sought good or evil during

---

63 See Cf. B. Libet, and others, 'Time of conscious intention to act in relation to onset of cerebral activity (readiness-potential). The unconscious initiation of a freely voluntary act', in: *Brain* 106(1983), 623–642; their conclusions have been questioned by J. Trevena, J. Miller, 'Brain preparation before a voluntary action: Evidence against unconscious movement initiation', in: *Consciousness and Cognition* 19 (2010), 447–456. See also: F. van der Meché, *Op de trap van Erasmus. De vrijheid van neuronen*. Rotterdam: Erasmus University Rotterdam, 2011.

64 Cf. E. Rannikko on the various current philosophical definitions of free will: 'Free will in terms of the power or ability of agents to act otherwise than they in fact do' and 'free will as a power by which one can act according to determinations of one's will'; E. Rannikko, *Liberium Arbitrium and Necessitas; A philosophical Inquiry Into Augustine's Conception of the Will* (Helsinki: Luther Agricola Society, 1997), 11–12.

65 S. Harrison, *Augustine's way into the will. The theological and philosophical significance of De Libero Arbitrio* (Oxford: Oxford University Press, 2006), 4.

66 Cf. Augustine, *sermo* 52; *De Trinitate* 15.17.31.

their lives. Calvin called double predestination a 'decretum horribile', a terrible decision.[67] The highest possible value was attached to God's predestination –however unfathomable –, a value greater than the free will of human beings. Paradoxically this did not imply that God's freedom conflicted with human freedom. People on earth were free to choose how to lead their lives. But they were bound by the conditions that God set for their contingent freedom, and they did not know what their future in the hereafter will be.

As we have seen on a number of occasions, increased awareness of the limitations of people as rationally and morally acting creatures has made it relatively simple to see the flaws of the *homo economicus* model. We have also argued that the insight into human limitations can be enriched and deepened by looking at theological sources. The indispensability of theology for economics is evident once more if we look at the concept of *bounded willpower*. The will is a theme that has attracted the attention of prominent economists. Very recently, D. McCloskey has contended that liberalism must be seen as a fulfilment of the Abrahamic equality of souls that causes human flourishing. By contrast with theologians like Tillich, she has pointed in this context to the intrinsic connection between the liberty of the human will 'under Abrahamic theology' and the liberty of human action under liberal economic ideology, although she has added that the will, 'constrained by ethical treatment of others and oneself and God', must be guided by virtues such as temperance, justice, courage, faith, hope and love when people engage in buying and selling.[68]

The evolution of Augustine's thinking about free will which was mentioned briefly in the third chapter offers us a suitable framework to enrich the notion of *bounded willpower* in two different ways. Augustine's penetrating description of what could be called *unbounded willpower* can help us to gain sharper focus on its opposite, *bounded willpower*. And what he wrote later in his life regarding the limited nature of the human will can make us realize the immensity and impact of *bounded willpower* on human existence and the need for outside forces to prevent people from becoming victims of their weakened will. In fact, no one else has ever such radical –and pessimistic –words on this impact.

Around the age of thirty-three Augustine wrote his *De libero arbitrio*. The title 'On Free Will' is misleading, as the three volumes of this work deal with

67 An important proof was Malachi 1: 2–3, which ascribes to God the statement that he hates Esau, who is as yet unborn, and loves his twin brother Jacob, who was naturally also still unborn. Cf. Romans 9: 13.

68 D. McCloskey, 'The Liberty of the Will in Theology Permits the Liberated Markets of Liberalism', in: *Journal of Economics, Theology and Religion*, vol. 1, no. 1 (2021), 81–108.

the origin of the evil human beings themselves commit or fall victim to. Just as in his early commentary on Paul's letter to the Romans, the *Expositio quarundam propositionem ex epistola ad Romanos*, Augustine in *De libero arbitrio* challenges the thinking of the Manicheans, who thought that the evil in the world had been caused both by a demiurge who had made creation and by the inferior material that this amateur used. Augustine vehemently opposes these claims and argues that evil should in fact be seen as a consequence of choices willingly made by humans. Free will has thus changed into the source of evil.[69]

Yet this is not what Augustine wants to emphasize in *De libero arbitrio*. To press home his point that humankind had the freedom to do good or evil, he gives a masterful description of the freedom that originally characterized the human will, the *unbounded willpower*, in other words. The first human being, 'adam' in Hebrew, was gifted with a sensible soul, good judgment and a free will. This will was free to the highest possible degree and unfettered because 'evil desires' ('cupiditas', 'libido', 'voluptas') could not get a hold over it.[70] According to the Creation narratives in the Bible book of Genesis, the human's primeval unbounded willpower was undermined by human being's desire to gain dominion. Much later, Augustine realized that this desire is outstanding proof of the reality of human freedom. As a matter of fact, in *De Civitate Dei* he says that the original free will was given to humans when they, being righteous, were able to refrain from sin, but because of that freedom were also able to sin.[71] Instead of putting it down to a compulsive disorder, Augustine therefore traces the first sin back to the freedom of humans, who initially were not forced into committing sin by anything or anyone. In doing so, Augustine stays faithful to an idea he had developed in his early work. The free will of the first human had already been infected by the desires just mentioned. Those desires paradoxically impeded the freedom of the will, which remains free, however, but is 'infected' by these 'disordered desires'. The boundedness of the will does not mean that its freedom is nullified by the ever-present risk of contagion. People are still supposed to be able to want to do the right thing and do it, no matter how difficult it has become.[72] In other words, they remain solely responsible for their deeds.[73] After all, moral judgments remain desirable and

69 Augustine, *Expositio quarundam propositionum ex epistula apostoli ad Romanos* 37.52; 54–56; *Ad Simplicianum* 1.2.7; 1.2.10.

70 Cf. Augustine, *De Genesi ad litteram* 9.14.25.

71 Augustine, *De civitate Dei* 22.30.

72 Augustine, *De libero arbitrio* 3.11.33; cf. *ibidem* 3.5.15–16; 3.11.33; cf. later *De natura boni* 3; 5; 8; *De ciuitate Dei* 8.15.2; 11.16.

73 Augustine, *Retractationes* 1.8.2.

presuppose a free will.[74] The freedom to choose implies moral responsibility. According to Augustine anyone who uses their reason and displays will power will be perfectly able to resist these disorganized desires.[75]

Precisely with the aim to accentuate the power of the free will, Augustine the discusses at great length passions like fear, which confuse people, or happiness, which often comes out of the blue and passes just as quickly. In his view, they constrain the freedom of the will. Vices, too, are among these passions. He states that greed does its stifling work. He believes that seeking favors equals submission. He also asks what other diseases inhabit the realm of the passions and come to dominate it.[76] Such words are often the prelude to a discussion in which he emphasizes that it is human beings' own responsibility to free themselves of these passions, as the will is sufficiently free to will the good. He is convinced that it is within human power to develop a good will.

As we have seen in the fifth chapter, in 395 Augustine discussed free will in the context of dependence on God's grace. He wrote in *De diuersis quaestionibus ad Simplicianum* that the human will and the ensuing good works can only become good once God's grace has descended upon a person. In other words: the bounded will is freed from its generally observed flaws, which are themselves the result of disorderly and constraining desires, by someone else whose actions purify and help the will. In a rhetorical question, a device Augustine (a former teacher of rhetoric) uses to touch his readers' minds more directly than a standard argument can, he asks if people are asking whether a good will is also a gift of God's grace, as he would be surprised to find anyone who dares deny this. Only the experience of goodness can transmit goodness, for instance by willing the good.[77]

From 395 onwards, therefore Augustine believes that anything that human beings want or intend to undertake is temporally and causally preceded by a gift, the grace of God.[78] It should be noted, however, that Augustine hastens to remind his readers in *Ad Simplicianum* of God's unknowability, impenetrability and ineffability.[79] The passages about God's incomprehensibility in all reflections on God's prescience and predestination in the first book of *Ad Simplicianum* are more crucial than their later reception has suggested.[80]

74 Augustine, *De libero arbitrio*, III, I,1-I,3.
75 Augustine, *De libero arbitrio*, I, X,20-XI,21
76 Augustine, *De libero arbitrio*, I, XI,22.
77 Augustine, *Ad Simplicianum* 1.2.7.
78 Cf. *ibidem* 1.2.1–1.2.2; 1.2.20.
79 See chapter 6. 2.
80 Augustine, *Ad Simplicianum* 1.2.16.

Several decades after *De diuersis quaestionibus ad Simplicianum*, a British monk, Pelagius, offered a grim response to Augustine's view on the relationship between the freedom of the will and the external influences required to improve and liberate the will. He was concerned that Augustine's thought on this matter would be taken as an invitation to portray human imperfection as inevitable, and thereby give people an easy excuse to explain away their sins.[81] The *fudge factor* almost seems a *theologoumenon*.

Pelagius therefore argued that the sin committed by the first man had not in fact set in motion a train of logic but was merely the sin of an individual whose mishap indeed set a miserable example, but did not affect later humankind.[82] The will remained untainted and sufficiently good to choose the good and attain perfection.[83] There was no need for a preceding grace, as that would imply that God would give what he ordered. To Pelagius this latter idea, which Augustine incidentally had articulated in a prayer in the *Confessiones*, was an unacceptable and vexing thought.[84]

The so-called Pelagian controversy, which involved more protagonists than just Augustine and Pelagius, was malicious at times. In the many writings he produced over this period, Augustine is tenacious, almost grim even, in his defense of his conviction that only the first man disposed of the ultimate free will.[85] This first man, however, became so damaged by the first sin, that the only thing humankind was left with was a free will prone to evil.[86] In *De gratia et libero arbitrio* ('On Grace and Free Choice'), on the other hand, Augustine emphasizes somewhat less pessimistically that God's freedom and mercy are not contradictory. In certain passages in this work, however, human freedom and divine actions indeed seem to conflict. In *De dono perseverantiae*, for example, Augustine leaves little room for the free will of the people of Sidon and Tyrus when he writes that it would not have helped them had they been able to believe, as they are not He 'whose dispositions are inscrutable and whose ways are mysterious' had not predestined them (cf. John 12, 37–40).[87] Ending this passage with an observation that recurs like a refrain throughout his work, Augustine nonetheless states that God's ways are mysterious and that

81 P. Brown, *Through the Eye of a Needle. Wealth, the Fall of Rome, and the Making of Christianity in the West, 350–550 AD* (Princeton-Oxford: Princeton University Press, 2012), 343–344.

82 Ogliari, *Gratia et Certamen*, 233–234.

83 Pelagius, *Ad Demetrias*, 2.1; 4.1.

84 Augustine, *Confessiones* 10. 30.45; 10. 37.60 cf. also *De dono perseverantiae* 20.53.

85 Augustine, *epistula* 217.12.

86 Augustine, *sermo* 156.12.

87 Augustine, *De dono perseverantiae* XIV,35.

the conclusion he presents may therefore perhaps not be entirely accurate. This is a clear reservation, one he is forced to make because he also frequently emphasizes that human free will and divine sovereignty are compatible. However paradoxical it may seem, he thinks God's actions and human freedom can coexist. In his early work *De Libero Arbitrio* and his late work *De Civitate Dei*, for example, it is obvious that human freedom entails freedom in God, rather than a freedom from God. He believes that human beings become truly liberated in their relationship with God, as they become free in a loving relationship with a fellow person, because such relationships make the tendencies within human beings that tend towards evil disappear.[88] In both cases, freedom is a gift.

Augustine's opponents thought that this contradicted with his earlier thoughts, the more so because in his *Expositio quarundam propositionum ex epistula ad Romanos*, and in the third book of *De libero arbitrio*, he had stated that perseverance was a virtue that human beings really had to develop themselves.[89] But even shortly before his death in 430 Augustine was still standing firm. In his *De praedestinatione sanctorum* and *De dono perseuerantiae* he admits that his early works contain errors and that the human will to do good, and the perseverance needed to do it, are gifts.[90] Even the latter virtue is a gift. People have nothing that they have not themselves received beforehand. Even their freedom is a gift.

A few decades ago, the Pelagian controversy became a source of inspiration for economists who saw Augustine's position as a welcome critique of meritocracy. Generally speaking meritocracy refers to the practice of assigning social positions or positions of power on the basis of people's accomplishments and personal track record. A recent study by Jo Littler very lucidly traces the various questions to which multifaceted meritocracy gives rise by outlining its historical genealogies in contemporary social theory and political rhetoric and its manifestations in popular culture. The varied expressions of neoliberal meritocracy have above all served to expand the gap between rich and poor; a gap which is then justified in narratives of neoliberal meritocracy which praise the rich, legitimize government by a wealthy elite and offer 'the false promise that the social ladder is consistent and there for us, if only we have enough nous and gumption to climb'. She argues therefore for a more plural

---

88 Augustine, *De libero arbitrio* III 3; *De ciuitate Dei* 5.10.

89 Augustine, *Expositio quarundam propositionum ex epistula apostoli ad Romanos* 60–62; *epistula* 226.3; 226.8.

90 J. Wetzel, 'Snares of Truth: Augustine on Free Will and Predestination', in: R. Dodaro, G. Lawless (ed.), *Augustine and his Critics. Essays in Honour of Gerald Bonner* (London-New York: Taylor & Francis Group, 2000), 124–141; especially 124.

understanding of merit 'which considers merit on a collective and not a purely individual basis – alongside mutual and co-operative forms of social reproduction which create greater parity in wealth, opportunity, care and provision'.[91]

Both the questions and the argument are consistent with the thinking of the political philosopher John Rawls. But he based his criticism of meritocracy more on Augustine's doctrine of grace. He recognized that Pelagius's concept of grace entailed the justification of an economic-retributive view of society that failed to account for the fact that people may have widely differing starting points, a fact of life they are unable to change in any way. Talents and the capacity to do certain things, for example, are given, while social origin, the financial position and social network of one's parents are factors a newborn has no influence over, but that are nevertheless powerful determinants of their subsequent development and career. In addition, in a competitive economy wages will be determined more by supply and demand than by the individual's moral actions. Similarly, it was later also noted that many people high up in the social hierarchy tend to see their position as a personal accomplishment, and fail to acknowledge that personal favors or sheer luck, for instance the circumstance that the favorite candidate did not apply or decline the offer may have played a key role, too.[92] Be that as it may, Augustine's position allowed Rawls to criticize the meritocratic social system that failed to acknowledge that economic inequality is indeed partly the result of non-meritocratic factors. [93] He associated meritocracy with individualism and egotism, which seriously hamper the awareness of external factors as co-determinants of success. Rawls therefore proposed replacing the *logic of merit* with a *justice of fairness* that takes into account that external factors are indeed determining factors for people's accomplishments.

In conclusion, the question remains what we can learn as theologians and economists from these theological positions in order to deepen and expand our understanding of the power and boundedness of the human will. Our presentation of the developments in Augustine's thinking about the free will – a thought process that took place at a crucial stage in the history of theology and also greatly influenced it – was too brief to show that main themes in this thinking are like a mirror. Through his theological-exegetical reflections upon

91 See J. Littler, *Against Meritocracy: Culture, Power and Myths of Mobility* (London- New York: Routledge, 2018), 23- 47, esp 41–47 (neoliberalism); 77–112 (social theory); 212–224; quotations 223, 224 respectively.

92 L. Bruni, P. Sartori, 'The Illusion of Merit, or Why Meritocracy is Not a Market Virtue', in press.

93 J. Rawls, *A Theory of Justice* (Cambridge Mass.: The Belknap Press of Harvard University Press, 1971), 17.

the absolute freedom of Adam's will in paradise, his *unbounded will power*, Augustine by way of contrast attempts to foster awareness in his readers that each one of them will already have acquired through their own experience. It is the realization that this perfectly free and unbounded will does not exist in this world of time and space, a realization that has been substantiated by recent research into *bounded will power*.

But Augustine goes one step further, and behavioral economists who have begun to study bounded will do so too: together they open theologians' eyes to the fact that orthodoxy produces more realistic people than heterodoxy. Augustine's intuition and its recent substantiation show that Pelagius was probably deeply honest, but naïve in his assumption that people can of their own accord free themselves of external influences or internal factors that hamper and taint their good will.[94] The intensity with which Augustine in later life describes the impact of the history of humankind on the free will that is already weakened is not testimony to patience, optimism or sparkling zest on his part, but does constitute proof of his realism, a realism that has been confirmed by studies into *bounded will power*. Conversely, we could also say that anyone who seeks a clear view on people's dependence on others, or on a force, like love or empathy, that cannot be easily verified empirically, would be well-advised to read Augustine's later work. It would help him or her to realize that human beings – their will, their reason and their morality – defy reduction to a model that serves as a basis for further development of theories in which the assumptions are specified. After his self-analysis in the *Confessiones* Augustine says that he himself is a question: 'Factus eram ipse mihi magna quaestio'.[95] It is a comment that suggests that he realized that anyone who has found an answer has not asked the right question.

## 5 Bonus: The Relationship between Happiness as an Economic Variable and Temperance as a 'Theological' Virtue

The Industrial Revolution brought about unprecedented economic growth, with a sharp reduction of poverty and increase of life expectancy as positive results. In his *Principles of Political Economy* (1848) John Stuart Mill contended that this growth would be a passing phenomenon. He assumed that as soon as material scarcity had been resolved and wealth was sufficient at the micro,

94 See for instance P. van Egmond, *'A Confession without an Pretence'. Text, context of Pelagius' defence of 417 AD*. (Amsterdam, 2012), 317–319; 352–354.

95 Augustine, *Confessiones* 4.4.9.

meso and macro levels, any aspirations to become even richer would vanish. Even John Maynard Keynes, in his *Economic possibilities for our grandchildren* (1930) assumed that one hundred years of economic growth would make scarcity a thing of the past forever. A society of contented, happy people would be the logical result, he stated, as they would have sufficient of everything they needed.

The underlying assumption of Mills' and Keynes' view of humankind is that people are happy when they have enough money and means to support themselves. But the criticism that can be made of the Pareto criterion *mutatis mutandis* also applies to Mills' and Keynes' anthropology. As we have seen above, the Pareto principle holds that overall wealth increases if the increase of wealth of the winners is sufficient to compensate the people who have fared worse.[96] We have argued that this is a noble principle, because it ensures that nobody loses out. But we have also observed that it clearly ignores the psychological mechanism that if one person becomes richer while a second person's wealth stays the same, this second person may still be discontented. It already hinted at the 'heavy price' economics had to pay 'for its self-imposed isolation from the other behavioral sciences'.[97] The psychologist is very much aware that people always think the grass is greener elsewhere, while the theologian knows that envy is a vice that has relentlessly determined human lives and world history from the beginning of humankind, with the murder of Abel by Cain as an early example. In addition, economics neglected the fact that habituation to a higher level of wealth leads to new avarice, which will decrease the happiness that was felt before the onset of habituation.[98] Neoclassical economic theorists correctly argue that the means people have at their disposal will at some point inevitably begin to feel inadequate, leading to discontent bordering on unhappiness.

This discontent can have disastrous consequences, as the so-called social encyclicals that various popes have issued have pointed out very poignantly. In *Rerum Novarum* (1891) Pope Leo XIII, who regarded happiness and prosperity as intrinsically connected, denounced the yawning wealth gap between underpaid workers and factory owners. All people should have sufficient to support themselves. As we saw earlier, Pope Francis in *Laudato si'* calls the limitless demand for consumer goods in the affluent Western world a root cause of climate change and decries the mechanism by which it is easier for the rich

96 Cf. Mock, 'Pareto Optimality', 808–809.

97 Bowles, 'Endogenous Preferences: The Cultural Consequences of Markets and other Economic Institutions', 102–105.

98 Graafland, *Het oog van de naald*, 139–148.

than for the poor to overcome the grave environmental consequences of naked consumerism. The economy, ecology and social justice are intimately related, and the ecological crisis is rooted in a moral crisis.[99]

It is clear that there is an intrinsic link between economic growth on the one hand and happiness on the other. This can be illustrated by two other examples. An exuberant demand for consumer goods –particularly in 'the affluent Western world' –could have serious repercussions for the environment, or even for world peace, as competition for resources could ignite armed conflict.[100] The awareness of these consequences is in itself enough to decrease 'happiness' around the world. It has been demonstrated that people's happiness increases when they no longer have to worry about balancing income and expenditure and about how to keep poverty at bay. In any country, the likelihood of an ordered life of well-being is increased when extra income is provided at the lower end of the distribution of incomes. The less vulnerable members of a society have to worry about sufficient income and possessions, the happier life will be in that country as a whole.

Not surprisingly this realization has led people in different countries, including France and the Netherlands, to argue that the assessment of the well-being of a society should not just be based on variables like national income or gross domestic product and gross national product.[101] Although relationships, trust, social cohesion, health and happiness are strongly influenced by economic developments, these non-economic components of welfare are still separate phenomena. That is why the general assembly of the United Nations (UN) in 2011 even passed a resolution to advocate measuring not just gross national product, but gross national happiness, too. Interest in happiness as a policy factor has proven to be on the rise.[102]

---

99 See chapter 4.4.

100 Cf. B. Goudzwaard, H. de Lange, *Beyond Poverty and Affluence: Toward an Economy of Care*. Grand Rapids. Michigan: Eerdmans, 1995. They offer a 'twelve-step program for economic recovery'.

101 Cf. J.E. Stiglitz, A. Sen, J.P. Fitoussi, *The Measurement of Economic Performance and Social Progress: Report by the Commission on the Measurement of Economic Performance and Social Progress*. Paris, 2009; Centraal Plan Bureau, *Memorandum Economische beleidsevaluaties en welvaart*. Den Haag: CPB, 2010; Centraal Plan Bureau, *Notitie Aspecten van brede welvaart in CPB-studies*. Den Haag: CPB, 2015; Planbureau voor Leefomgeving, Sociaal Cultureel Planbureau, Centraal Planbureau, *Naar een Verkenning Brede welvaart*. Den Haag: PBL, SCP, CPB, 2017.

102 R. Veenhoven, 'Het grootste geluk voor het grootste aantal. Geluk als richtsnoer voor beleid', in: *Sociale Wetenschappen* 2002 (4), 1–43, especially 12–18.

We must now address the question what 'happiness' means. Long ago theologians reflected on the possibility and characteristics of eternal happiness. It was hardly imaginable on earth, but according to Thomas Aquinas and others, happiness would reach its fulfilment in the so-called *visio beatifica*. This *visio* entailed a 'seeing' or realization that would only come after death; neither the gift of trust or faith, nor human reason include the *visio*. The *visio beatifica* amounted to a perfect 'existence' in which the human longing for a meaningful and good life had come to full fulfilment in the seeing of God.[103] In more recent times happiness –on earth –has been a chief research interest of psychologists eager to find out what people feel when they are happy, of neuroscientists, who study the relationship between incentives like rewards and happiness, and of economists who wish to discover out what people value in their quest for happiness. They have all worked energetically. As the Harvard professor of psychology Daniel Gilbert, author of the bestseller *Stumbling on Happiness*, put it in an interview: 'Papers on happiness are published in *Science*, people who study happiness win Nobel prizes, and governments all over the world are rushing to figure out how to measure and increase the happiness of their citizens.'[104]

The definition of happiness used was not univocal, however. In a broader sense it was connected with quality of life. Politicians attempted to create preconditions like security, judicial fairness and good healthcare, all meant to guarantee the quality of life citizens enjoy. Happiness in the narrower sense chiefly concerns the abilities each individual has to make something out of his or her life, abilities that have to do with the absence of functional impediments and the capacity for personal growth. Just as with the preconditions for happiness in the broader sense, this capacity for life is not the same as happiness in the narrower sense. But the presence of these preconditions and abilities will increase the chances that people will begin to think, judge and act in such a way that they become increasingly happy.[105] More specifically it was established that good physical and mental health, a safe neighborhood, freedom

103 See for example Thomas Aquinas, *Summa Theologiae* I-II, quaestiones 2–5; especially *Summa Theologiae* I-II, q.2. a.8; I-II, q.3. a.8.Cf. also *Summa Theologiae* I, q.12. a.4.

104 G. Morset, 'The Science behind the Smile. An interview with Daniel Gilbert', in: *Harvard Business Review* 2012, no. 1 (January-February issue), 3–8, quotation 3–4. https://hbr.org/2012/01/the-science-behind-the-smile

105 R. Veenhoven 'Wat is geluk?', in G. van Liemt (ed.), *Het rendement van geluk. Inzichten uit wetenschap en praktijk* (Den Haag 2014), 18–26 (SMO); L. Bormans (red.), *Geluk. The World Book of Happiness*. Tielt: Lannoo Uitgeverij, 2010. www2.eur.nl/fsw/research/veenhoven World Database of Happiness.

and autonomy of opinions and lifestyle, good relationships, meaningful work or daytime activities and material wealth all contribute to happiness.[106]

Economists have thus indeed paused to consider the meaning of the word happiness. It did not take them long to acknowledge that happiness is hard to measure. It is a notion with both a rational and an emotional component and a high degree of subjective perception. The questionnaires used to try and gauge the amount and intensity of happiness in relationship to income or life events were rather disparate.[107]

Few thought that theologians could be of help to economists who sought to establish a link between economic processes and increased happiness. They do not seem obvious candidates that could deepen or broaden the notion of happiness as defined for economic research purposes. They seem to disqualify themselves by assuming, as we have just seen, that happiness is not to be found on earth. In a centuries-old devotional hymn to the Virgin Mary, *Salve Regina*, still sung around the world, the earth is even compared to a vale of tears. Even as a young man, Augustine already complained that, if we could, all of us would like to keep our bodies healthy and free of complaints, but that human beings certainly do not live the way they would want to live due to the vulnerability of the body.[108] In his view, the desire for happiness could only be truly fulfilled by a happiness that is not transitory. And such a thing does not exist on earth, where all things are in flux and transitory.[109] As a sixty-year-old, Augustine still held that life in the *seculum*, the dimension of time and space, is not free from suffering. And suffering is often self-inflicted. In his view, a certain amount of justice can be attained by abandoning one's own pursuit of profit in favor of the common good.[110] But this willingness to sacrifice one's own interests is thin on the ground.[111] Regardless of whether Augustine is cynical or realistic –or

106 R. Veenhoven, 'Het grootste geluk voor het grootste aantal: Geluk als richtsnoer voor beleid', in: *Sociale Wetenschappen* (2002), no. 4, 1–43., especially 10–12.

107 N.J.A. van Exel, *Waarde(n)volle economie. Over geluk, welvaart en morele dilemma's. Rede in verkorte vorm uitgesproken bij de aanvaarding van het ambt van bijzonder hoogleraar Economics & Values aan de Erasmus School of Economics, Erasmus Universiteit Rotterdam, vanwege de Vereniging Trustfonds EUR, op 30 juni 2017* (Rotterdam: ESE 2017), 8, 18–20.

108 Augustine, *De Trinitate* 13.7.10.

109 Augustine, *De Beata Vita* II, 11.

110 R. Markus, *Saeculum: History and Society in the Theology of St Augustine* (Cambridge: Cambridge University Press, 1970), 72–104.

111 Augustine, *De civitate Dei* XIX, 6 (670–671); *De Civitate Dei* II: 21 (52–54); cf. D. Burt, *Friendship and Society. An Introduction to Augustine's Practical Philosophy* (Grand Rapids-Cambridge: Wm. B. Eerdmans Publishing, 1999), 127–129; Cf. P. van Geest, *Waarachtigheid. Augustine over levenskunst* (Zoetermeer: Meinema, 2011), 122–123.

both –it does not seem that study of his work could help economists in their quest for a more nuanced discussion of happiness.

Lastly, the advice of none other than Jesus himself that we should not worry unduly about tomorrow's clothing and food, because 'Each day has enough trouble of its own' serves as an antidote to our tendency to worry in times of uncertainty. This scriptural wisdom (Matthew 6: 34) seems less useful, however, when it comes to devising a suitable measuring instrument for the interaction between happiness on the one hand and variables like job satisfaction, productivity, economic crises, 'conscious capitalism' or the economic yield of happy people on the other.

But still. The past decades have seen a surprisingly substantial body of research on the interplay between modesty and moderation on the one hand and happiness on the other. It has been shown that these characteristics, behaviorally speaking, have a positive effect on health, on the emotions, self-efficacy or the capacity to learn to respect others, avoid conflict and enter into positive relationships with others. Studies have shown that modesty and moderation safeguard people against overly risky behavior in the public domain and in economic interactions, and against making (bad) decisions in reaction to 'ego threats'.[112] Very recent research shows that a certain degree of emotional intelligence and a sense of self-esteem can foster happiness through modesty and moderation, and that depression can be traced back to low scores on these characteristics.[113]

The 39 questions of the *Modest Behavior Scale* (MBS) relate to characteristic individual behaviors like downplaying one's strong points when receiving praise for them, praising the person one is criticized by, or an overall reluctance to speak about oneself.[114] As it happens, the meaning of the word modesty can be traced back to the Latin word *modestus* (i.e. exercising moderation, being sensible, controlled, appropriate), which during the middle ages became linked to *moderantia* (moderation). Many layers of meaning can be identified in the way the two terms and their synonyms are used in the works of the early Christian theologians. We will use Augustine's interpretation of moderation as our final argument for the indispensability of theology for economics when it

112 C.R. Colvin, J. Block, D.C. Funder, 'Overly positive self-evaluation and personality: negative implications for mental health', in: *Journal of Personality and Social Psychology* 68(1995), no. 6, 1152–1162; D. Dunning, C. Health, J. Suls, 'Flawed self-assessment', in: *Psychological Science in the Public Interest* 5(2004), no. 6, 69–106.

113 Ch. Zheng, Y. Wu, 'The More Modest You are, the Happier You are: The Mediating Roles of Emotional Intelligence and Self-esteem', in: *Journal of Happiness Studies. An Interdisciplinary on Subjective Well-Being* 21(2020), vol. 5, 1603–1615.

114 Ch. Zheng, Y. Wu, 'The More Modest You are, the Happier You are', 1606.

comes to developing a richer language –and a more multifaceted thinking –for reflection on economic processes that does not see the human being as a mere *homo economicus*, but as a relational being who may come to greater happiness by practicing moderation.

In 386 Augustine contributed to the late antique discussion on the art of living, happiness and the order of life by publishing a slim volume called *De beata vita* (On Happiness).[115] One of the booklet's premises is the idea, widely supported at the time, that a sense of moderation in everything one does, thinks or feels is not just good, but also leads to happiness. Socrates believed that a life of moderation was a virtuous life.[116] Unknowingly foreshadowing the neoclassical economic theory that assumed that available means will always be experienced as inadequate, Democritus of Abdera (460–370 BC) warned that greater desires lead to greater needs which will, when pursued or gratified excessively, take those involved from happiness to unhappiness.[117] An immoderate need for riches, Epicurus said, in fact amounts to poverty.[118] Philodemus was aware that possession brings worry, and poverty entails even more worry, and he wrote that wealth is preferable to poverty, but only up to the point from which it begins to cause its own worries.[119] The stoic motto *ne quid nimis* ('nothing to excess, everything with moderation') is the operational principle that reflects these insights. Finally, Cicero, too, calls temperance (*temperantia*) one of the most important aspects of virtue (*virtus*).[120]

Even Luke is very direct and unambiguous in his Gospel. He leaves no room for doubt especially in his practical guidelines. Like Horace before him in *Andria* 1.1.34 and Augustine after him - both of whom refer to the *ne quid nimis* principle - he instructs his readers to keep right measure, for instance when he writes that John advises his audience not to demand more money than the appointed rate (Lk. 3: 12–13).

Relying on insights from the late classical philosophy in particular, Augustine in *De beata vita* illustrates Philodemus's reflections on moderation as the road to happiness with a wonderful example. He mentions Orata, who, although immeasurably rich, is still in the clutches of the same feelings as someone who is incredibly poor and needy. As it happens Orata and his unnamed poor counterpart are both gripped by fear: the poor person because lack of possessions

115 Augustine, *De beata vita* I, 6.
116 Diogenes Laërtius, *Vitae philosophorum* 1.41; 1.93; 2.32.
117 Democritus, *Fragmenta* 319 (219).
118 Epicurus, *Sententiae Vaticanae* 25.
119 Philodemus, *Peri oikonomias* 12.
120 Augustine, *De beata vita* II, 8.

implies lack of food, Orata because he realizes that the quirks of fate could rob him of all he owns.[121] Fear is the inexorable fate of someone who begins to see *opulentia* as a goal and a benchmark of success, rather than as simply a way to build a balanced life. People who fail to exercise the right degree of moderation will lose their equilibrium in life and will be ridden by fears. It follows from this that everything in life that is excessive is defective, because it lacks right measure.[122]

Augustine is indebted to the stoic *ne quid nimis* principle when he argues that both excess and shortage are shortcomings because in both cases right measure is lost.[123] Like Cicero he sees a fruitful life as the result of temperance and self-control.[124] In fact, Augustine remained faithful to the *ne quid nimis* principle for the rest of his life, as can be seen, for example, in *Enarratio IV in Psalmum* 118.1 or in his definition of greed in *In epistolam Iannis ad Parthos*: 'Greed is 'to want more than is needed'.[125] The apostles and the philosophers were united in their critique of greed because it means eschewing moderation.[126] Augustine's words in *Enarratio IV in Psalmum* 118.1, for example, have recently been succinctly summarized by Pope Francis:

> On the other hand, no one can cultivate a sober and satisfying life without being at peace with him or herself ... Inner peace is closely related to care for ecology and for the common good because, lived out authentically, it is reflected in a balanced lifestyle together with a capacity for wonder which takes us to a deeper understanding of life.[127]

Finally, in *De beata vita*, Augustine argues that people are harming themselves by their lack of moderation. He employs a clever semantic strategy for this, linking the meaning he assigns to the word 'limit' (*modus*) to that which this notion had acquired in the earlier philosophical schools. Without robbing the 'neoplatonic' word of its meaning he adds a particular layer of meaning to it.[128] Observing the proper measure (*modus*), he says, implies a good form of living, as it keeps

121 Augustine, *De beata vita* IV. 26.
122 *ibidem.*
123 Augustine, *De beata vita* IV, 32.
124 Augustine, *De beata vita* IV, 31: 'temperantia', 'modestia'.
125 Augustine, *In epistolam Ioannis ad Parthos* 8.7.
126 Augustine, *sermo* 177.2.
127 Francis, *Laudato si'*, 225.
128 *De beata Vita* IV.33–34. Cf. G. Madec, 'Si Plato viveret... Augustin, De vera religione 3.3', in: *Néoplatonisme: Mélanges offerts à Jean Trouillard* (Fontenay-aux-Roses: École Normale Supérieure, 1981), 231–247, especially 232–235.

a person free from fear. He uses 'the highest measure' (*summus modus*) to refer to a 'reality' that fully transcends human beings in time and space and beyond: God. In his view God the Father is the One in whom all measures, weights and numbers are hidden and from whom the order comes forth by which all things in creation relate to each other. In this way, Augustine tries to clarify that moderation in life creates an openness to larger wholes that, undetermined by fear, foster insight into the whole in which one finds oneself.[129]

Augustine is thus one of the most outspoken interpreters of the late antique and early Christian idea that moderation is a path to being *beatus*: to being free from sorrow.[130] Both explicitly and implicitly his work entails an invitation to come to a more profound understanding of the word 'happiness'. Implicitly he states that the excessive pursuit of fame, wealth and honor leads to misfortune, as it leads to fear, and hence to isolation. Explicitly he writes that happiness is only experienced as a corollary of the awareness of being part of a whole: nature, a human community. Much later, in *De ciuitate Dei*, he would clearly show, as we have seen, that someone who won't accept that tragedy and suffering are inherently part of human existence, forgoes the tranquility of mind that is paradoxically also linked to happiness.

129 Augustine, *De beata vita* IV.6; IV.25.

130 For the meaning of 'beatus' see A. Blaise, *Dictionnaire Latin-Français des auteurs chrétiens* (Strasbourg: Le Latin Chrétien, 1954), 100.

CHAPTER 7

# Epilogue

## 1 Market, Model, Morality and Anthropology

Like any untested schematic portrayal of reality, an economic theory is only one particular representation of things. This is what books by economists tell us. We have learned from books by theologians that such representations are rooted in implicit assumptions, expectations, biases, selective perceptions and psychological or even sociopathological factors. To give one concrete example: in the first centuries of Christianity Christ was not portrayed as a crucified human being, but as a king who, with solemn dignity, stretches out his hands to the corners of the earth and in doing so covers the cross from which he is suspended. This representation can be traced back to early Christians' sensitivity to the spirit of their times. The Greek philosopher Celsus, drawing from both the platonic and the stoic schools of thought, phrased it very poignantly in the second century. In his polemic *Alèthès logos* ('Word of Truth') he mocked Christians for their belief that an almighty god had revealed himself in a 'weak' crucified figure like Jesus of Nazareth. His ridicule did not leave Christians unmoved: they adjusted their representation of the Lord to placate the prejudices of the spirit of the times, as they would do again during the Middle Ages, when the plague was rampant and the crucified figure of Christ acquired the features of a person in agony, followed many centuries later by a return to the representation of Christ as King when fascism and national socialism were on the rise.

The discussion of books in which economic theories are proposed as a part of the empirical observation of reality showed that the underlying assumptions of economics are strongly determined by tacit expectations and biases. To give a concrete example: in his *Wealth of Nations*, Adam Smith occasionally uses the metaphor of 'the invisible hand' to indicate that serving one's self-interest will also benefit the common good, as it increases production and hence prosperity. The words he uses can be related to both the spirit of the times and his world view. Living at the time of eighteenth-century Deism, Smith set out to create an orderly and unified representation of creation and of social reality around him. In his view, the patterns that are visible in nature and in the social and economic order create a platform for a good and happy life, provided people are prepared to shape their lives according to the principles these orders suggest. In this way Adam Smith managed to evoke a sense

 | DOI:10.1163/9789004501706_008

of order and harmony based on a model, a theory. A theory that is food for thought, just as the representation of an unportrayable God or a Crucified God is food for faith.

In this book we have tried to resist the temptation to study all the metaphors that past and present neo-classical economists, post-Keynesians, monetarists, microeconomists, macroeconomists and behavioral economists have employed or still employ to dress up their theories to make people believe that their representation or model of reality in fact coincides with reality itself. Theologians, on the other hand, are fortunately unable to capture 'the reality' of God in any representation of Him. In fact, Augustine, in his *sermo* 117, writes: 'si comprehendis, non est Deus', in other words: anyone who tries to capture God in a concept, image or notion can be certain of one thing: all their efforts will be in vain, as God defies description. Similarly –and again: fortunately –economists, too, are unable to capture the reality that is constituted by the consumer and producer behavior in models and diagrams, even though these do allow them to identify certain patterns, just as it helps theologians to speak about God to prevent the numinous from becoming so mysterious that no one knows any longer that life is shrouded in a Mystery.

What we intended to do when we began this treatise was to take up the challenge that economists have thrown at theologians: to help devise a new model of the human phenomenon. Economists themselves are critical of the view of the human being as an exclusively rational being who, armed with consistent preferences, acts purposively and purely out of self-interest. They no longer want it, and this rejection means a definite farewell to the ideal of a conclusive theory of humankind.

In the reflection on wealth, trade, money and interest as it developed during the history of Christian theology, the scholastic economists saw economic interaction as an expression of personal relationships that were morally justified because they were fundamentally conditioned by the virtues of charity and justice. Honesty and justice were seen as indispensable for the production, distribution and consumption of goods. In addition, the economy was always linked to personal choices that were presumed to be marked by justice and benevolence towards others. The goods and factor markets were seen as a system of natural patterns in which personal motives were irrelevant. In a similar way Reformation theologians kept searching for an intrinsic relationship between morality and market, a search driven by the conviction that every human being was created in God's image.

In a sense, economic and theological insights thus remained closely intertwined. This was continued in the thinking of Adam Smith (1723–1790), the founder of economics as a separate discipline. Just like other moral philosophers of his era, Smith considered the economy to be subservient to virtues like moderation. He also realized that love of self and charity are not mutually exclusive. Charity builds upon love of self – that was his idea. Although Smith's *The Wealth of Nations* is often quoted to justify the pursuit of self-interest as the only relevant motive in the economy, he also explicitly quotes the golden rule of ethics in his book: always do to others what you would have them do to you (Matthew 7:12). In this way he exploded the idea that love of self and charity were incompatible. This was an assumption that had characterized much moralistic philosophical and theological literature for centuries. Smith's brilliant and liberating discovery changed the world. Human prosperity, creativity and innovation thrived. The combination of liberty, love of self and charity proved to be a better foundation for trust in reciprocity than moralism alone had been. And because self-love is kept in check by charity, Smith argues, the combination has a civilizing effect. In nearly the same spirit, Coase formulated his famous theorem, which lays out two conditions for the creation of wealth through cooperation. The first is that individual deciders must base their choices on the common interest of the entire household, rather than on their own interest. When making choices they must take into account all costs and benefits for all stakeholders. They thus internalize all the external effects their behavior has on all stakeholders. The second condition is that the gains of cooperation must be shared in such a way that all involved benefit. This condition ensures that the whole takes into account the interests of each individual. Each individual is more than compensated for their contribution to the whole. If we apply this to the body metaphor, every organ takes care of the body, while the body takes care of every organ.

In spite of Smith and Coase, economics eventually broke away completely from the family from which it had sprung. At the root of the economic equivalent of the Copernican revolution stood the ideas of the Italian economist Vilfredo Pareto (1848–1923): no longer would the economy revolve around ethics, but the reverse became the norm. Instead of deriving right choices from ethical considerations, ethical values were henceforth derived from the way people made choices. Economics became a positive, empirical science that refused to take its orders from philosophy or ethics. The foundation of economics as an autonomous field of study was rational choice theory. The *homo rationalis* –a human being who makes rational choices –distances him- or herself from the utility ethics of the *homo economicus*. Rational human beings do as they please and need no more than their own rationality to decide what seems right to them.

The practitioners of behavioral economics, increasingly numerous, began to apply the concept of scarcity to the attention and willpower of the individual. They no longer saw human beings as unlimitedly rational. The traditional view of humankind economists had thus far adhered to–the rational *homo economicus* with stable preferences –became the subject of growing criticism. While the *homo economicus* often still holds sway in economics classrooms, boardrooms and policy making, the rational choice model that dominated the twentieth century is past its prime. The search was on for a model of human beings in which they would no longer be seen as the sum of their transactions in anonymous markets. After the Industrial Revolution, economists started to become increasingly interested in transactions in markets. To many economists, it is the highest form of cooperation, as material interests run parallel. People who do not know each other personally can still collaborate productively. But economists also began to see competition and anonymous market processes as an impoverished form of human cooperation.[1] People should therefore, they argued, primarily be seen as the sum of relationships in which they are not interchangeable with competitors and in which an intrinsic motivation to further the interest of others rather than strategic considerations would be decisive. Not surprisingly this has primarily become an issue in what is called relational economics. In addition, behavioral economists and 'relational economists' in particular recognize that social values like justice and reciprocity could play an important part in explaining human behavior, conflict and cooperation. The economy no longer revolves around established institutions such as legislation and financial triggers only, but also around soft institutions that influence the preparedness to harm or serve others. As a consequence of these developments, increasingly there is room in economics for centuries-old notions from the humanities, like virtues, values, trust, personal motives and love.

## 2 Language and Reflection on Economic Processes

As a result of the rapprochement between economics and the humanities, reputed economists are now reflecting on notions like 'gratuity', 'trust' and 'inner motives and intentions'. These notions are discussed at length in Scriptural and patristic sources in passages and treatises that deal with mercy, faith and the interaction between the fear that purifies and the love that makes perfect. These sources are studied by theologians. To put it boldly, this in itself should be enough to make theologians indispensable to economists, but we

1 R. Sapolsky, *Behave. The Biology of Humans at our Best and Worst.* London: Vintage, 2017.

are obviously not the only ones. In any case theologians may well be able to contribute to the development of a richer language, and a richer way of thinking for a reflection on economic processes in which human beings are chiefly seen as relational beings who eventually find happiness and fulfillment in the benevolent, altruistic or even loving treatment by others, including others in the public domain and in economic interaction. Just like religion and faith, empathy and love are relevant not just in the privacy of our homes, but also in the outside world.

Economists certainly do not need theologians to realize that the reality of the human phenomenon is more complex than the models suggest, models they quite rightly developed to gain a grip on real-life issues. Their awareness of the discrepancy between models and reality had already been raised by studies by economists and psychologists that questioned the dominance of the *homo economicus*. They did this by reflecting on notions like *bounded rationality*, *bounded morality* and *bounded willpower*, thus reaching a deeper understanding of human beings as economic actors. At this point our suggestion, again a bold one, is to let theologians contribute to acquiring even deeper insight into the causes and consequences of the human inability to evaluate all the consequences of a decision, or the human inability to do – or even want – the right thing. Our understanding of the depth, scope, complexity and implications of *bounded rationality*, *bounded morality* and *bounded willpower* could be enhanced by consulting theological sources which describe the inadequacy of reason and love as a path to knowledge, which bring the multifaceted nature of sin to light in full detail, and which outline the immensity and intensity of the limitations or weakness of human willpower. Works by negative theologians, mirrors of confession, medieval theological-economic treatises, and especially the works of Augustine, are veritable treasure troves that invite us on almost every page to further reflection on our limitations as humans, a kind of deep thinking that could help economists in their search for a richer and fuller anthropology as the foundation for their theoretical models.

The works discussed here are just a handful of examples from the history of theology. There are countless other works that could help us to expand our knowledge of the causes, consequences and immensity of *bounded morality*, *bounded rationality* and *bounded willpower*. There are numerous other theological works that testify to deep and fruitful thinking about things such as human dignity. It is a human aspect that can not be reduced to the social contexts in which human beings prove themselves, maintain themselves, are repressed or are victorious. It is intrinsic to each individual human existence, and is as such inalienable. At the same time human dignity is a quality gained through respectful interaction with others, and lost by encroaching on the intrinsic dignity of others by exploiting them in any way. The works of theologians who write about dignity are indeed food for economic thought.

The same could be said of theologians who write about hope. Over the last decades, various disciplines have rediscovered hope. This virtue, which implies desire and probability, is now the subject of research in psychology, psychiatry, economics, conflict studies, health care studies, ecology, philosophy and theology.[2] A survey of 1,936 publications on hope in *Web of Science* reveals differences in approach and definition between the various academic disciplines, as well as regards the internal and external sources of hope, social and individual experiences of hope, internal and external effects, and the specific objects or sources of hope.[3] Even though the subject of hope is very diverse, the historical contributions in the recently published volume *Historical and Multidisciplinary Perspectives on Hope* show that the descriptions of hope proposed in antique and medieval philosophy, scholastic theology, the Enlightenment and postmodernism in fact have many aspects in common.[4]

Over the last decades, behavioral economists in particular have pointed out that hope plays an important role in economic life and can be fostered by measurable developments in the field of innovation, productivity and entrepreneurship, and that lack of hope is correlated to apathy.[5] Empirical economic research confirms that despair can hinder economic growth, and that hope is the very force that drives workers to perform better and to choose to invest and grow. A survey held among 8,453 young people between 11 and 15 years of age in 495 villages in India, for example, showed that girls are more optimistic and more successful in school if there is a woman among the school's managers.[6] Hope and trust in people and in the future that is intertwined with them are drivers of innovation and growth that should not be underestimated, as they

2 See S. C. van den Heuvel, *Historical and Multidisciplinary Perspectives on Hope* (Springer: Open Acces, 2020), 99- 261.

3 Cf. E. Pleeging, J. van Exel, M. Burger, 'Characterizing Hope: An Interdisciplinary Systematic Review of the Characteristics of Hope', forthcoming.

4 Cf. S. Gravlee, 'Hope in Ancient Greek Philosophy', in: S. C. van den Heuvel, *Historical and Multidisciplinary Perspectives on Hope* (Springer: Open Acces, 2020), 3–24; M. Webber, J. Kok, 'Early Christian Thinking on Hope', in: *ibidem*, 25–45; A. Pinsent, 'Hope as a Virtue in the Middle Ages, in: *ibidem*, 47- 60; R. T. Michener, 'Post-Kantian to Postmodern Considerations of (Theological) Hope', in: *ibidem*, 77- 95. These contributions focus on integration of hope into virtue ethics as human expectations are radically changing due to the changing times.

5 M. Burger, E. Pleeging, 'Hope in Economics', in: S. C. van den Heuvel, *Historical and Multidisciplinary Perspectives on Hope* (Springer: Open Acces, 2020), 165–178.

6 L. Beaman, E. Duflo, R. Pande, T. Topalova, 'Female Leadership Raises Aspirations and Educational Attainment for Girls: A Policy Experiment In India', in: *Science* 335 (6068) – (Febr. 2012), 582–586.

foster the setting of more positive goals, weighing of chances and assessment of progress.[7]

Other research on the basis of data from the United States demonstrates that income growth not only affects subjective wellbeing (SWB) and perspectives on the future, but also affects the power of hope that ensures that goals are reached more efficiently.[8] Finally, a study among 1,000 respondents in the Netherlands has revealed that the 'willingness to pay' (WTP) institutions that contribute to solving climate change problems is correlated with a certain form of hope. This form is a kind of hope nourished not only by knowledge of the gravity of the situation, but also by understanding and concern.[9]

Both theoretical and applied economic research of hope thus shows that this force is an inestimable motive for innovation and growth, because it has a positive effect on goal setting, the weighing of opportunities and the assessing of progress.[10]

Philosophers have been consulted frequently, and rightly so. Immanuel Kant associated hope with rational expectations about the future and did not regard it as one of the passions.[11] The Marxist philosopher Ernst Bloch said that hope does not just entail imagination or dreams, but that 'educated, learned hope' (docta spes) also implies the ability to set ourselves real goals for the improvement of our (in Bloch's view: capitalist) fate in this concrete world.[12] It is precisely their emphasis on a hope filtered by reason which proves that the economy is not only determined by rational motives or objective circumstances such as income and safety – it is a point that has been made

---

7 See P. Nullens, M. Burger, S. van den Heuvel, E. Pleeging, 'Hoop als drijfveer', in: H. Commandeur, P. van Geest, F. Langerak (eds.), *Management en Organisatie.* Themanummer: *Inzicht in drijfveren III* (Deventer: Kluwer, 2016), 79–91 (*Management en Organisatie* 70–5\6).

8 E. Pleeging, M. Burger, J. van Exel, 'Hope Mediates the Relation between Income and Subjective WellBeing', in: *Happiness Studies* (2020). https://doi.org/10.1007/s10902-020-00309-6

9 E. Pleeging, J. van Exel, M. Burger, S. Stavropoulos, 'Hope for the future and willingness to pay for sustainable energy', in: *Ecological Economics* 181 (2021) 106900. See also their 'hope barometer', a gauge they developed to permit organizations to measure hope. https://www.thehopeproject.nl/nl/the-hope-barometer/; https://www.thehopeproject.nl/nl/over-ons/

10 See also P. Nullens, M. Burger, S. van den Heuvel, E. Pleeging, 'Hoop als drijfveer', in: H. Commandeur, P. van Geest, F. Langerak (eds.), *Management en Organisatie.* Themanummer: *Inzicht in drijfveren III* (Deventer: Kluwer, 2016), 79–91 (*Management en Organisatie* 70–5\6).

11 B. Böser, 'Enlightenment Views of Hope', in: S.C. van den Heuvel (ed.), *Historical and Multidisciplinary Perspectives on Hope* (Springer: Open Access, 2020), 61–75.

12 E.H. Erikson, *Childhood and society.* (New York: Norton, 1950); E. Bloch, *Das Prinzip Hoffnung: In fünf Teilen.* Frankfurt: Suhrkamp, 1977.

frequently in this book. But it also demonstrates that a writer like Augustine can be a useful interlocutor. We have observed above that he also regarded the passions as a salutary force as long as they are filtered by reason: reason turns fear into prudence, for instance. The pathway he has developed to ensure that hope is both filtered and forceful can offer incentives to economists who are studying hope.

Throughout the centuries, theologians too have devoted much thought to hope, the theologal virtue and force that should ideally be the pre-eminent constitutive element in Christian identity. In the *Epistle to the Romans*, one of the most important sources of Christian theology of all times, hope is described as redemptive. 'For in this hope we were saved,' Paul says (Rom. 8:24), while one of his prominent interpreters, Augustine, argues that it is hope that truly turns people into Christians. [13] The endless series of authors –prophets, evangelists, apostles and their interpreters –from the Jewish and Christian tradition who have expressed their hope for better times, particularly in times of hopelessness and repression, is a potential gold mine for economists who seek to reflect on the immensity and intensity of hope as a force that has the potential to transform humankind and society.[14] Study of the way in which hope has been conceptualized in Christianity can help to broaden anyone's frame of reference.

## 3 Conclusion: Keynes's Take on the Economist and the Theologian

It can even be inferred from the words of the great economist John Maynard Keynes that economists and theologians are compatible: '.... the master-economist must possess a rare combination of gifts. He must reach a high standard in several different directions and must combine talents not often found together. ... He must understand symbols and speak in words. He must contemplate the particular in terms of the general, and touch abstract and concrete in the same flight of thought. He must study the present in the light of the past for the purposes of the future. No part of man's nature or his institutions must lie entirely outside his regard.'[15]

13 Augustine, *De civitate Dei* 6.9.

14 J. Moltmann, *Ethik der Hoffnung*. Gütersloh: Gütersloher Verlagshaus, 2010.

15 J.M. Keynes, *Essays in biography* (London: MacMillan, 1933), 170; quoted in: H. van Dalen, K. Koedijk, 'Gevraagd: een nieuwe kijk op economie', in: H. van Dalen, K. Koedijk (eds), *Nieuwe Kijk op Economie Gevraagd* (Tilburg: Tilburg University Press, 2012), 64–69, quote 67.

Keynes's profile of the 'master-economist' could be taken to apply *mutatis mutandis* to theologians as well. They too should possess a rare combination of skills. They will have to be as precise as a philologist who is preparing a critical edition of a text or dissecting its redactional layers. They will have to think as methodically as a lawyer, as they are supposed to be well-versed in canon law. They must be as empathetic as a top clinical psychologist, because as pastoral psychologists they will have to guide people to understanding and liberation. And above all, they will have to love people, because the God they study, and in whom they may also believe, has been described as Love. This God therefore can not be credibly brought to human beings by simply presenting them with a set of propositions about God. Theologians will nevertheless have to know these propositions well, and this means they will have to possess the disposition of the historian of mentalities who charts and evaluates the historic development of ideas and convictions. It goes without saying that theologians will have to be versed in the interpretation of symbols found in Scripture and tradition, and they will have to be able to abstract details from the history of the church and of theology and interpret them against the larger backdrop of history and vice versa. And it is absolutely essential that no aspect of human nature should lie outside their field of vision. Most theologians realize this, and church history has taught them that they must be wary of having an overly optimistic view of human nature. In fact, perhaps they *will* have a somewhat rosy outlook, because despair is hell, as Augustine said, and as we have seen. Keynes's words were indeed interdisciplinary.

# Bibliography

## Primary Sources


*S. Ambrosii de Helia et Ieiunio*. A commentary, with an Introduction and Translation. Ed. J.M. Buck. Washington, D.C.: Catholic University of America, 1929 (*The Catholic University of America, Patristic Studies* XIX).

Augustine, *Confessionum libri XIII*. Ed. L. Verheijen (*Corpus Christianorum Series Latina* 27).

Augustine, *Contra duas epistulas Pelagianorum*. Ed. K. Urba, J. Zycha (*Corpus Scriptorum Ecclesiasticorum Latinorum* 60), 421–570.

Augustine, *Contra secundam Iuliani responsionem imperfectum opus*. Ed. M. Zelzer, (*CSEL* 85/1).

Augustine, *De beata vita*. Ed. P. Green (*CCSL* 29).

Augustine, *De civitate Dei*. Ed. B. Dombart, A. Kalb (*CCSL* 48).

Augustine, *De diversis quaestionibus ad Simplicianum*. Ed. A. Mutzenbecher (*CCSL* 44).

Augustine, *De dono perseverantiae*. Ed. J. Chéné, J. Pintard (*Bibliothèque augustinienne. Oeuvres de Saint Augustin* 24).

Augustine, *De doctrina christiana*. Ed. J. Martin (*CCSL* 32), 1–167.

Augustine, *De Genesi ad litteram*. Ed. J. Zycha (*CSEL* 28.1), 1–435.

Augustine, *De gratia Christi et de peccato originali libri duo*. Ed. K. Urba, J. Zycha (*CSEL* 42), 123–206.

Augustine, *De gratia et libero arbitrio*. Ed. J. Chéné, J. Pintard (*Bibliothèque augustinienne. Oeuvres de Saint Augustin* 24).

Augustine, *De libero arbitrio*. Ed. W.M. Green (*CCSL* 29), 205–321.

Augustine, *De ordine*. Ed. W.M. Green (*CCSL* 29).

Augustine, *De opere monachorum*. Ed. J. Zycha (*CSEL* 41).

Augustine, *De Trinitate*. Ed. W. Mountain, F. Glorie (*CCSL* 50).

Augustine, *Enarrationes in Psalmos I-L; LI-C; CI-CL*. Ed. E. Dekkers, J. Fraipont (*CCSL* 38–40).

Augustine, *Epistulae*. Ed. A. Goldbacher (*CSEL* 34).

Augustine, *Epistulae*. Ed. A. Goldbacher (*CSEL* 44).

Augustine, *Expositio quarundam propositionum ex epistula apostoli ad Romanos*. Ed. J. Divjak (*CSEL* 84).

Augustine, *In epistolam Johannis ad Parthos, Tractatus VII*, 5–7, in: P. Agaësse (intr., ed., trans.), *Commentaire de la première épître de S. Jean*. Paris: Cerf, 1961.

Augustine, *In Johannis euangelium tractatus CXXIV*. Ed. R. Willems (*CCSL* 36).

Augustine, *Retractationum libri II*. Ed. A. Mutzenbecher (*CCSL* 57).

Augustine, *Sermo Casinensi* I, 33, in: *Sancti Augustini Sermones post Maurinos repertos*. Ed. G. Morin (Roma 1930), 401–412 (*Miscellanea Agostiniana* 1).

Augustine, *Sermo Dolbeau* 15, in: François Dolbeau (ed.), *Augustin d'Hippone: Vingt-six Sermons au Peuple d'Afrique*. Paris: Études Augustiniennes, 1996 (= *Collection des Études Augustiniennes Série Antiquité* 147).

Augustine, *Soliloqviorvm libri duo*. Ed. W. Hörmann (*CSEL* 89).

Benedictus XVI, *Caritas in Veritate* (http://w2.vatican.va/content/benedict-xvi/nl/encyclicals/documents/hf_ben-xvi_enc_20090629_caritas-in-veritate.html).

Democritus, *Fragmenta*. Ed. F.G.A. Mullach. Berlin: G. Besseri, 1843.

Denzinger, H., *Kompendium der Glaubensbekenntnisse und kirchlichen Lehrentscheidungen*. Verbessert, erweitert, ins Deutsche übertragen und unter Mitarbeit von Helmut Hoping herausgegeben von Peter Hünermann. Freiburg: Herder, 1991[37].

Diogenes Laërtius, *Vitae philosophorum*. Ed. G. Hübner. Leipzig: Teubner, 1828.

Diogenes Laërtius, *Leven en leer van beroemde filosofen*. Transl. R. Ferwerda. Budel: Damon, 2008.

Epicurus, *Sententiae Vaticanae*, in: id. *Epicurea*. Ed. H. Usener. Leipzig: Teubner, 1887.

Erasmus, *Collected Works of Erasmus* (Toronto: University of Toronto Press, 1991), vol. 61, *Patristic Scholarship. The edition of St. Jerome*. Ed. J.F. Brady – J.C. Olin (Toronto: University of Toronto Press, 1992), vol. 1.

Erasmus, *Exhortation à la lecture de l'Évangile*. Ed. A. Vanautgaerden. 2 vols. (Turnhout: Brepols, 2005). vol. 1: *Le texte Latin*. Edition, annotation et introduction J.-F. Cottier. Traduction J.-F. Cottier - A. Vanautgaerden (Turnhout: Brepols, 2005), 104–108.

Erasmus, *Hieronymi Vita in S. Hieronymi Stridonensis Opera Omnia* (Frankfurt am Main-Leipzig, 1684), vol. 1.

Franciscus, *Laudato Si'*, http://www.vatican.va/content/francesco/en/encyclicals/documents/papa-francesco_20150524_enciclica-laudato-si.html

Franciscus, *Evangelii Gaudium*, http://www.vatican.va/content/francesco/en/apost_exhortations/documents/papa-francesco_esortazione-ap_20131124_evangelii-gaudium.html

Gabriel Biel, *Integerrimi profundissimique viri Magistri Gabrielis Biel ex Spira: Sacratissimarum litterarum licenciati: florentissimi gymnasij Tubingensis dum in humanis esset ordinarij lectoris resolutissimi Tractatus de potestate et utilitate monetarum* (Oppenheim: Köbel, 1516).

Gabrielis Biel, *Collectorium circa quattuor libros Sententiarum*. Auspiciis Hanns Rückert. Collaborantibus Martino Elze Volker Sievers et Renata Steiger. Ediderunt Wilfridus Werbeck et Udo Hofmann. Tübingen: J.C.B. Mohr (Paul Siebeck), 1973–1992. 4 vols. vol. IV/2, *Libri quarti pars secunda* (*dist. 15–22*) (Tübingen: J.C.B. Mohr (Paul Siebeck), 1977), 175–189.

*Gaudium et Spes* 27, in: *Vaticanum II. Conciliedocumenten. Latijnse tekst en nieuwe Nederlandse vertaling*. Antwerpen: Halewijn, Baarn: Adveniat, 2019.

Giles of Lessines, *De usuris in communi et de usuram contractibus* IX en III, in: Thomas Aquinas, *Opera* (Parma Edition), vol. 17, 413–436.

Gregorius Magnus, *In homilia in euangelia*. Ed. J.-P. Migne (*Patrologia Latina* 76).

Irenaeus, *Adversus Haereses*. Ed. in: Bernhard Mutschler: *Das Corpus Johanneum bei Irenäus von Lyon. Studien und Kommentar zum dritten Buch von Adversus Haereses*. Tübingen: Mohr Sibeck, 2006 (*Wissenschaftliche Untersuchungen zum Neuen Testament* 189).

*Joannis Calvini opera quae supersunt omnia*. Ed. E. Cunitz, J.-W. Baum, E.W.E. Reuss. Brunsvigae: C.A. Schwetschke, 1863. 59 parts in 58 vols. Vol. 8.

John Calvin, *Responsio ad Sadoleti epistulam* (1539), in: *Ioannis Calvini Opera Selecta*. Ed. P. Barth). vol. I (München: Kaiser Verlag, 1926), 457–490.

John Calvin, *Commentaries on the last four books of Moses, arranged in the form of a Harmony*. Vol 3. Edinburgh: Calvin Translation Society, 1855.

Johannes Duns Scotus, *Opus Oxoniense*, in: *Opera Omnia*. vol. 10 (Lyon, 1639); [reprint Hildesheim: Olms, 1968].

Johannes Eriugena, *Periphyseon*, II, 597D-598A. Ed. E. Jeauneau (*Corpus Christianorum Continuatio Mediaevalis* 162).

John Paul, *Centesimus Annus* (http://w2.vatican.va/content/john-paul-ii/en/encyclicals/documents/hf_jp-ii_enc_01051991_centesimus-annus.html).

Leo XIII, *Quod apostolici muneris* 11, in: Denzinger, H., *Kompendium der Glaubensbekenntnisse und kirchlichen Lehrentscheidungen*. Verbessert, erweitert, ins Deutsche übertragen und unter Mitarbeit von Helmut Hoping herausgegeben von Peter Hünermann (Freiburg: Herder, 1991[37]), 3133.

Leo XIII, *Rerum Novarum*, http://www.vatican.va/content/leo-xiii/en/encyclicals/documents/hf_l-xiii_enc_15051891_rerum-novarum.html

Leucippus, Democritus, *The Atomists, Leucippus and Democritus: Fragments*. Text and Translation with a Commentary by C.C.W. Taylor. Toronto-Buffalo-London: University of Toronto Press, 1999.

Nicolas Oresme, *De Origine et Natura Iure et Mutacionibus Monetarum* (*De Moneta of Nicholas Oresme and English Mint documents*). Translated with introduction and notes by Ch. Johnson. London-Edinburgh-Paris-Melbourne-Toronto-New York: Thomas Nelson and Sons, 1956 (*Medieval texts*).

Olevianus, C., Ursinus, Z., *Catechismus oder christlicher Underricht, wie der in Kirchenund Schulen der Churfürstlichen Pfaltz getrieben wirdt*. Heidelberg: J. Mayer, 1563.

Our World in Data, https://ourworldindata.org/grapher/average-real-gdp-per-capita-across-countries-and-regions (2018).

Pelagius, *Epistula ad Demetriadem*. Ed. J.P. Migne (PL 30), 15–45.

Pelagius, *Libellus fidei*, in; P. J. van Egmond, 'A Confession without Pretence': *Text and Context of Pelagius' Defence of 417 AD*. Amsterdam, 2012.

Pico della Mirandola, *Rede over de menselijke waardigheid.* Vertaald en van aantekeningen voorzien door Michiel Op de Coul, met een inleiding en nawoord van Jan Papy. Groningen: Historische Uitgeverij, 2008 (*Filosofie & Retorica* 2).

Richardus of Middleton, *Super quator libros Sententiarum.* 4. Vols. Brescia, 1591.

Smith, A., *The Theory of Moral Sentiments.* Ed. K. Haakonssen. Cambridge: Cambridge University Press, 2002 (*Cambridge Texts in the History of Philosophy*).

Smith, A., *The Theory of Moral Sentiments.* Glasgow Editions, 1759. Ed. D.D. Raphael, A.L. Macfie. Oxford: Clarendon Press, 1976.

Smith, A., *An inquiry into the Nature and Causes of the Wealth of Nations.* Ed. R.H. Campbell, A.S. Skinner. Oxford: Clarendon Press, 1976 [original: 1776].

Tertullian, *De idolatria.* Ed. J.H. Waszink, J.C.M. van Winden. Leiden: Brill, 1987.

Tertullian, *De patientia.* Ed. J.W. Ph. Borleffs. Den Haag: Daamen, 1948.

*The Shepherd of Hermas in Latin. Critical Edition of the Oldest Translation Vulgata.* Ed. C. Tornau – P. Cecconi. Berlin-Boston: Walter de Gruyter, 2014. (*Texte und Untersuchungen zur Geschichte der altchristlichen Literatur* 173).

S. Thomae Aquinatis, *Opera omnia iussu impensaque Leonis XIII P. M. edita.* vol. 6–7: *Prima secundae Summae theologiae.* Roma: Ex Typographia Polyglotta S.C. de Propaganda Fide, 1891–1892.

S. Thomae Aquinatis, *Sancti Thomae Aquinatis Opera omnia.* Ed. R. Busa. Stuttgart-Bad Canstatt: Fromman-Holzboog, 1980.

Xenophon, *Oikonomos.* Ed. K. Schenkl. Berlin: Weidmann, 1876.

## Secondary Sources

Ackoff, R.L., 'From data to wisdom', in: *Journal of Applied Systems Analysis* 16 (1989), 3–9.

Aertnys, J., *Theologia Moralis secundum doctrinam S. Alfonsi de Ligorio doct. Ecclesiae.* Torino: Marietti, 1950. 2 vols. (*Collectio Urbaniana* 12).

Aertnys, J., *Theologia Pastoralis complectens Practicam Institutionem Confessarii.* Paderborn: Ferdinand Schöning, 1901.

Agteres, S., 'Pistis and Fides as Civic and Divine Virtues: A Pauline Concept through Greco-Roman Eyes', in: C. Breytenbach (ed.), *Paul's Graeco-Roman Context* (Leuven: Peeters, 2015), 541–559. (*Bibliotheca Ephemeridum Theologicarum Lovaniensium* 277).

Akerlof, G., 'Loyalty filters', in: *The American economic review* 73 (1983), no. 1, 54–63.

Akerlof, G.A., Shiller, R., *Animal Spirits: How Human Psychology Drives the Economy, and Why it Matters for Global Capitalism.* Princeton-New Jersey: Princeton University Press, 2009.

Akerlof, G.A., Shiller, R., *Phishing for Phools: The Economics of Manipulation & Deception.* Princeton-New Jersey: Princeton University Press, 2015.

Amort, E., [*Historia indulgentiarum*] *De origine, progressu, valore, ac fructu indulgentiarum, necnon de dispositionibus ad eas lucrandas requisitis, accurata notitia, historia, dogmatica, polemica, critica* (Venetiis: apud Joannem Baptistam Recurti, 1733), 355–410.

Angenendt, A., *Geschichte der Religiosität im Mittelalter*. 3. Auflage. (Darmstadt: Wissenschaftliche Buchgesellschaft, 2005), 652–657.

Ariely, D., *The honest truth about dishonesty: how we lie to everyone – especially ourselves*. Durham, NC: Duke University Press, 2012.

Ballor, J., 'Theology and Economics: A Match Made in Heaven?', in: *Journal of Interdisciplinary Studies* 26 (2014), no. 1/2, 115–134.

Banzhaf, S., 'Economics and Theological Ethics: An Environmental Economist Replies to his Queen', in: *Journal of Economics, Theology and Religion* (*JETR*), in press.

Bateman, B.H., Banzhaf, H.S., (eds). *Keeping Faith, Losing Faith: Religious Belief and Political Economy*. Durham, N.C.: Duke University Press, 2008.

Bavel, B. van, *The Invisible Hand? How Market economies have emerged and declined since AD 500*. Oxford: Oxford University Press, 2016.

Bavel, T. van, 'The influence of Cicero's Ideal of Friendship on Augustine', in: J. den Boeft (ed.), *Augustiniana Trajectina. Communications présentées au colloque international d'Utrecht (13–14 novembre 1986)* (Paris: Etudes Augustiniennes, 1987), 59–72 (*Collection des Études augustiniennes. Série Antiquité* 119).

Beaman, L., Duflo, E., Pande, R., Topalova, P., 'Female Leadership Raises Aspirations And Educational Attainment for Girls: A Policy Experiment In India', in: *Science* 335 (6068) – (Febr. 2012), 582–586.

Beed, C., Beed, Cl., 'Economics and Theology', in: *Journal of Interdisciplinary Economics* 21 (2009), no. 2, 143–161.

Bell, D., *The Economy of Desire: Christianity and Capitalism in a Postmodern World*. Ada, MI: Baker Academic, 2012.

Bell, D., 'Justification and Salvation', in: S. Schwarzkopf (ed.), *The Routledge Handbook of Economic Theology* (New York: Routledge, 2020), 64–71.

Benjamin, W., Fragment 74, 'Kapitalismus als Religion', in: W. Benjamin, *Gesammelte Schriften*. Ed. R. Tiedemann, H. Schweppenhäuser (Frankfurt am Main: Suhrkamp Verlag, 1991), 100–103.

Berlin, I., *Against the current: Essays in the history of ideas*. Ed. H. Hardy (New York: Viking Press, 1980), 25–79.

Bermon, E., 'La théorie des passions chez saint Augustin', in: B. Besnier, P.F. Moreau, L. Renault (ed.), *Les passions antiques et médiévales* (Paris: Presses Universitaires de France, 2003), 173–197 (*Théories et critiques des passions* 1).

Biéler, A., *Calvin's Economic and Social Thought*. Geneva: World Alliance of Reformed Churches, World Council of Churches, 2005.

Biemond, A.J., Commandeur, H., Geest, P. van, '*Homo dignus*. Erkenning van de intrinsieke waardigheid van de mens in de organisatie', in: *Management en Organisatie* 72–6 (2018), 26–39.

Blaise, A., *Dictionnaire Latin-Français des auteurs chrétiens*. Strasbourg: Le Latin Chrétien, 1954.

Blaug, M., 'The fundamental theorems of modern welfare economics, historically contemplated', in: *History of Political Economy* 39 (2007), no. 2, 185–207.

Bloch, E., *Das Prinzip Hoffnung: In fünf Teilen*. Frankfurt: Suhrkamp, 1977.

Blosser, J., 'Christian Freedom in Political Economy. The Legacy of John Calvin in the thought of Adam Smith', in: P. Oslington (ed.), *Adam Smith as Theologian* (New York-London: Routledge, 2011), 46–60.

Bormans L., *Geluk. The World Book of Happiness*. Tielt: Lannoo, 2010.

Böser, B., 'Enlightenment Views of Hope', in: S.C. van den Heuvel (ed.), *Historical and Multidisciplinary Perspectives on Hope* (Springer: Open Access, 2020), 61–75.

Bouckaert, L., Zsolnai, L., (eds), *The Handbook of Spirituality and Business*. London: Palgrave McMillan, 2011.

Boumans, M., Davis, J., *Economic Methodology: Understanding Economics as a Science*. London: Palgrave Macmillan, 2010.

Bovenberg, A.L., van Geest, P.J.J., Hengstmengel, J., Rupert, J. en Commandeur, H.R., *Simultaan Behartigen van Belangen. De liefde als de samenbindende kracht voor de economie*. Amsterdam: Boom, 2020.

Bovenberg, L., 'Economics as a discipline of hope', in: P. Nullens, S.C. van den Heuvel (eds.), *Driven by Hope: Economics and Theology in Dialogue* (Leuven: Peeters Publishers, 2018), 21–40 (*Christian Perspectives on Leadership and Social Ethics* 6).

Bovenberg, L., 'Finance: A Relational Perspective', in: C. van Beuningen, K. Buitendijk (eds.), *Finance and the Common Good* (Amsterdam: Amsterdam University Press, 2019), 79–97.

Bovenberg, L., 'Jezus Christus als econoom', in: P. van Geest, M. Poorthuis, Th. Wagenaar, A. Warringa (eds.), *Maak vrienden met de Mammon. Over de levensbeschouwelijke dimensie in de economie* (Almere: Parthenon, 2013), 56–77.

Bovenberg, A.L., 'Vrijhandel vanuit relationeel perspectief: kansen en bedreigingen', in: *Christen Democratische Verkenningen* 2017, no. 3, 53–63.

Bovenberg, L., 'Markteconomie is ondergeschikt aan menselijke relaties', in: P.J. Dijkman, a.o. (eds.), *Menselijke waardigheid* (Amsterdam: Boom, 2011), 97–104 (*CD Verkenningen* 2011–4).

Bovenberg, B., Geest, P. van, *Kruis en munt. De raakvlakken tussen economie en theologie*. Utrecht: Kok Boekencentrum Uitgevers, 2021.

Bowles, S., 'Endogenous Preferences: The Cultural Consequences of Markets and other Economic Institutions', in: *Journal of Economic Literature* 36 (March 1998), 75–111.

Bowles, S., *The moral economy. Why Good Incentives Are No Substitute for Good Citizens.* New Haven-London: Yale University Press, 2016.

Braudel, F., *Beschaving, economie en kapitalisme (15de-18de eeuw)*. Amsterdam: Contact, 1989. 2 vols. [transl.].

Brennan, H.G., Waterman, A.M.C., 'Introduction', in: H.G. Brennan, A.M.C. Waterman (eds), *Economics and Religion: Are They Distinct?* (Boston: Kluwer, 1994), 3–15.

Brennan, G., Waterman, A.M.C., 'Christian Theology and Economics: Convergence and Clashes', in: I. Harper, S. Gregg (eds), *Christian Theology and Market Economics* (Cheltenham: Edward Elgar, 2008), 77–93.

Brewer, H., 'Die kirchliche Privatbusse im christlichen Altertum', in: *Zeitschrift für katholische Theologie* 45 (1921), 1–42.

Brown, P., *Through the Eye of a Needle. Wealth, the Fall of Rome, and the Making of Christianity in the West, 350–550 AD*. Princeton-Oxford: Princeton University Press, 2012.

Bruni, L., 'Economics and Vulnerability: Relationships, Incentives, Meritocracy', in: P. Rona, L. Zsolnai (eds.), *Economics as Moral Science* (New York: Springer International Publishing, 2017), 107–128.

Bruni, L., 'The Samaritan's Trust Game', in: *Journal of Economics, Theology and Religion* 1(2021), in press.

Bruni, L., *Civil Happiness: Economics and Human Flourishing in Historical Perspective* (London: Routledge, 2006), 34–117.

Bruni, L., *Gli imperi di sabbia. Logiche del mercato e beatitudini evangeliche*. Bologna: Edizioni Dehoniana, 2016.

Bruni, L., *Il mercato e il dono. Gli spiriti del capitalismo*. Milano: Università Bocconi, 2015.

Bruni, L., *Il prezzo della gratuità*. Roma: Città Nuova, 2006.

Bruni, L., *La sventura di un uomo giusto. Una rilettura del libro di Giobbe*. Bologna: Edizioni Dehoniana, 2016.

Bruni, L., Oslington, P., Zamagni, S., 'Economics and theology special issue: introduction', in: *International Review of Economics* 63 (2016), no. 1, 1–5.

Bruni, L., *Reciprocity, altruism and civil society*. London: Routledge, 2008.

Bruni, L., Smerilli, A., *Benedetta Economia*. Roma: Città Nuova, 2008.

Bruni, L., Smerilli, A., *De ongekende kant van de economie. Gratuïteit en markt.* Nieuwkuijk: De nieuwe stad, 2014.

Bruni, L., Smerilli, A., *L'altra metà dell'economia. Gratuità e mercati*. Roma: Città Nuova, 2014.

Bruni, L., Stanca, L., 'Watching Alone: Relational Goods, Television, and Happiness', in: *Journal of Economic Behavior and Organization* 65 (2008), 506–528.

Bruni, L., Sugden, R., 'Fraternity: why the market need not to be a morally free zone', in: *Economics and Philosophy* 24 (2008), no. 1, 35–64.

Bruni, L., Sugden, R., 'Reclaiming virtue ethics for economics', in: *Journal of Economic Perspectives* 27 (2013), no. 4, 141–164.

Bruni, L., Sugden, R., 'The road not taken: how psychology was removed from economics, and how it might be brought back', in: *Economic Journal* 117 (2007), 146–173.

Bruni, L., *The Economy of Salvation. Ethical and Anthropological Foundations of Market Relations in the First Two Books of the Bible*. Cham: Springer, 2019.

Bruni, L., *The Economy of Salvation. Ethical and Anthropological Foundations of the Market Relations in de First Two Books of the Bible*. Heidelberg: Springer Verlag, in press (*Virtues and Economics* 4).

Bruni, L., *The Genesis and the Ethos of the market*. Basingstoke: Palgrave Macmillan, Houndmills, 2012.

Bruni, L., *The Wound and the Blessing: Economics Relationships and Happiness*. New York: New City Press, 2012.

Bruni, L., Zamagni, S, 'In a Space of Questions: A Reflection on Religion and Economics at the Beginning of the Twenty-First Century', in: *History of Political Economy* 43 (2011), no. 2, 389–411.

Bruni, L., Zamagni, S., *Civil Economy: Efficiency, Equity, Public Happiness*. Bern: Peter Lang, 2007.

Bruni, L., Zamagni, S., Becchetti, L., *Dall'homo oeconomicus all'homo reciprocans*. Bologna: Il Mulino, 2010.

Buchanan, J., 'The Samaritan's dilemma', in: E.S. Phelps (ed.), *Altruism, Morality and Economic Theory* (New York: Russel Sage Foundation, 1975), 71–85.

Burger, M., Pleeging, E., 'Hope in Economics', in: S.C. van den Heuvel, *Historical and Multidisciplinary Perspectives on Hope* (Springer: Open Access, 2020), 165–178.

Burt, D., *Friendship and Society. An Introduction to Augustine's Practical Philosophy*. Grand Rapids-Cambridge: Wm. B. Eerdmans Publishing, 1999.

Byers, S., 'Augustine's debt to Stoicism in the Confessions', in: J. Sellars (ed), *The Routledge Handbook of the Stoic Tradition* (New York: Routledge, 2016), 56–69.

Canning, R., *The Unity of Love for God and Neighbour in St. Augustine*. Louvain: Peeters, 1993.

Cantoni, D., 'The Economic Effects of the Protestant Reformation: Testing the Weber Hypothesis in the German Lands' [Job Market Paper] https://web.archive.org/web/20121119001845/ http://www.people.fas.harvard.edu/~cantoni/cantoni_jmp_2_7_1.pdf.

Carvalho, J.P., Sriya, I., Rubin, J., (eds), *Advances in the Economics of Religion*. London: Palgrave Macmillan., 2019.

Casper, B., Hemmerle, K., Hünermann, P., *Theologie als Wissenschaft. Methodische Zugänge*. Freiburg im Breisgau: Herder, 1970.

Cavanaugh, W., *Being Consumed: Economics and Christian Desire*. Grand Rapids: Eerdmans, 2008.

Centraal Planbureau, *Notitie Aspecten van brede welvaart in CPB-studies*. Den Haag: CPB, 2015; Centraal Planbureau, *Memorandum Economische beleidsevaluaties en welvaart*. Den Haag: CPB, 2010.

Clark, Ch., 'Catholicism and Economics: Towards a «Deeper Reflection on the Nature of the Economy and Its Purposes»', in: *The American Journal of Economics and Sociology* 7 (2019), no. 2, 409–441;

Coase, R., 'The relevance of transaction costs in the economics analysis of law', in: F. Parisi en C. Kershaw Rowley (eds.), *The origins of law and economics: essays by the founding fathers* (Cheltenham, UK: Edward Elgar, 2005), 200.

Coase, R., *The Firm, the Market and the Law*. Chicago: University of Chicago, 1988.

Coase, R.H., 'The Problem of Social Cost', in: *Journal of Law and Economics* 3 (1960), 1–44.

Colvin, R., Block, J., Funder, D.C., 'Overly positive self-evaluation and personality: negative implications for mental health', in: *Journal of Personality and Social Psychology* 68 (1995), no. 6, 1152–1162.

Cook, R.M., 'Speculations on the Origins of Coinage', in: *Historia: Zeitschrift für Alte Geschichte* 7, no. 3 (1958), 257–262.

Cornillon, J., *Tout en commun ? La vie économique de Jésus et des premières générations chrétiennes*. Paris: Cerf Patrimoines, 2020.

Dahling, J.J., Whitaker, B.G., Levy, P.E., 'The Development and Validation of a New Machiavellianism Scale', in: *Journal of Management* 35 (2009), no. 2, 219–257.

Dalen, H. van, Koedijk, K., 'Gevraagd: een nieuwe kijk op economie', in: H. van Dalen, K. Koedijk (eds.), *Nieuwe Kijk op Economie Gevraagd* (Tilburg: Tilburg University Press, 2012), 64–69.

Damasio, A.R., *Descartes' error: emotion, reason and the human brain*. London: Penguin Books, 1994.

Damme, E. van, 'Liefde, geluk en economische wetenschap', in: *Economisch Statistische Berichten* 101 (2016), 57–61.

Damme, E. van, 'Verwevenheid van recht en economie', in: M. Groenhuijsen, E. Hondius, A. Soeteman (eds.), *Recht in Geding*. Den Haag: Boom Juridische uitgeverij, 2014.

Damme, E. van, 'Waarom doceren wij ouderwetse economie?', in: A.L. Bovenberg, R. Haan (eds.), *Preadviezen van de Koninklijke Vereniging voor de Staathuishoudkunde 2016: Economieonderwijs* (Amsterdam: Koninklijke Vereniging voor de Staatshuishoudkunde), 161–171.

Dean, J.M., Waterman, A.M.C.,(eds), *Religion and Economics: Normative Social Theory*. Dordrecht: Kluwer Academic Publishers, 1999.

Decock, W., 'Lessius and the Breakdown of the Scholastic Paradigm', in: *Journal of the History of Economic Thought* 31(2009), vol.1, 57–7.

Decock, W., 'The Catholic Spirit of Capitalism? Contrasting Views on Profit-Making Through Capital Investment in the Age of Reformations', in: W. Decock, J. Ballor, M. Germann, L. Waelkens (eds.), *Law and Religion: The Legal Teachings of the Protestant and Catholic Reformation* (Göttingen: Vandenhoeck und Ruprecht, 2014), 22–44.

Delumeau, J., *Le péché et la peur: La culpabilisation en Occident, 13e-18e siècles*. Paris: Fayard, 1983.

Denaux, A.J., *De plaats van theologie in universiteit, kerk en samenleving. Afscheidsrede, uitgesproken door Adelbert Denaux, bij zijn afscheid als decaan van de Tilburg School of Catholic Theology, op 14 december 2012* (Tilburg: Tilburg University Press, 2012), 10–21.

Dideberg, D., 'Amor', in: C. Mayer (ed.), *Augustinuslexikon* (Basel-Berlin: Schwabe Verlag, 1986-…), vol. 1, col. 294–300.

Dideberg, D., 'Caritas', in: C. Mayer (ed.), *Augustinuslexikon* (Basel-Berlin: Schwabe Verlag, 1986-…), vol. 1, col. 730–743.

Dierksmeier, C., 'Scholastic Business Ethics: Thomas Aquinas Versus William of Ockham', in: C. Lütge (ed.), *Handbook of the Philosophical Foundations and Business Ethics* (Dordrecht - New York: Springer, 2013), 159–178.

Dierksmeier, C., 'Thomas von Aquin über Gerechtigkeit als globale Wirtschaftstugend', in: R. Schönberger (eds), *Die Bestimmung des Menschen und die Bedeutung des Staates. Beiträge zum Staatsverständnis des Thomas von Aquin* (Baden: Nomos, 2017), 195–226 (*Staatsverständnisse* 103).

Dinter, A., Heimbrock, A.-G, Söderblom, K. (eds), *Einführung in die Empirische Theologie: gelebte Religion erforschen.* Göttingen: Vandenhoeck & Ruprecht, 2007 (*Empirical theology* 38).

Dunning, D., Health, C., Suls, J., 'Flawed self-assessment', in: *Psychological Science in the Public Interest* 5 (2004), no. 6, 69–106.

Dur, R., 'De economie van de liefde', in: *ESB Gedrag* 99 (2014), 780–782.

Eijffinger, S., 'De val van de economie en de economie van het verval', in: *Nexus* 64 (1999), 41–48.

Ekkart, R.E.O., 'De Leidse Bibliotheek in 1610', in: *De Boekenwereld* 1 (1984–1985), 13–17.

Ellemers, N., *Morality and the Regulation of Social Behavior. Groups as Moral Anchors*. New York: Routledge, 2017.

Elster, J., 'Emotions and economic theory', in: *Journal of Economic Literature* 36 (1998), 47–74.

Erikson, E.H., *Childhood and society*. New York: Norton, 1950.

Everett, J.R., *Religion in Economics. A Study of John Bates Clark, Richard T. Ely, Simon N. Patton.* New York: King's Crown, 1946.

Exel, van, N.J.A., *Waarde(n)volle economie. Over geluk, welvaart en morele dilemma's. Rede in verkorte vorm uitgesproken bij de aanvaarding van het ambt van bijzonder hoogleraar Economics & Values aan de Erasmus School of Economics, Erasmus Universiteit Rotterdam, vanwege de Vereniging Trustfonds EUR, op 30 juni 2017*. Rotterdam: ESE, 2017.

Fehr, E. en Gächter, S., 'Fairness and Retaliation: The Economics of Reciprocity', in: *Journal of Economic Perspectives* 14 (2000), no. 3, 159–182.

Fergusson, D., *The Providence of God: A Polyphonic Approach* (Cambridge: Cambridge University Press, 2018), 110–133 (*Current Issues in Theology* 11).

Fiedrowicz, M., 'Ciues sanctae ciuitatis Dei omnes affectiones rectas habent' De ciuitate Dei 14,9): Terapia delle passioni e preghiera in S. Agostino', in: *L'etica cristiana nei secoli III e IV: eredità e confronti* (Roma: Institutum patristicum augustinianum, 1996), 431–440 (*Studia Ephemeridis Augustinianum* 53).

Fikkert, B., Rhodes, M., 'Homo Economicus Versus Homo Imago Dei', in: *Journal of Markets and Morality* 20 (2017), no. 1, 101–127.

Finley, M.I., *The Ancient Economy*. London: Chatto & Windus, 1973.

Fitzgerald, J., 'Chapter 2: Early Greek economic thought', in: D.B. Hollander, Th.R. Blanton IV, J.T. Fitzgerald (eds.), *The Extramercantile Economies of Greek and Roman Cities. New Perspectives on the Economic History of Classical Antiquity* (London-New York: Routledge, 2019), 30–48 (*Routledge Monographs in Classical Studies*).

Flasch, K., *Logik des Schreckens. Augustinus von Hippo. De diversis quaestionibus ad Simplicianum* I 2. Mainz: Dieterich, 1990.

Florensky, P., *Early Christian Writings 1903–1909*. Translation B. Jakim. Grand Rapids: Eerdmans, 2017.

Franses, Ph.H., 'Een woord vooraf', in: S. Phlippen, G. Werner (eds.), *Canon van de economie* (Rotterdam: ESE, 2015), 8–11.

Friedman, B.M., *Religion and the Rise of Capitalism*. New York: Knopf, 2021.

Galie, P.J., Bopst, C., 'Machiavelli & modern business: Realist thought in contemporary corporate leadership manuals', in: *Journal of Business Ethics* 65 (2006), no. 3, 235–250.

Geest, P. van, '*Ante omnia igitur opus est Dei timore converti* (*doctr. chr.* 2.7.9). Augustine's Evaluation of Fear', in: A. Dupont, G. Partoens, M. Lamberigts (eds.), *Tractatio scripturarum. Philological, Exegetical, Rhetorical and Theological Studies on Augustine's Sermons* (Louvain: Peeters, 2012), 443–464 (*Instrvmenta Patristica et Medievalia. Research on the Inheritance of Early and Medieval Christianity* 65 - *Ministerium Sermonis* II).

Geest, P. van, 'Armoede en menselijke waardigheid. Het Magisterium van de katholieke kerk over de wisselwerking tussen beide – Poverty and human dignity: The magisterium of the Catholic Church on the interaction between the two', in: *Tydskrif vir Geesteswetenskappe/Journal of Humanities* 60 (2020), no. 3, 646–658.

Geest, P. van, 'Onenigheid en tweesporenbeleid. De visie op en omgang met slaven in de katholieke kerk tot de achttiende eeuw', in: *Nieuw Letterkundig Magazijn* 38 (december 2020), 6–11.

Geest, P. van, 'Patristics among the tulips. Interdisciplinarity as a chance for theology and patristics', in: *Gregorianum* 95 (2014), 73–94.

Geest, P. van, *Waarachtigheid. Augustinus over levenskunst* (Zoetermeer: Meinema, 2011), 122–123.

Geest, P. van, 'Gabriel Biel, Brother of the Common Life and *alter Augustinus*? Aim and Meaning of his *Tractatus de communi vita clericorum*', in: *Augustiniana* 58(2008), 305–357.

Geest, P. van, 'Sed ea quae obscura sunt praetermitto' (*Speculum* 108). Augustine' selection of Scriptural quotations as proof of his desire to effect a confrontation', in: *Rivista Augustinianum* 57 (2017), 493–513.

Geest, P. van, *The Incomprehensibility of God. Augustine as a Negative Theologian.* Leuven-Dudley: Peeters, 2010 (*Late Antique History and Religion* 4).

Geest, P. van, 'The Fundamental Paradox in Luke's Perception of Money and Property', in: L.J.B. Lietaert Peerbolte, A. van Wieringen (eds), *On the road with Luke-Acts. Perspectives from biblical Texts and Early Christian Writings.* (Leiden: Brill, 2021), in press (*STAR*).

Génicot, E., *Theologiæ Moralis Institutiones.* Louvain-Bruxelles: Museum Lessianum-Dewit, 1931.

Gerbner, K., *Christian Slavery. Conversion and Race in the Protestant Atlantic World.* Philadelphia: University of Pennsylvania Press, 2019.

Gigerenzer, G., 'Moral Satisficing: Rethinking Moral Behavior as Bounded Rationality', in: *Topics in Cognitive Science* 2 (2010), 528–554.

Gilles, D., 'Le remède et le venin, « Vrai mal dont Dieu tire de bons effets » Prohibition de l'usure et valorisation de l'intérêt à Port-Royal', in: L. Brunori, S. Dauchy, O. Descamps, X. Prévost (eds.), *Le Droit face à l'économie sans travail.* vol. 2: *L'approche internationale* (Paris: Classiques Garnier, 2020), 107–133 (*History of Law* 7).

Gneezy, U., Rustichini, A., 'A fine is a price', in: *Journal of Legal Studies* 29 (2000), 1–17.

Gonzalez, J.L., *Faith and Wealth. A History of Early Christian Ideas on the Origin, Significance, and Use of Money.* San Francisco: Harper & Row, 1990.

Goodenough, O., Gruter Cheney, M., 'Is Free Enterprise Value in Action?', in: P. Zak (ed.), *Moral Markets. The Critical Role of Values in the Economy* (Princeton-Oxford: Princeton University Press, 2008), xxiii–xxx.

Goudzwaard, B., de Lange, H., *Beyond Poverty and Affluence: Toward an Economy of Care.* Grand Rapids, Michigan: Eerdmans, 1995.

Graafland, J., *Het oog van de naald. Over markt, geluk en solidariteit.* Kampen: Ten Have, 2007.

Graafland, J.J., 'Do Markets Crowd Out Virtues?', in: *Journal of Business Ethics* 91 (2009), 1–19.

Graafland, J.J., *Economics, Ethics and the Market. Introduction and Applications.* London-New York: Routledge, 2007.

Gravlee, S., 'Hope in Ancient Greek Philosophy', in: S.C. van den Heuvel, *Historical and Multidisciplinary Perspectives on Hope* (Springer: Open Access, 2020), 3–24.

Haan, R., *Vergeten vragen. Humanisme in economisch-theologisch perspectief.* Vught: Skandalon, 2016.

Haas, G.H., *The Concept of Equity in Calvin's Ethics.* Waterloo, Ontario: Wilfrid Laurier UP, 1997.

Hadot, I., 'Amicitia', in: C. Mayer (ed.), *Augustinuslexikon* (Basel-Berlin: Schwabe Verlag, 1986-…), vol. 1, col. 287–293.

Haidt, J., 'The emotional dog and its rational tail: a social intuitionist approach to moral judgment', in: *Psychological review* 108 (2001), 814–834.

Hamman, A.-G., Études patristiques. *Méthodologie, liturgie, histoire, théologie.* Paris: Beauchesne, 1991 (*Théologie historique* 85).

*Handbuch der Ablässe* (Roma: Libreria Editrice Vaticana, 2008), 17–24; 27–81.

Harrison, S., *Augustine's way into the will. The theological and philosophical significance of De Libero Arbitrio.* Oxford: Oxford University Press, 2006.

Hartrop, A., 'Why is Engagement between Christian Theologians and Economists Difficult?', in: J. Kidwell, S. Doherty, (eds), *Theology and Economics: A Christian Vision of the Common Good* (New York: Palgrave & McMillan, 2015), 11–26.

Hay, D., Menzies, G. 'Is the Model of Human Nature in Economics Fundamentally Flawed? Seeking a Better Model of Economic Behavior', in: J. Kidwell, S. Doherty, *Theology and Economics: A Christian Vision of the Common Good* (New York: Palgrave Macmillan, 2015), 183–198.

Helliwell, J.F., Layard, R. en Sachs, J., *World Happiness Report.* New York: United Nations, 2015.

Helmer, É., 'Platon et Aristote ou les pouvoirs politiques de la monnaie', in: *Revue du Mauss* 2015/2 (n° 46), 363–384.

Henderson, J., Pisciotta, J.L., (eds.), *Faithfull Economics. The Moral Worlds of a Neutral Science.* Waco: Baylor University Press, 2005.

Hengstmengel, J., 'Trade', in: D. Hunter, P. van Geest, B.J. Lietaert Peerbolte (eds.), *Brill Encyclopedia of Early Christianity* (Leiden: Brill), in press.

Hengstmengel, J., 'Wealth-Poverty', in: D. Hunter, P. van Geest, B.J. Lietaert Peerbolte (eds.), *Brill Encyclopedia of Early Christianity* (Leiden: Brill), in press.

Hengstmengel, J., *De homo economicus. Een familiegeschiedenis.* Amsterdam: Boom, 2020.

Hengstmengel, J., 'The Paradox of Value in the Teaching of the Church Fathers', in: *European Journal of the History of Economic Thought*, in press.

Hermans, Chr.,'Epistemological reflections on the connection between ideas and data in empirical research into religion', in: L.J. Francis, M. Robbins, J. Astley, *Empirical Theology in Texts and Tables. Qualitative, Quantative and Comparative Perspectives* (Leiden: Brill, 2009), 73–99 (*Empirical studies in theology* 17*ibidem*, 73–99.

Hirschfeld, M., *Aquinas and the Market. Towards a Humane Economy* (Harvard: Harvard University Press, 2018), 34–65.

Hirschman, A., *The Passion and the Interests* (Princeton, New Jersey: Princeton University Press, 1977), 9–66.

Holman (ed.), S.R., *Wealth and Poverty in Early Church and Society* (Grand Rapids: Baker Academic, 2008), (*Holy Cross Studies in Patristic Theology and History*).

Hoogen, A. van den, 'The Relationship between Economics and Theology', in: *Jahrbuch Fur Kontextuellen Theologien* 4 (1996), 39–57.

Hovind, C., *Godonomics. How to Save Our Country – and Protect Your Wallet – Through Biblical Principals of Finance* (Colorado Springs: Mutnomah Books, 2013), passim.

Hutchison, T., *Before Adam Smith: The Emergence of Political Economy, 1662–1776*. New York: Basil Blackwell, 1988.

Iannaccone, L.R., Sims Bainbridge, W., 'Economics of Religion', in: J. Hinnells (ed.), *The Routledge Companion to the Study of Religion* (Abingdon: Routledge, 2010), 461–75.

Irwin, D.A., *Against the Tide: An Intellectual History of Free Trade*. Princeton NY: Princeton University Press, 1996.

Jackson, P., Fleischer, Chr., 'Religion and Economics. A Literature Review', in: *Religions and Development Working Paper 3*. University of Birmingham, 2007.

Johnson, Ch., 'Introduction', in: *De Moneta of Nicholas Oresme and English Mint documents*. Translated with introduction and notes by Ch. Johnson (London, 1956), ix–xii (*Medieval texts*).

Jüngen, J., 'UB wordt E-learning center: de eurolib-projecten van de UB-EUR', in: *Informatie professional* 7 (2003), no. 10, 18–23.

Kabir, H.M., (ed), *Handbook of Empirical Research on Islam and Economic Life*. Cheltenham/Northampton: Edward Elgar, 2017.

Kabir, H.M., Lewis, M.K., (eds), *Handbook on Islam and Economic Life*. Cheltenham/Northampton: Edward Elgar, 2014.

Kahneman, D., *Thinking, Fast and Slow*. London: Penguin Books, 2011 (Dutch Translation: *Ons feilbare denken*. Antwerpen-Amsterdam: Business Contact, 2015).

Kahneman, D., 'A perspective on judgment and choice: Mapping bounded rationality', in: *American Psychologist* 58 (2003), no. 9, 697–720.

Kahneman, D., 'A psychological perspective on economics', in: *American Economic Review* 93 (2003), no. 2, 162–168.

Kern, W., Pottmeyer, H.J., Seckler, M., (eds.), *Handbuch der Fundamentaltheologie*. vol. 4: *Traktat theologische Erkenntnislehre*. Tübingen: Francke, 2000.

Keynes, J.M., *A Tract on Monetary Reform*. London: Macmillan & Co, 1923.

Keynes, J.M., *Essays in biography*. London: Macmillan, 1933.

*Klaar om te wenden. De academische bestudering van religie in Nederland: een verkenning*. Amsterdam: KNAW, 2015.

Kloppenborg, J.S., 'Fiscal Aspects of Paul's Collection for Jerusalem', in: *Early Christianity* 2 (2017), vol. 8, 153–198.

Koehn, D., Wilbratte, B., 'A Defense of a Thomistic Concept of the Just Price', in: *Business Ethics Quarterly* 22 (3), 501–526.

Kooi, C. van der, 'Protestant thinking on markets, morality and money: Calvin, Kuyper, and the Ecumenical Movement', in press.

Kooi, K. van der, *Als in een spiegel. God kennen volgens Calvijn en Barth*. Kampen: Kok, 2002.

Kooi, C. van der, *As in a Mirror. John Calvin and Karl Barth on Knowing God. A Diptych*. Leiden/Boston: Brill, 2005 [translation of: *Als in een spiegel*].

Kooi, C. van der, 'Calvin and the Ban on Usury', in: M. Wijlens, V. Shmaliy, S. Sinn (eds), *Churches and Moral Discernment*. Vol 2: *Learning from History* (Geneva: WCC, 2021), 40–49 (*Faith and Order Paper* 229).

Labellarte, A., (ed.), *Nicola Oresme. Trattato sull'origine, la natura, il diritto e i cambiamenti del denaro*. Bari: Stilo Editrice, 2016.

Ladaria, L., Turkson, P., *Oeconomicae et pecuniariae quaestiones*. Roma: Libreria Editrice Vaticana, 2018.

Landreth, H., Colander, D., *History of Economic Thought*. Boston-Toronto: Houghton Mifflin Company, 2006. [Fourth edition].

Lang, P.H.D., 'Private Confession and Absolution in the Lutheran Church: A Doctrinal, Historical, and Critical Study', in: *Concordia Theological Quarterly* 56 (1992), no. 4, 241–261.

Lange van Ravenswaay, J.M., *Augustinus totus noster. Das Augustinverständnis bei Johannes Calvin*. Göttingen: Vandenhoeck & Ruprecht, 1990 (*Forschungen zur Kirchen- und Dogmengeschichte* 45).

Langholm, O., *The Legacy of Scholasticism in Economic Thought: Antecedents of Choice and Power*. Cambridge: Cambridge University Press, 1998.

Langholm, O., *Economics in the Medieval Schools: Wealth, Exchange, Value, Money and Usury according to the Paris Theological Tradition, 1200–1350*. Leiden: Brill, 1992.

Levine, A., (ed.), *The Oxford Handbook of Judaism and Economics*. Oxford: Oxford University Press: 2010.

Libet, B., a.o., 'Time of conscious intention to act in relation to onset of cerebral activity (readiness-potential). The unconscious initiation of a freely voluntary act', in: *Brain* 106 (1983), 623–642.

Littler, J., *Against Meritocracy: Culture, Power and Myths of Mobility*. London- New York: Routledge, 2018.

Long, D.S., Fox, N.R., *Calculated Futures: Theology, Ethics, and Economics*. Waco: Baylor University Press, 2007.

Lossky, V., 'Les éléments de théologie négative, dans la pensée de saint Augustin', in: *Augustinus Magister (Congrès International Augustinien, Paris, 21–24 Septembre 1954)* Paris: Études Augustiniennes, 1954. 2 vols. vol. 1, 575–581.

Lubac, H. de, *Augustinisme et Théologie moderne*. Paris: Cerf, 1965 (*Théologie. Études publiées sous la direction de la faculté de théologie S.J. de Lyon-Fourvière* 63).

Lucassen, J., Moor, T. de, Luiten van Zanten, J., 'The return of the guilds. Towards a global history of the guilds in pre-industrial times', in: *International Review of Social History* 53 (2008), 5–18.

Lupieri, E., 'Businessmen and merchants will not enter the places of my Father', in: J. von Hagen, M. Welker (eds.), *Money as God? The Monetization of the Market and its Impact on Religion, Politics, Law, and Ethics* (Cambridge: Cambridge University Press, 2016), 379–413.

Madec, G., 'Si Plato viveret ... Augustin, De vera religione 3.3', in: *Néoplatonisme: Mélanges offerts à Jean Trouillard*. Fontenay-aux-Roses: École Normale Supérieure, 1981.

Maghrebi. N., a.o. (eds), *Handbook of Analytical Studies in Islamic Finance and Economics*. Berlin: De Gruyter, 2020.

Mäkeler, H., 'Nicolas Oresme und Gabriel Biel. Zur Geldtheorie im späten Mittelalter', in: *Scripta Mercaturae. Zeitschrift für Wirtschafts und Sozialgeschichte* 37 (2003), 56–94.

Már Jónsson, E.M., *Le miroir. Naissance d'un genre littéraire*. Paris: Les Belles Lettres, 1995.

Markus, R., *Saeculum: History and Society in the Theology of St Augustine* (Cambridge: Cambridge University Press, 1970), 72–104.

Marshall, N., *The penitential discipline of the primitive church for the first four hundred years after Christ: together with its declension from the fifth century, downwards to its present state*. Oxford: Parker, 1844.

Mathur, V.K., 'How Well Do We Know Pareto Optimality?', in: *The Journal of Economic Education* 22 (1991), 172–178.

Maxwell, J.F., *Slavery and the Catholic Church: The history of Catholic teaching concerning the moral legitimacy of the institution of slavery* (London: Barry Rose Publishers, 1975), 50–110.

McCarraher, E., *The Enchantments of Mammon. How Capitalism became the Religion of Modernity* (Cambridge, MA-London: The Belknap Press of Cambridge University, 2019), 6–13; 663–679.

McCloskey, D., *Bourgeois Equality. How Ideas, not Capital or Institutions, Enriched the World*. Chicago: The University of Chicago Press, 2016.

McCloskey, D., *The Bourgeois Dignity. Why Economics Can't Explain the Modern World*. Chicago: The University of Chicago Press, 2011.

McCloskey, D., *The Bourgeois virtues. Ethics in an Age of Commerce*. Chicago: The University of Chicago Press, 2007.

McCloskey, D., *The Vices of Economists: The Virtues of the Bourgeoisie*. Amsterdam: Amsterdam University Press, 1996 (Dutch translation: *De zondeval der economen: over wetenschappelijke zonden en burgerlijke deugden*. Amsterdam: Amsterdam University Press, 1997).

McCloskey, D., 'The Liberty of the Will in Theology Permits the Liberated Markets of Liberalism', in: *Journal of Economics, Theology and Religion*, vol. 1, no. 1 (2021), 81–108.

McCleary, R., (ed.), *Oxford Handbook of the Economics of Religion*. Oxford: Oxford University Press, 2011.

McCleary, R., Barro, R.J., *The Wealth of Religions. The Political Economy of Believing and Belonging*. Princeton/Oxford: Princeton University Press, 2019.

Meeks, M.D., *God the Economist: The Doctrine of God and Political Economy* (Minneapolis: Fortress, 1989).

Meché, F. van der, *Op de trap van Erasmus. De vrijheid van neuronen*. Rotterdam: Erasmus University Rotterdam, 2011.

*Medieval Handbooks of Penance: A Translation of the Principal Libri Poenitentiales*. Translated by J. McNeill, H.M. Gamer. New York: Columbia University Press, 1990.

Meens, R., *Het tripartite boeteboek. Overlevering en betekenis van vroegmiddeleeuwse biechtvoorschriften (met editie en vertaling van vier tripartita)*. Utrecht: Verloren, 1994. (*Middeleeuwse Studies en Bronnen* 41).

Menger, K., *Principles of Economics*. Auburn-Alabama: Ludwig von Mises Institute, 2007 [reprint].

Michener, R.T., 'Post-Kantian to Postmodern Considerations of (Theological) Hope', in: S.C. van den Heuvel, *Historical and Multidisciplinary Perspectives on Hope* (Springer: Open Access, 2020), 77–95.

Milbank, J., *Theology and Social Theory: Beyond Secular Reason* (Malden-Oxford: Blackwell Publishing, 2006. second edition), 278–326.

Mill, J.S., *Three Essays on Religion. Nature, the Utility of Religion and Theism*. London: Longmans, Green, Reader and Dyer, 1874.

Mixon, F.G., 'Introduction to the Symposium on the Economics of Religion', in: *Forum for Social Economics*, 49 (2020), no. 4, 345–356

Mock, W.B.T., 'Pareto Optimality', in: D.K. Chatterjee (ed.), *Encyclopedia of Global Justice* (Dordrecht: Springer, 2011), 808–809.

Moltmann, J., *Ethik der Hoffnung*. Gütersloh: Gütersloher Verlagshaus, 2010.

Monroe, A.E., *Monetary Theory before Adam Smith* (Harvard: Harvard University Press, 2014 [reprint]), 14f (*Harvard Economic Studies* 25).

Moor, de, T., *Homo Cooperans. Instituties voor collectieve actie en de solidaire samenleving*. Utrecht: Universiteit Utrecht, 2013 [inaugural adress].

Moriss, A., *Economics as Religion from Samuelson to Chicago and Beyond*. Pennsylvania: Pennsylvania State University Press, 2001; id. 'What Is Economic Theology', in:

*Princeton Seminary Bulletin* 25 (2004), no. 1: 58– 79; Ph. Goodchild, *Credit and Faith*. Lanham: Rowman & Littlefield, 2019; id. *Economic Theology: Credit and Faith* II. Lanham: Rowman & Littlefield, 2020; S. Schwarzkopf, *The Routledge Handbook of Economic Theology*

Morriss, A., 'Understanding Economics through Theology: Reflections on Robert Nelson's Economics as Religion', in: *Case Western Reserve Law Review* 56 (2006), no. 3. R.H. Nelson, *Reaching for Heaven on Earth. The Theological Meaning of Economics*. Savage: Rowman & Littlefield, 1991.

Morset, G., 'The Science Behind the Smile An interview with Daniel Gilbert', in: *Harvard Business Review* 2012, no. 1 (January-February issue), 3–8; https://hbr.org/2012/01/the-science-behind-the-smile.

Mullainathan, S., Thaler, R., 'Behavioral Economics' (October 2000). *NBER Working Paper No. w7948*. (https://ssrn.com/abstract=245733).

Nell-Breuning, O. von, 'Zur Kritik des wirtschaftlichen Liberalismus', in: id., *Wirtschaft und Gesellschaft heute*. vol. 1. *Grundfragen* (Freiburg im Breisgau: Herder 1956), 103–122.

Nell-Breuning, O. von, *Unsere Verantwortung. Für eine solidarische Gesellschaft*. Freiburg im Breisgau: Herder, 1987.

Noonan, J.T., *The Scholastic Analysis of Usury*. Cambridge, MA: Harvard University Press, 1957.

Nooteboom, B., *Trust, Forms, foundations, functions, failures and figures*. Cheltenham: Edward Elgar, 2002.

Nooteboom, B., *Vertrouwen. Opening naar een veranderende wereld*. Utrecht: Klement, 2017.

Novak, M., *The Spirit of Democratic Capitalism*. New York: Simon & Schuster, 1982.

Novak, M., *Toward a Theology of the Corporation*. Washington: AEI, 1981.

Nullens, P., Burger, M., Heuvel, S. van den, Pleeging, E., 'Hoop als drijfveer', in: H. Commandeur, P. van Geest, F. Langerak (eds.), *Management en Organisatie*. Themanummer: *Inzicht in drijfveren III* (Deventer: Kluwer, 2016), 79–91 (*Management en Organisatie* 70–5\6).

Obadia, L., Wood, D.C., (eds). *The Economics of Religion: Anthropological Approaches*. Bingley: Emerald, 2011.

Ogliari, D., *Gratia et certamen. The relationship between grace and free will in the discussion of Augustine with the so-called semipelagians*. Leuven: Peeters, 2003 (*Bibliotheca Ephemeridum Theologicarum Lovaniensium* 169).

Opdebeeck, H., 'Rediscovering a Personalist Economy', in: P. Rona, L. Zsolnai (eds.), *Economics as Moral Science* (New York: Springer International Publishing, 2017), 69–79.

Oslington, P., (ed.) *Economics and Religion*. 2 vols. Cheltenham/Northampton: Edward Elgar, 2003.

Oslington, P., (ed.), *Handbook of Christianity and Economics*. New York: Oxford University Press, 2014.

Oslington, P., 'A theological economics', in: *International Journal of Social Economics* 27 (2000), 32–44.

Oslington, P., Williams, P.S., Hirschfeld, M., 'Introduction. Recent Developments in Economics and Religion', in: P. Oslington, P.S. Williams, M. Hirschfeld (eds), *Recent Developments in Economics and Religion* (Cheltenham: Edward Elgar Publishing, 2018), 1–23 (*The international Library of Critical Writings in Economic Series* 341).

Oslington, P., 'Economics and Biblical Studies', in: C. Matthews (ed.), *Oxford Bibliographies in Biblical Studies*. New York: Oxford University Press, 2015.

Pannenberg, W., *Wissenschaftstheorie und Theologie*. Frankfurt am Main: Suhrkamp, 1987 (reprint).

Pareto, V., *Manual of Political Economy. A Critical and Variorum Edition*. A. Montesano, A. Zanni, L. Bruni, J.S. Chipman, M. McLure (eds.). Oxford: Oxford University Press, 2014.

Perna, M.L., 'Genovesi Antonio', in: M. Caravale (ed.), *Dizionario biografico degli italiani* (Catanzaro, 2000). Vol. 53, 148–149.

Pessers, D., *Liefde, solidariteit en recht. Een interdisciplinair onderzoek naar het wederkerigheidsbeginsel*. Amsterdam: Universiteit van Amsterdam, 1999.

Piketty, Th., *Capital et idéologie*. Paris: Seuil, 2019.

Pinsent, A., 'Hope as a Virtue in the Middle Ages', in: S.C. van den Heuvel, *Historical and Multidisciplinary Perspectives on Hope* (Springer: Open Access, 2020), 47–60.

Planbureau voor Leefomgeving, Sociaal Cultureel Planbureau, Centraal Planbureau, *Naar een Verkenning Brede welvaart*. Den Haag: PBL, SCP, CPB, 2017.

Pleeging, E., Exel, J. van, Burger, M., 'Characterizing Hope: An Interdisciplinary Systematic Review of the Characteristics of Hope', in press.

Pleeging, E., Burger, M., Exel, J. van, 'Hope Mediates the Relation between Income and Subjective Well-Being', in: *Happiness Studies* (2020). https://doi.org/10.1007/s10902-020-00309-6.

Pleeging, E., Exel, J. van, Burger, M., Stavropoulos, S., 'Hope for the future and willingness to pay for sustainable energy', in: *Ecological Economics* 181 (2021) 106900.

Rannikko, E., *Liberium Arbitrium and Necessitas; A philosophical Inquiry into Augustine's Conception of the Will*. Helsinki: Luther Agricola Society, 1997.

Ratzinger, J., *Theologische Prinzipienlehre. Bausteine zur Fundamentaltheologie*. München: Wewel, 1982.

Rawls, J., *A Theory of Justice*. Cambridge Mass.: The Belknap Press of Harvard University Press, 1971. (revised edition 1999).

Reiss, J., *Philosophy of economics: A contemporary introduction*. London-New York: Routledge, 2013.

Richter, G., *Oikonomia. Der Gebrauch des Wortes Oikonomia im Neuen Testament, bei den Kirchenvätern und in der theologischen Literatur bis ins 20. Jahrhundert*. Berlin: de Gruyter, 2013 [reprint].

Rick, S., Loewenstein, G., 'The role of emotion in economic behavior', in: M. Lewis, J.M. Haviland-Jones, L. Feldman Barret (eds.), *Handbook of emotions* (New York: Guilford Press, 2008), 138–156.

Rist, J., 'Augustine on Free Will and Predestination', in: *Journal of Theological Studies* 20 (1969), 420–447.

Rist, J., *Augustine. Ancient Thought Baptized*. Cambridge: Cambridge University Press, 1994.

Robbins, L., *An essay on the nature and significance of economic science*. [second edition, revised and extended]. London: Macmillan & Co, 1945.

Rocca, G.P., *Speaking the Incomprehensible God: Thomas Aquinas on the Interplay of Positive and Negative Theology*. Washington D.C.: Catholic University of America Press, 2004.

Rodrik, D., *Economics Rules: The Rights and Wrongs of the Dismal Science*. New York: Norton, 2015.

Rothbarth, M.N., *Economic Thought Before Adam Smith. An Austrian Perspective on the History of Economic Thought* (Auburn, Alabama: Ludwig von Mises Institute, s.l.), 99–133.

Rubin, J., 'Introduction to the special issue on the economics of religion', in: *Journal of Demographic Economics* 86 (2020), no. 3, 2007–211.

Schelkens, K., Geest, P. van, Gennip, J. van, *Het Katholicisme in Europa. Een geschiedenis*. Amsterdam: Boom, 2021. Second edition.

Schilderman, 'Truth and method in empirical theology', in: L.J. Francis, M. Robbins, J. Astley, *Empirical Theology in Texts and Tables. Qualitative, Quantative and Comparative Perspectives* (Leiden: Brill, 2009), 27–41 (*Empirical studies in theology* 17).

Schüle, A., 'Do not sell your soul for money; economy and eschatology in biblical and intertestamental tradition', in: J. von Hagen, M. Welker (eds.), *Money as God? The Monetization of the Market and its Impact on Religion, Politics, Law, and Ethics* (Cambridge: Cambridge University Press, 2016), 365–378.

Schulze, L., *Calvin and "social ethics": his views on property, interest and usury*. Pretoria: Kital, 1985.

Schumpeter, J., *History of Economic Analysis* [edited from manuscript by Elizabeth Boody Schumpeter] London-Boston-Sydney: Allen & Unwin, 1986 (paperback edition).

Schwarzkopf, S. (ed.), *The Routledge Handbook of Economic Theology*. New York: Routledge, 2020.

Schwarzkopf, S., 'An Introduction to Economic Theology', in: id., *The Routledge Handbook of Economic Theology* (New York: Routledge, 2020), 1–15.

Seabright, P., *The Company of Strangers. A Natural History of Economic Life*. Princeton: Princeton University Press, 2010.

Sedláček, T., *Economics of Good and Evil. The Quest for Economic Meaning from Gilgamesh to Wall Street*. Oxford: Oxford University Press, 2011.

Sedláček, T., *De economie van goed en kwaad. De zoektocht naar economische zingeving van Gilgamesj tot Wall Street*. Schiedam: Scriptum, 2015.

Sellars, W., *Empiricism and the Philosophy of Mind* (London: Routledge & Kegan Paul, 1963), 127–196.

Sen, A., 'Rational fools: A critique of the behavioral foundations of economic theory', in: *Philosophy & Public Affairs* 6 (1977), no. 2, 317–344.

Sen, A., *Development as freedom*. Oxford: Oxford Paperbacks, 2001.

Sen, A., *On ethics and economics* (*The Royer Lectures*). Oxford: Blackwell, 1987.

Simon, H., 'A Behavioral Model of Rational Choice', in: *The Quarterly Journal of Economics* 69 (1955), no. 1, 99–118.

Simon, H.A., 'Motivational and Emotional Controls of Cognition', in: *Psychological Review* 74 (1967), no. 1, 29–39.

Simon, H.A., 'Rational Choice and the Structure of the Environment', in: *Psychological Review* 63 (1956), no. 2, 129–138.

Simon, H.A., 'Rational Decision Making in Business Organizations', in: *The American Economic Review* 69 (1979), no. 4, 493–513.

Simon, H.A., 'Rationality as process and as product of thought', in: *American Economic Review* 68 (1978), no. 2, 1–16.

Simon, H.A., *Models of bounded rationality*. Cambridge, MA: MIT Press, 1982.

Sløk, C., 'Guilt', in: S. Schwarzkopf (ed.), *The Routledge Handbook of Economic Theology* (New York: Routledge, 2020), 72–80.

Solomon, R., 'Free Enterprise, Sympathy and Virtue', in: P. Zak (ed.), *Moral Markets. The Critical Role of Values in the Economy* (Princeton-Oxford: Princeton University Press, 2008), 16–41.

Spanneut, M., 'Le stoïcisme et saint Augustin', in: P. Courcelle, *Forma futuri. Studi in onore del Cardinale Michele Pellegrino* (Torino: Bottega d'Erasmo, 1975), 896–914.

Spanneut, M., 'L'impact de l'apatheia stoïcienne sur la pensée chrétienne jusqu'à Saint Augustin', in: A. Gonzáles Blanco (ed.), *Cristianismo y aculturación en tiempos del Imperio Romano* (Murcia: Universidad de Murcia, 1990), 39–52 (= *Antigüedad y cristianismo* 7).

Stackhouse, M.L., 'Weber, Theology and Economics', in: P. Oslington (ed.), *Oxford Handbook of Christianity and Economics* (Oxford: OUP, 2014), 107–336.

Stark, R., *The Victory of Reason: How Christianity Led to Freedom, Capitalism and Western Success*. New York: Random House Publishing Group, 2005.

Stigler, G., *Memoirs of an Unregulated Economist*. New York: Basic Books, 1988.

Stiglitz J.E., Sen, A., Fitoussi, J.P., *The Measurement of Economic Performance and Social Progress: Report by the Commission on the Measurement of Economic Performance and Social Progress*. Paris, 2009.

Tanner, K., *Christianity and the New Spirit of Capitalism*. New Haven: Yale University Press, 2019.

Tawney, R., *Religion and the Rise of Capitalism. A Historical Study*. Peter Smith: Reprint Edition, 1962, 317.

Teske, R.J., 'Properties of God and the Predicaments in *De Trinitate* V', in: *The Modern Schoolman* 59 (1981–1982), 1–19.

Todeschini, G., 'Usury in Christian Middle Ages. A Reconsideration of the Historiographical Tradition (1949–2010)', in: F. Ammannati (ed), *Religione e istituzioni religiose nell' economia Europea. 1000–1800 - Religion and Religious Institutions in the European Economy. 1000–1800. Atti della Quarantaquattresima Settimana di Studi 8–12 maggio 2011* (Firenze: Firenze University Press, 2012), 119–130.

Trevena, J., Miller, J., 'Brain preparation before a voluntary action: Evidence against unconscious movement initiation', in: *Consciousness and Cognition* 19 (2010), 447–456.

Uhlaner, C.J., 'Relational Goods and Participation: Incorporating Sociability into a Theory of Rational Action', in: *Public Choice* 62 (1989), no. 3, 253–285.

Van Stichel, E. van, 'Gaudium et Spes: From a Personalist to a Trinitarian Anthropology and Its Implications for Reflecting on the (Global) Economy', in: *Journal of Catholic Social Thought* 12 (2015), no. 2, 227–244.

Veenhoven, R., 'Wat is geluk?', in: G. van Liemt (ed.), *Het rendement van geluk. Inzichten uit wetenschap en praktijk* (Den Haag: SMO, 2014), 18–26.

Veenhoven, R., 'Het grootste geluk voor het grootste aantal. Geluk als richtsnoer voor beleid', in: *Sociale Wetenschappen* (2002), no. 4, 1–43.

Viale, R. (ed.), *Routledge Handbook of Bounded Rationality*, London: Routledge, Taylor & Francis Group, 2020.

Vink, M., 'Freedom and Slavery: The Dutch Republic, the VOC World, and the Debate over the World's Oldest Trade', in: *South African Historical Journal* 59 (2007), no. 1, 19–46.

Vinod H.D., (ed.), *The Oxford Handbook of Hindu Economics and Business*. Oxford: Oxford University Press, 2012.

Wagner-Tsukamoto, S.A., *Is God an Economist? An Institutional Economic Reconstruction of the Old Testament*. Basingstoke, UK - New York: Palgrave Macmillan, 2009.

Waterman, A.C.M. 'On Economics, Theology, and Religion', in: *Journal of Economics, Theology and Religion* 1 (2021), no. 1, in press.

Waterman, A.M.C., 'The Beginning of 'Boundaries': The Sudden Separation of Economics from Christian Theology', in: G. Erreygers (ed), *Economics and Interdisciplinary Research* (London: Routledge; Block, 2001), 41–63.

Weaver, G.R., Reynolds, S.J., Brown, M.E., 'Moral intuition: Connecting current knowledge to future organizational research and practice', in: *Journal of Management* 40 (2014), no. 1, 100–129.

Webber, M., Kok, J., 'Early Christian Thinking on Hope', in: S.C. van den Heuvel, *Historical and Multidisciplinary Perspectives on Hope* (Springer: Open Access, 2020), 25–45.

Weber, M., *The Protestant Ethic and the Spirit of Capitalism*. London: Unwin University Books, 1930.

Welby, J., *Dethroning Mammon. Making Money Serve Grace. The Archbishop of Canterbury's Lent Book 2017*. London-Oxford-New York-New Delhi-Sydney: Bloomsbury Publishing, 2017.

Wetzel, J., 'Snares of Truth: Augustine on Free Will and Predestination', in: R. Dodaro, G. Lawless (ed.), *Augustine and his Critics. Essays in Honour of Gerald Bonner* (London-New York: Taylor & Francis Group, 2000), 124–141.

Wilthagen, T., Aarts, E., Valcke, P., *Tijd voor interdisciplinariteit. Een essay over de meerwaarde van samenwerking voor wetenschap, universiteit en maatschappij*. Tilburg: Tilburg University Press, 2018.

Wirzba, N., *The Paradise of God: Renewing Religion in an Ecological Age*. Oxford: Oxford University Press, 2003.

Zak, P., 'Value and Values: Moral Economics', in: P. Zak (ed.), *Moral Markets. The Critical Role of Values in the Economy* (Princeton-Oxford: Princeton University Press, 2008), 259–279.

Zeeuw, A. de, *Integrating Economics and the Environment. Valedictory Adress delivered by Aart de Zeeuw as Professor of Environmental Economics at Tilburg University on 22 september 2017* (Tilburg: Tilburg University, 2017), 8–21.

Zheng, Ch., Wu, Y., 'The More Modest You are, the Happier You are: The Mediating Roles of Emotional Intelligence and Self-esteem', in: *Journal of Happiness Studies. An Interdisciplinary on Subjective Well-Being* 21 (2020), vol. 5, 1603–1615.

# Index of Names

# Index of Subjects